Reading for Learning

NCTE Editorial Board

Reading for Learning

Using Discipline-Based Texts to Build Content Knowledge

Heather Lattimer
University of San Diego

NCTE

NATIONAL COUNCIL OF TEACHERS OF ENGLISH
1111 W. KENYON ROAD, URBANA, ILLINOIS 61801-1096

Copy Editor: Erin Trainer

Production Editor: Carol Roehm

Interior Design: Jenny Jensen Greenleaf

Cover Design: Jenny Jensen Greenleaf

Cover Images: Thompson-McClellan Photography

NCTE Stock Number: 08437

Library of Congress Cataloging-in-Publication Data

Lattimer, Heather, 1971–
    Reading for learning : using discipline-based texts to build content knowledge / Heather Lattimer.
        p. cm.
    Includes bibliographical references and index.
    ISBN 978-0-8141-0843-7 (pbk)
    1. Content area reading. I. National Council of Teachers of English. II. Title.
    LB1050.45.L38 2010
    428.4071—dc22

                                                                      2010029958

Mom and Dad,
From Green Eggs and Ham *to dinner table debates,*
thank you for inspiring a love for reading.

Contents

Acknowledgments

Many, many thanks to the teachers who allowed me to visit their class-
rooms and learn from their expertise. Special thanks to Diana Combs,
Jaime Enochs, Tom Fehrenbacher, Rebecca Gemmell, Erica Heinze-
man, Peter Jana, Mary Kraus, Roni Krautheim, Ian Law, Stacey Lopaz, Rob
Meza-Ehlert, Kim Moerman, Mary McBride, Sean Neil, Mike Paredes, Doug
Robbins, Annette Saavedra, Marc Shulman, Susan Stark, Chris Steussy, Tom
Volle, Sara Watts, and Jennie Wheeler.

Thanks also to educational leaders who opened the doors of their schools,
especially Ben Daley, Ana Diaz-Booz, Cheryl Hibbeln, Jennifer Husbands,
Laurie Mosier, Rob Riordan, Bobbi Samilson, Cheryl Seelos, Beth Smith, Don
Wopperer, and Karen Wroblewski.

A debt of gratitude is owed to university colleagues who provided support
and encouragement. Special thanks to Donna Barnes, Barbara Brooks, Sandy
Buczynski, Adele Chandler, Nona Conner, Paula Cordeiro, Linda Dews, Kathy
Estey, Steve Gelb, Bobbi Hansen, Lea Hubbard, Nori Inoue, Tedi Kostka, Judy
Mantle, Maria Menezes, Sarina Molina, Reyes Quezada, and Joi Spencer. Appreciation also goes to my university students for pushing my thinking, challenging me to clarify my explanations, and allowing me to travel along on their
educational journeys.

Thank you to the staff at NCTE, particularly Kurt Austin, Janet Brown,
and Sharon Roth, for your enthusiasm in initiating this book project and your
patience in seeing it through to fruition. Thank you to NCTE's production team,
especially Carol Roehm and Erin Trainer, for crafting a beautiful final product,
and Pat Mayer, for designing the cover. And many, many thanks to Jennifer
Roberts for providing great feedback, unflinching honesty, and unwavering
support as the first reader on early drafts.

It would not be possible to undertake the challenge of writing a book without a fantastic support network at home. Special thanks to Ashley Crow, JoAn

Johnson, Marilyn and Maurice Loucks, and most especially, Grandma Carol and Bampa for sharing time, care, and love with my boys.

Finally, a most important note of gratitude to my husband, Joe, and our sons, Andy, Matthew, and James. Thank you for your patience and encouragement . . . and for dragging me out from behind the computer to go for bike rides by the ocean, compete in family domino tournaments, and curl up with a good bedtime story.

Introduction

For too long, content learning and reading instruction have been mired in a false dichotomy. The perception, and often the policy, has been that we have to make a choice between teaching reading *or* teaching content. The following recently observed announcement illustrates this misperception in action:

> The principal cleared her throat and the room quieted. Faculty members shifted their attention away from summer vacations and toward the start of the school year. After a few brief introductions and announcements, the professional growth focus for the year was announced. "Our reading scores dropped again last year," the principal began. "We are at risk of being designated as underperforming. Therefore, this year, all teachers will need to be teachers of reading." A hand in the back immediately shot up. "Does this mean that teaching reading takes precedence over teaching all other content?" a science teacher challenged. The principal hesitated for a moment, knowing that she was about to alienate a significant portion of her faculty, including some of her best teachers. "Yes. Unfortunately, reading must take priority. We will have to set aside some of our content teaching in favor of teaching our students how to read."

"Every teacher is a teacher of reading" started out with good intentions. It responded to the reality that all too often, students in middle and high school are unable to read and understand grade-level texts about subjects such as math, science, history, and the arts. It was intended to help students become better readers and learners across content areas (Fisher & Ivey, 2005). However, despite good intentions and a great deal of money, time, and effort, the "Every teacher is a teacher of reading" initiative has failed to result in reading gains, and it has not changed the way most content teachers practice their craft (see, for example, Lesley, 2004/2005; O'Brien, Stewart, & Moje, 1995).

There are many possible explanations for this failure, but at least one problem and cause for concern has to do with the unnecessary tension that the "Every teacher is a teacher of reading" mantra sets up. Many educators, like the principal in the previous vignette, see the choice as being about teaching content *or* reading. Content teachers, most of whom studied for years to become experts in their content area and few of whom have deep knowledge of literacy development, have been understandably frustrated by the demand that content take a backseat to general reading comprehension instruction. Many content teachers have resisted the push to become "teachers of reading," responding that the demands of their content, the standards set out by the state, and the increasingly common subject-specific tests required of their students leave no time for reading comprehension instruction (O'Brien, Stewart, & Moje, 1995).

The battle lines that have been drawn, however understandable in light of the manner in which content reading policies have been carried out, are unnecessary. There doesn't have to be a choice between reading *or* content. Reading and content can, and should, go hand in hand to support subject-area learning. This book is designed to provide a window into how to make that possible. It draws on research on cognition and learning, reading research, subject-specific research in history, science, math, and the arts, as well as on classroom practice and observation. It suggests practical, classroom-tested approaches to support students in developing content-specific understanding by using authentic, subject-appropriate readings. The goal is not to remake content teachers into reading teachers. Instead this book sets out to support content teachers in teaching students to access and use readings to deepen content understanding.

A note to teachers of English language arts (ELA): Although much of the discussion in this book focuses on exploring discipline-based texts that fall outside of the realm of literature, this book is for you too. Content standards across nearly all states, recommendations by the National Council of Teachers of English (NCTE) and the International Reading Association (IRA), and the 2010 Common Core State Standards all encourage ELA instruction that includes reading instruction in nonfiction, expository, persuasive, procedural, and technical texts. Bringing science-focused articles, historical documents, arts journals, charts, and math puzzles into the ELA classroom can be a wonderful way to meet these required standards.

Discipline-based texts can help develop students as readers who can navigate multiple genres and can also prepare them as writers who recognize the interplay between purpose, audience, and structure. Bringing readings from other disciplines into the ELA classroom also facilitates cross-content collaboration, an approach that has been found to raise both student achievement and teacher satisfaction (Bolak, Bialach, & Dunphy, 2005; Flowers, Mertens, & Mulhall, 1999). You are encouraged to read this book alongside colleagues from other disciplines, discuss common practices and content-specific differences, and identify ways to support one another's work in the classroom.

The Intersection between Reading and Content Learning

Sam Wineburg has spent much of his academic career studying how historians work. His examination of expert historians in the midst of practicing their craft reveals the centrality of the use of texts to historians' work as well as the unique character of reading in history. Accessing historical documents, according to Wineburg, is absolutely central to studying the past. "Reading," he writes, "is not merely a way to learn new information, but becomes a way to engage in new kinds of thinking" (2001, p. 80). In a later article, Wineburg and colleagues explain further:

> Understanding history requires understanding the processes integral to constructing historical narratives—the ways that historians analyze and compare fragmented, sometimes contradictory sources to create evidence-based narratives and conclusions. At the heart of these processes is reading—but reading informed by the ways of knowing in the discipline. (Martin, Wineburg, Rosenzweig, & Leon, 2008, p. 140)

To study history without reading and critically analyzing historical documents would be disingenuous. The same is true of most subject areas. Scientists, mathematicians, engineers, social scientists, artists, and performers all engage with texts that are appropriate to their content areas. Scientists do not develop theories or plan experiments out of thin air; they build on previous research, working to replicate, refute, refine, or reimagine earlier findings and apply that learning to new situations. Mathematicians, both theoretical and applied, read and study problems, look for patterns in data sets, and communicate, question, and defend proposed solutions. Artists and performers read to contextualize their work—to learn what came before and connect with the larger social, environmental, and political realities within which they work.

Yet for much of the history of US education, K–12 teaching focused on the acquisition of knowledge. Students in elementary, middle, and high school, it was believed, needed to learn "the facts" before they were ready to engage in subject-specific research and investigation; that should be left to the experts. It was under this conception of learning that content and reading were separated; content learning was about the acquisition of factual knowledge, while reading was about skill development. The two were not necessarily seen as related, nor were they understood to be mutually beneficial.

As we learn more about the nature of learning, it has become increasingly clear that true content learning is not simply about knowledge acquisition, rather it is about constructing understanding (Bransford, Brown, & Cocking,

2000; Vygotsky, 1978). If we want students to understand the causes of World War II, for example, we should not simply teach "the facts." Instead, we should engage students in the process of uncovering the historical narrative. We should provide them with multiple primary and secondary sources, encourage them to critically analyze the texts, and provide structures within which they can debate their interpretations with peers to develop their own understanding of the causes of the war.

Under this conception of learning, reading is not separate from content learning, but is intimately connected. Texts are used to provide the material that students can explore, debate, analyze, and evaluate as they fit together multiple pieces of evidence to construct an understanding of the big ideas of history, science, mathematics, and the arts. Teachers move from being "knowledge givers" to "knowledge facilitators" (Grant, 2003); they frame debates and inquiries, select texts and activities, and structure opportunities for student engagement with the material. We are no longer teaching students that the core ideas of history, science, math, and the arts are "fixed and stable forever, dropped out of the sky readymade" (VanSledright, 2004, p. 232). Instead, we are inviting students to engage in the processes and practices of the disciplines, allowing them to see behind the proverbial curtain and to participate in the fascinating, challenging, and often messy process by which experts continue to generate knowledge in their fields. We see an example of this kind of teaching in the following classroom vignette. The names of all teachers and students in this text have been changed to honor their privacy.

Reading for Learning in the Science Classroom

When students arrived in Ms. Nguyen's tenth-grade biology classroom, they found that the desks had been rearranged to accommodate a large, blue ice chest sitting on the floor in the middle of the room. As they quieted down and took their seats, they could hear strange noises coming from inside the chest. Wasting no time, Ms. Nguyen called for their attention as soon as the bell rang. "I need a volunteer," she announced. A few students somewhat reluctantly raised their hands. Ms. Nguyen sized up her potential volunteers through squinted eyes and then selected Eric, a young man who had a big personality and could usually be counted on to be a good sport. As Eric moved toward the center of the room, the noises coming from the ice chest grew louder. There was a repeated scratching sound along with an occasional whine or growl.

"Thanks for volunteering, Eric," Ms. Nguyen began. "I'd like you to put on this blindfold and then stick your hand inside the ice chest."

Eric started to walk back to his seat. "I don't want to do that. I don't know what's in there. It might bite my hand off."

"Come back," Ms. Nguyen said encouragingly. "It is perfectly safe. You aren't going to get hurt. Trust me." Eric continued to look skeptical. "What would it take for me to convince you to reach in?" Ms. Nguyen continued. "What evidence do you need before you are willing to trust my assertion that the ice chest is safe?"

Eric thought about it for a moment. "Can I look inside?" Ms. Nguyen shook her head. "Can I pick up the chest and shake it?" Ms. Nguyen agreed and Eric shook the chest. There was something inside. A few dull thuds could be felt as Eric moved the chest around, but there were no howls of protest. It didn't seem to be alive. "Can I poke a stick inside if I keep my eyes closed?" Again Ms. Nguyen nodded her head. Eric covered his eyes and grabbed a ruler from a nearby desk and opened the lid a crack. The stick encountered what seemed to be a paper sack in one area of the cooler and on the other side a small hard object attached to the bottom. As Eric probed around a bit more the ruler struck some sort of button or knob on the object and the scratching and whining noises suddenly stopped. Eric grinned. "Okay, now I'm ready to reach inside, Ms. Nguyen." He did so, withdrawing a paper sack of cookies as well as a small audio recorder that had been taped to the bottom of the cooler.

"Very nicely done, Eric," Ms. Nguyen commented as Eric passed around the bag of cookies and returned to his seat. "I like that you were skeptical at first and that you wanted to investigate the evidence before you were willing to reach right

in to the cooler. As you deduced, I was telling the truth when I said that you wouldn't be hurt, but you were smart to question my assertion. That is what good scientists do. When someone has a new discovery or a colleague announces a new medical treatment, scientists initially remain skeptical. They question and probe, they attempt to replicate experiments, and they try to find other explanations or evidence that might have been missed. Good scientists are constantly asking, "How do we know when to accept an explanation as scientifically valid?"

"Today we're going to investigate another assertion that was made over two hundred years ago. And I want you to follow Eric's example and be similarly skeptical. Take a look at the statement on the screen" [see Figure 0.1]. "What do you think—would you allow this man to place fluid from a 'diseased pustule,' an infected sore, under your skin?"

"No way," a student sitting next to Eric immediately spoke out. "I wouldn't do it. I mean, he's asking to make me sick. If I'm not sick now, why would I want to take something that could make me sick?"

How do we know when to accept an explanation as scientifically valid?

It is 1796. A man comes to your farm with a strange request. He wants to cut your arm and place fluid from the pustule of a diseased person under your skin. He says that the fluid will cause you to develop a rash on your arms but promises that it will prevent you from getting a more serious disease. Do you accept his offer? Why or why not?

FIGURE 0.1. Ms. Nguyen challenged her students to consider when an explanation was scientifically valid.

"And why should we believe him?" another student wanted to know. "Do we know who this person is?"

"I want to know what diseases he's talking about," commented a young woman near the front of the room. "I mean, if one was like a cold and the other was like Ebola, I might be willing to try it. But I'd want to see more evidence first."

"Good points," Ms. Nguyen agreed. "I'll fill you in a bit more and then provide you with some evidence to analyze. The man in this account is Edward Jenner, a country doctor in England. The fluid that he wants to place under your skin is from a cowpox pustule. And the more serious disease that he is hoping to prevent is smallpox, a highly contagious disease that has killed hundreds of thousands of people. Based on his previous observations, Dr. Jenner thinks he has found a way to prevent smallpox. He thinks that if he intentionally gives people cowpox, they'll be safe from smallpox. In 1796 he was ready to test

his assertion. He went to a local farmer and asked if he could inoculate the man's son, James Phipps, with fluid from the cowpox pustule of a local milkmaid. Then, after the cowpox had run its course, Dr. Jenner wanted to intentionally infect James with fluid from a smallpox pustule." Ms. Nguyen paused to make sure everyone was following.

"I want you to act as advisors to Mr. Phipps. I'm passing around a handout that includes some of the scientific evidence that Dr. Jenner had collected to support his explanation of the connection between cowpox and smallpox. The evidence is written in Jenner's own words from 1798 and was published in a text called *An Inquiry into the Causes and Effects of the Variolae Vaccinae, or Cowpox*. There are also spaces on the paper for you to respond to this text [see sample, Figure 0.2]. I want you to interrogate Jenner's observations, much as his colleagues did at the time. Ask questions, consider other explanations, shake them around, and poke a stick at them. And then decide: Do you know enough to accept

Excerpts from *An Inquiry into the Causes and Effects of the Variolae Vaccinae, or Cowpox* (Jenner, 1798)

Dr. Jenner's Observations	Explanation	Questions / Concerns
"This disease has obtained the name of the cow-pox. It appears on the nipples of the cows in the form of irregular pustules… Inflamed spots now begin to appear on different parts of the hands of domestics employed in milking."	The infection spreads from the cow's udder to the hands of the milkers.	Why only the hands? Do they get sick in the rest of their body too?
"Case II.- Sarah Portlock… was infected with the cow-pox when a servant at a farmer's in the neighbourhood, twenty-seven years ago. In the year 1792… she nursed one of her own children who had accidentally caught [smallpox], but no indisposition ensued."	Her body had resistance to small pox because she had cowpox.	Did everyone who had cowpox have resistance to smallpox? Was she just lucky?
"Case III.- John Phillips, a tradesman of this town, had the cowpox at so early a period as nine years of age. At the age of sixty-two I inoculated him [with fluid from a smallpox pustule]… It very speedily produced a sting-like feel in the part. A [fever] appeared, which on the fourth day was rather extensive, and some degree of pain and stiffness were felt about the shoulder; but on the fifth day these symptoms began to disappear, and in a day or two after went entirely off, without producing any effect on the system."	His case of smallpox was milder because he had cowpox.	If the cowpox gives you immunity why did he get sick at all? Why did John get sick and Sarah stay healthy?

FIGURE 0.2. Ms. Nguyen's students responded to excerpts from Jenner's written observations about cowpox as a vaccine.

Dr. Jenner's assertion? Can we accept his explanation as scientifically valid?"

The class worked through the first two pieces of evidence together. Before she asked students to read on their own, Ms. Nguyen wanted to provide them with some clues for accessing the eighteenth-century language. She also wanted to model for them the kinds of critical questions they should be considering as they read. She read each quote aloud and then engaged students in the process of thinking through the explanation. "Let's take it one sentence at a time," she suggested, and then used prompts like these to guide students: "Tell me what it means in your own words." "Pay attention to his choice of words." "How is he relating those two pieces of information?" "What do you think he's asserting?" Once satisfied that students understood the intent of Jenner's statement, Ms. Nguyen pushed them to consider alternative explanations: "Are there any other ways that information could be interpreted?" "What evidence might Dr. Jenner have missed?" "Is this conclusive proof?"

Ms. Nguyen then released students to work with peer partners to read through and interrogate the remaining quotes. She moved around the room to answer questions about unfamiliar language, encourage thoughtful collaboration between peers, and remind students to probe for weaknesses in the evidence and consider alternative explanations (see question prompts, Figure 0.3). "I want them to hear those questions in their heads," she told me after the class had ended. "I want them to practice using them now so that when they encounter journal articles or reports of science in the popular media later they can critically analyze the claim and the evidence."

She went on to explain the thinking behind this lesson more generally: "Dr. Jenner's treatise is a great example of scientific inquiry at work," she told me. "He states his claim and then methodically lays out his evidence, case by case. It's a lot less dense than a modern medical journal article, but it follows the same basic principles. It's great for beginning biology students because they can read the cases and analyze the evidence just like Jenner's contemporaries likely did. And it also helps us to springboard into our unit on viruses and the immune system. By the time they open their textbooks, these students have already developed an initial understanding of immune

---

Interrogating Science Texts: Questions to Consider

1. **Comprehend the statement**
   - What has been observed?
2. **Understand the explanation**
   - How are the observations connected?
   - What is the author asserting?
3. **Interrogate the text**
   - Are there other ways that the observations could be explained?
   - What evidence might we be missing?

FIGURE 0.3. Ms. Nguyen provided students with prompts to guide their work with Jenner's text.

reactions. They're able to make connections between Jenner's work and present-day scientific understanding. It makes the content reading much more meaningful."

After about twenty minutes, a change in the noise level in the room indicated that most students had finished interrogating the reading. Ms. Nguyen called the class together. "What do you think?" she queried. "Does Dr. Jenner's evidence support his assertion? Should we accept his explanation that being inoculated with cowpox will protect people against smallpox?"

"I think so," a student near the back of the room volunteered. "The cases seem pretty convincing. In each of them someone gets sick with cowpox and then later doesn't get sick with smallpox."

"I don't know," another student countered. "The results weren't always consistent. Some people who'd had cowpox didn't get sick at all with smallpox, while others got high fevers. How can you be sure that you would be safe?"

"Okay, yeah, some of the people got sick," a young woman responded. "But at least no one died of the disease. The worst that happens in each of these cases is a bad fever and rash. We know smallpox was deadly. So even if the cowpox makes you only partially resistant, it's still worth it if it keeps you alive."

The discussion went on like this for several minutes with consensus growing that the preponderance of the evidence was in Dr. Jenner's favor. Ms. Nguyen then returned to her earlier question. "Based on these observations, would you allow Dr. Jenner to inoculate you with cowpox? What would you advise Mr. Phipps? Should he let Dr. Jenner inoculate his son?"

The students hesitated. Although most believed that the connection between cowpox and smallpox had merit, they were still hesitant to act on this belief. "I think maybe I'd want him to do it to someone else first," one student said, speaking for much of the class. "Someone nearby. Then I could watch and see what happened for myself before I'd agree to do it."

Ms. Nguyen explained that Dr. Jenner did indeed go on to vaccinate James Phipps with cowpox, which caused a slight fever but no great illness. Later, when he was repeatedly exposed to smallpox, James Phipps showed no signs of infection. This event, along with the other evidence that Dr. Jenner had collected, eventually helped to convince the Royal Medical Society that vaccination with cowpox would protect people against smallpox, and in 1840 the British government began providing the vaccinations free of charge. In 1980 the World Health Organization declared that smallpox had been eradicated.

Before the bell rang to end the period, Ms. Nguyen had one final request. "I want to go back to the question that framed our discussion: How do we know when to accept an explanation as scientifically valid? Dr. Jenner faced a lot of skepticism and a lot of questions, but it turned out that he was right about cowpox and smallpox. Should people just have accepted what he said? Or were they right to question him? When should we decide that a claim is scientifically valid?"

"I think that they should have questioned him," a young woman near the front of the room commented.

"Just because someone says it is true, you can't automatically believe it. If we did that then there'd be a lot of problems because a lot of people could make mistakes or jump to conclusions that weren't valid."

"I agree," responded a young man. "It's like someone said earlier, you can't just believe it because there's one or two examples. You have to question and you have to be able to see lots of evidence."

Eric, the young man who had volunteered to reach his hand inside the ice chest at the beginning of the period, got the last word. "I don't know that we can ever know for sure that something is going to be absolutely true all of the time. But if there's a lot of evidence and if a lot of scientists examine the evidence and ask questions and no other possibilities seem likely, then it seems like you have to accept it. If we never accepted new explanations then we'd never have any progress."

Characteristics of Classrooms That Support Reading for Learning

Content classrooms that effectively use reading to support content learning, such as the one profiled in the preceding vignette, share several common characteristics. These characteristics, which will be described in the following sections, are grounded in educational theory and research. They don't look the same in every classroom or content area, but they inform the manner in which teachers plan and organize instruction and assess student learning across disciplines. These characteristics provide a foundation for the concepts, strategies, and classroom examples that are described in the later chapters of this book. An understanding of these characteristics helps teachers integrate reading as a critical part of content teaching and learning and prevents strategies from becoming isolated activities.

The Goal Is Understanding

In the widely read curriculum design text *Understanding by Design*, educators Grant Wiggins and Jay McTighe (2005) differentiate between knowledge and understanding. Knowledge, they argue, is having command of a set of facts that can be used to respond on cue to prompting by others. Understanding, on the other hand, is less concerned about individual pieces of knowledge and is more focused on mastery of the core concepts of a discipline. Someone who has understanding is able to strategically interact with new information and ideas, recognize the meaning and relevance of material, make connections, ask questions, and articulate the reasoning behind their assertions.

important to have both

Content reading that supports content learning provides opportunities for students to develop their understanding. The texts that are selected and the lessons that are designed to incorporate those texts work in support of learning about and interacting with the core concepts of the discipline. Reading is not done simply in the service of acquiring information; indeed, if that is the only purpose for reading, it can be argued that there are more efficient and effective means of gathering facts (Fisher & Frey, 2008). Instead, content reading for content learning opens opportunities for students to build conceptual understanding through critical analysis and application.

In the earlier example, Ms. Nguyen responded to the goal of building understanding by encouraging her students to interrogate Dr. Jenner's assertions. She wanted them to develop a conceptual understanding of viruses and the immune system and to understand the nature of scientific inquiry. Many students graduate from high school not realizing that science is a process and that our understanding of science is always evolving. This unfortunate reality is a by-product of courses and texts that present scientific knowledge as something to be memorized and regurgitated (J. J. Gallagher, 2007). Ms. Nguyen designed her lesson to counter that perception. By exposing her students to Dr. Jenner's writing and having them interrogate his claims, she provided opportunities for them to recognize that the theories we accept as valid today were once up for debate. She reinforced this lesson during subsequent class meetings by providing opportunities to examine other scientific studies, both past and present, and encouraging students to maintain a similarly skeptical stance when they were collecting and analyzing data in their own lab activities. For those students who decide to pursue advanced study of science in college and beyond, this kind of work prepares them to participate in the discourse of the scientific community. And for all students, regardless of what field they choose to pursue, critical reading of texts teaches them to be thoughtful consumers of popular scientific information and more appreciative of the rigorous examination that ideas are subjected to before they are recognized as accepted theories.

Teaching for understanding requires that teachers have a clear vision of their learning goals when planning lessons, selecting texts, and implementing instruction. Ms. Nguyen's lesson was powerful not only because she had found a great text, but also because she was able to engage students with that text in a manner that supported her learning goals. She followed what Wiggins and McTighe (2005) describe as a "backward design" approach, beginning her planning with the end in mind. She knew she wanted students to understand the core concept of scientific inquiry. She crafted a powerful essential question around which to build her lesson: "How do we know when to accept an explanation as scientifically valid?" And then she planned learning experiences that would allow her students to explore this question with richly layered materials appropriate to her content standards. Wiggins and McTighe advocate for the use of essential questions as a means to maintaining a deliberate focus on the big ideas of the discipline. Other strategies for maintaining focus on core concepts when planning instruction and selecting texts include organizing around case studies, an approach increasingly common in medicine, law, and other professional schools, and building units that focus on project-based learning (Thomas, 2000; Markham, Larmer, & Ravitz, 2003).

Instruction Is Inquiry Driven

Classrooms that use reading to support content learning are grounded in an inquiry stance. Inquiry approaches to instruction build on work by cognition researchers, including Bruner (1966), Piaget (1971), and Vygotsky (1962), who argue that learning does not take place by transmission of information from teacher to student, but rather through student engagement with new ideas and information in a manner that allows the construction of individual and community understanding. Facilitating this construction of understanding in the classroom means that we, as teachers, need to ask authentic questions or pose real-world problems that are appropriate to our field and engaging for our students. And that we then need to allow students to investigate those questions and problems through reading, writing, problem solving, discussion, and debate (Brooks & Brooks, 1999).

Ms. Nguyen's use of the Jenner text illustrates the application of an inquiry approach. Before the students began reading, she posed a dilemma: "There's a deadly disease out there. Do you take a risk and expose yourself to a potential treatment?" She encouraged students to take a position in response to the dilemma. She required them to interrogate potential supporting evidence in the reading. And, in subsequent lessons, she helped students make connections between the Jenner text and current informational readings on present-day scientific knowledge. During these lessons, students read materials not to answer questions at the end of the textbook, but to respond to a real concern and to weigh the validity of potential evidence.

Strong inquiry provides guided opportunities for students to engage with an authentic question or concern, learn more about that question or concern, connect their new learning to their existing schema, and respond in a manner that is appropriate for the content and audience. Engaging students in inquiry provides real reasons for reading texts and engaging with classroom material. It increases students' motivation for reading by tapping into intrinsic curiosity and a desire to learn rather than relying solely on extrinsic threats and rewards (Deci, 1996; Jensen, 2005). Reading the text matters not just because a teacher tells them to read it, but because the texts address compelling questions that have resonance both within and beyond the classroom.

Reading Opportunities Are Authentic

In classrooms where content reading supports content learning, reading opportunities reflect the real-world work of practitioners within the discipline. Students read texts and ask questions that approximate what the experts do. In history classrooms, for example, students don't just read the history textbook; they engage with primary source documents as well. In a math class, knowledge gained from reading procedural texts applies beyond the problem set at the end of the chapter and connects to real-world applications. Texts are read critically, with an understanding that no text is neutral, that every reading contains bias, and that readers need to consider multiple interpretations (Alvermann, Moon, & Hagood, 1999; G. Johnson, 1999).

The concept of authenticity within the school setting has gained popularity in recent years in response to several important influences. Nancie Atwell, in her seminal work *In the Middle* (1998), built on research by Donald Graves (2003) and Donald Murray (2003), among others, to emphasize the idea that students should read and write as real-world readers and writers. She encouraged classroom structures and instructional techniques that would allow for students to talk about their reading, receive focused strategy lessons, revise and publish their writing, and, perhaps most important, have time to read, write, talk, and think within the school day.

Deborah Meier (2002), working to recraft secondary education at Central Park East Secondary School in New York, and Ted Sizer (2004), founder and director of a network of small schools called the Coalition of Essential Schools, emphasized the role of authenticity in assessment. They called on schools to engage students in real-world projects, portfolios, and presentations—to use performance-based assessments to drive the curriculum in the school rather than continue to be beholden to external and artificial tests. *agree!*

Increasingly, content educators have followed the examples of Atwell, Meier, and Sizer and have suggested that engaging students as historians, scientists, mathematicians, and artists will provide more meaningful learning opportunities and better prepare students to participate in academic and professional communities. Nearly all discipline-based state standards, as well as content standards adopted by national professional associations such as the National Council of Teachers of Mathematics (NCTM), National Science Teachers Association (NSTA), and the National Council for the Social Studies (NCSS), include specific process standards that address the need to prepare students in the *ways of thinking* within the discipline.

In the preceding example, Ms. Nguyen worked to introduce her students to ways of thinking appropriate to science. They read and responded to Dr. Jenner's recorded observations, weighed the evidence, and considered alternatives. Such practices align with the work of scientists reviewing research studies prior to publication. Before findings are accepted as credible and are ready for publication, they must go through a peer-review process and be scrutinized against scientifically acceptable norms. Although Ms. Nguyen's students certainly weren't Jenner's peers, they nevertheless were engaging in a similar process.

Instruction Is Explicit

Content teachers who effectively use reading to support content learning provide explicit instruction in the skills, strategies, and ways of thinking used within the discipline. Many of us, steeped in our fields for years of study (and having chosen our fields because we were comfortable and confident within the subject area), don't realize just how much cognitive skill goes into the process of investigating a topic, solving a problem, or reading a content-specific text. We assume that if we can do it, students should be able to do it too if we provide them with easier investigations, less rigorous problems, or shorter texts. But simply assigning "easier" material does not necessarily make the cognitive tasks less complex, nor support students in learning the skills they need to become proficient in the skills, strategies, and ways of thinking of the discipline. Kylene Beers, a reading researcher who works with underperforming students, writes,

> It is important to remember that we can teach students how to comprehend texts. We shouldn't assume that if we simply explain what something means, students will automatically know how to comprehend other texts. To help dependent readers become independent readers, we must teach them what many of us, as independent readers, do with seemingly little effort. We must teach them strategies that will help them understand texts. (2003, pp. 40–41)

Effectively teaching students how to comprehend and respond to a text involves the following elements.

A Clear and Narrow Focus

Readers don't have to read, analyze, apply, and respond to a whole text all at once. The strongest learning occurs when students have multiple opportunities to engage with challenging texts and can gradually work to uncover meaning. Focus students' reading on a single task for each reading. In Ms. Nguyen's class, students read first to paraphrase information into their own words, and then returned for a second reading to evaluate the strength of the evidence and consider alternate explanations. By focusing on one cognitive task at a time, students are able to dig deeper into material and develop a stronger understanding of the texts and content concepts (J. Allen, 1995, 2000).

Opportunities for Modeling and Application

If students are to begin to approximate the behaviors and ways of thinking of content experts, they need to see content experts at work. In the classroom, this means that we must model our processes of reading, thinking, and making sense of texts. We need to think out loud about our process, guiding students through the steps that we go through to make meaning of text. Nancie Atwell refers to this type of classroom demonstration as "taking off the top of my head," and describes it as a critical part of making the invisible and often confusing process of reading accessible for students (1998). Ms. Nguyen took off the top of her head by modeling the questions that a good reader asks. She encouraged student input through an interactive read-aloud and then provided opportunities for them to use the same questions to guide their independent reading. Close connection between the teacher's model and targeted application opportunities helps set up students for success in using reading to support content learning.

Assessment *for* Learning

There is a critical difference between assessment *of* learning and assessment *for* learning. Traditionally in content classrooms we have used the former approach. We teach a series of lessons, assign a number of readings or problem sets, and then give a final assessment. That test, essay, or project is assumed to represent a student's learning, the student is assigned a grade, and then we move on to the next unit. The difficulty with this approach is that too much gets wrapped up in that one final assessment. Success is determined by multiple factors, including how well students took notes, read texts, and listened to lectures and how well they were able to represent their understanding on the test, essay, or project, as well as how they felt that day and how distracted they were from the conversation they just had in the hallway during passing period. It can be nearly impossible, based on an end-of-unit summative assessment, to parse out what students know and are able to do, what new challenges they are prepared for, and where they might need additional support. Not to mention the fact that, at the end of the unit, it's time to move on and there's not usually an opportunity to go back and respond to student strengths and needs from the previous unit anyway.

Assessment *for* learning, also known as formative assessment, describes activities that take place as a regular part of classroom instruction and that allow us to assess student learning in progress. Assessments for learning help us recognize what students have mastered and where they need help. They allow us to respond by working to shore up areas of weakness and build on areas of strength within the unit before we move on to new concepts or skill learning. Educational Testing Service researchers Leahy, Lyon, Thompson, and Wiliam note,

> In a classroom that uses assessment to support learning, the divide between instruction and assessment blurs. Everything students do . . . is a potential source

of information about how much they understand. The teacher who uses assessment to support learning takes in this information, analyzes it, and makes instructional decisions that address the understandings and misunderstandings that these assessments reveal (2005, p. 19).

Teachers who effectively use reading to support content learning build assessment for learning into their classrooms. They use assessment to identify challenges in comprehension, recognize where conceptual understanding breaks down, and track student progress in learning to analyze texts and apply learning. Ms. Nguyen, for example, was able to use students' responses to Dr. Jenner's quotes to assess how well they could read and understand the technical writing used in the text, consider explanations, and ask critical questions. That information helped her to recognize students' strengths and weaknesses, design future whole-class instruction, and provide targeted support to individuals or groups of students who needed additional assistance.

Thinking about Thinking

It is likely impossible to fully prepare students with all of the scientific, mathematical, historical, artistic, and other discipline-related knowledge that they might need throughout their lives. Even if time were not an issue and students came ready to learn every day, there is simply too much subject-area knowledge for students to learn everything. What we can do, however, is teach students how to learn within our disciplines. This requires teaching processes, showing them how to inquire, and modeling the processes of content experts. It also requires stepping back with some regularity to have students reflect on their own learning and development. At the end of Ms. Nguyen's lesson, she asked students to reflect on the essential question, How do we know when to accept an explanation as scientifically valid? In later lessons, after the class interrogates other journal articles or analyzes their own research data, she would revisit the question, and would push students to reflect on their evolving understanding by asking: How has your thinking changed? What caused the change? What questions or concerns do you still have? The metacognitive process of thinking about thinking, recognizing and responding to strengths and weaknesses in our own learning, and adapting our knowledge and skills to fit new circumstances helps students learn more within the confines of our classroom and empowers them to become independent learners once they leave us.

A Preview of What's to Come

The chapters that follow in this text provide specific suggestions for effectively using reading to support learning in the content classroom. Chapter 1 addresses text selection and the need to choose readings that are central to the focus of study, authentic to the content, and accessible for students. Chapter 2 focuses on preparing students to be successful in their reading by providing a context and purpose. Chapter 3 examines four ways to support comprehension. Chapter 4 addresses the development of academic language. And Chapter 5 describes techniques for moving beyond basic comprehension to deepen students' conceptual understanding through analysis and application. Each of these chapters includes specific strategies and classroom examples that detail strategies in use. At the end of Chapters 2 through 5, you'll find a special section that addresses assessment strategies, learnings, and next steps for the classroom examples highlighted in the chapter.

The ideas and information in the chapters build on a solid foundation of reading research and learning theory. In addition, they reflect my experience as a classroom teacher, instructional coach, and education professor. Over the past fifteen years, I've taught high school history and middle school math. I've also worked as a math resource teacher and a literacy coach, and I currently teach at the university level. Since leaving my own secondary school classroom seven years ago, I've been privileged to have the opportunity to observe, teach, co-teach alongside, and provide support for middle and high school teachers in a range of disciplines.

Having a diverse set of experiences working in a range of roles and content areas has helped me to appreciate the multiple ways in which content teachers can be effective. The strategies profiled in this text are not one-size-fits-all prescriptions. The examples are not recipes to be copied. Teachers should adapt the ideas and approaches to fit the demands of their content areas and the particular needs of their students. There are many ways to support student learning in the classroom. I hope that this text will provide a few new ideas to add to your repertoire.

Selecting Texts

What You'll Find in This Chapter

Selecting texts: The chapter begins with a discussion of text selection and provides three criteria to consider when selecting texts: content, authenticity, and accessibility.

Classroom vignette: Teaching in the Cracks in the History Classroom

Preparing texts: The second section of the chapter discusses strategies for preparing texts to make them more accessible for students.

Classroom vignette: Preparing Texts in the Civics Classroom

The role of the textbook: The final section of the chapter discusses the challenges and opportunities presented by textbooks. Strategies and examples are provided for effectively using the textbook as a resource in the content classroom.

Classroom vignettes: Using the Textbook as a Resource (in Social Studies, Science, Math, and History)

Selecting Texts

As a beginning teacher, I was assigned to teach two different courses: tenth-grade world history and ninth-grade area studies. The tenth-grade course came with a class set of textbooks and a sizable collection of publisher-produced reproducible textbook support materials. The ninth-grade course came with no text and no support materials. As a novice teacher, not having a textbook was intimidating. I was on my own to figure out what to do with those students every day. But it was also liberating. I was free to choose what we studied and to design the curriculum and select the readings that best fit with the students' interests and abilities and best met the goals of the course. As that first year went along, I noticed that my ninth-grade students were generally more engaged and responsive during class; and at the end of the year, they demonstrated greater academic growth than the tenth graders. Although there were certainly many possible explanations for this difference, I'm convinced that having access to a wider range of reading materials and having opportunities to read and interact with content texts that fit their interests and abilities played a significant role in supporting the ninth graders' engagement and success in learning.

Teaching is about design (Wiggins & McTighe, 2005). Teachers design learning experiences to support students in meeting the goals of the content, the school, and the state standards. As teachers, we have unique expertise: we are at the nexus of understanding the needs of our students and the demands of the content. No one is better positioned to craft learning experiences that support the academic growth of the particular students in our classrooms. That's a weighty responsibility, but it is also a wonderful opportunity. If we position ourselves as the design experts in our classrooms, then we get to take ownership of our planning and instruction.

One critical component of instructional design is text selection. The texts that we choose can have a significant impact on the success, or failure, of a lesson. Texts that are purposefully selected, that allow students to further their understanding of the content being studied, and that are engaging and accessible can go a long way toward providing a meaningful learning experience for students. On the other hand, texts that are too difficult, too long, too boring, too biased, or too tangential are unlikely to engage even the most dedicated students in meaningful learning. If we are to be successful designers, we need to be as thoughtful about the texts we select as we are about preparing for other aspects of our lessons.

This idea seems obvious, but in an age of standardized tests and mandated curricula it can appear difficult to achieve. Many teachers rely on survey texts to expose students to material they may not get to in class. Some districts and administrators require the use of specific text materials that "cover" the standards. While sometimes assigning such texts is necessary, if we limit content reading to these materials we are limiting students' opportunities for learning. Textbooks and other survey reading materials are notoriously difficult to read and rarely hold the reader's interest over the course of a chapter or unit (Barr, 2006). Students are unlikely to develop meaningful understanding of the core concepts in the text or retain the information and ideas it contains if the assigned reading prioritizes breadth over depth and is not connected, in some meaningful way, to interactive debate, analysis, or discussion.

On a recent Saturday afternoon, I struck up a conversation with a high school–age referee at the field where my middle son had a soccer game. She was personable and outgoing when I asked her about school. She explained that she'd always been a good student, but that things were really hard this year. Her teachers were assigning twenty to thirty pages of reading per night for each class. "I try to do it," she explained, "but it's really frustrating. I feel like I can't keep up. There's just too much and I can't remember most of what I read." I then asked her about her favorite class. Her eyes lit up. "I love my science class," she enthused. "We do all kinds of projects. Like right now we're doing a C.S.I. project where we have to investigate a crime scene and do research on the different kinds of tests that investigators do to solve the crime." "So do you have reading for that class?" I asked. "Yeah. There's a lot of reading, and not just the textbook, but lab reports and journals and stuff. But it's interesting. It's like there's a purpose for reading it."

This student's science teacher had found a way to "teach in the cracks" (Short, Schroeder, Kauffman, & Kaser, 2005). Rather than limiting course readings to the survey texts and mandated curricula, he was successfully carving out time and space to go beyond the required material and introduce texts that were authentic to the content and meaningful to the students. Nichols (2009) describes this as layering texts, engaging students in multiple readings on the same topic to build deep conceptual understanding. This process may start with the required reading material and then go on to other, richer texts that provide more detail, new ideas, and alternative perspectives. Although time limitations and various district requirements prevent all topics from being taught in such a manner, if we dig "postholes" on even just a few topics, students will begin to recognize the rich possibilities of learning within our disciplines (Brown, 1996; Scheurman, 2008).

Teaching in the Cracks in the History Classroom

For his annual westward expansion unit, Mr. Gonzalez organizes his planning and instruction around the concept of progress. He challenges his eighth-grade students to consider the essential question, "Is progress always a good thing?" Students are encouraged to think carefully about this concept as they examine the Lewis and Clark expedition, the settlement of the Great Plains, and the expulsion of Native Americans. By looking at the question in multiple contexts and through multiple lenses, Mr. Gonzalez hopes that students will come to understand that progress has costs as well as benefits and that not all individuals and groups gain from progress in equal measure.

Mr. Gonzalez supports his careful unit planning with purposeful text selection. "I have a lot of students who are struggling readers, and we only have a limited amount of time for this unit," he explains. "So I have to be thoughtful in what I choose for readings."

He begins the unit with an interactive reading of the district-mandated textbook. Because many students struggle with the text, Mr. Gonzalez actively guides their reading, directing them toward the information and ideas that best connect with his unit focus. "I use the textbook to lay a foundation for the documents to come," he explains.

The class then engages in reading a range of historical documents that provide multiple perspectives on the concept of progress. Readings include a first-person account by a homesteader who was part of the great westward resettlement, an account of the Trail of Tears from a Cherokee perspective, a portion of the Indian Removal Act legislation, and an excerpt from a historian's analysis of the new status women and former slaves achieved in the West. The texts offer in-depth accounts of the diverse experiences of Americans during westward expansion and encourage students to consider the concept of progress through multiple lenses. In addition, they provide opportunities for Mr. Gonzalez to address issues of bias, point of view, and the students' role as active readers.

Mr. Gonzalez admits that the process of purposefully selecting texts can be time consuming, but believes that it is worth the effort. "I have more fun and the kids have more fun with these texts. And they learn more. At the end of the unit, we have a debate about whether or not westward expansion was a good thing. That's when I can tell that they've really developed an understanding of the time period and internalized the texts. They become incredibly passionate arguing on behalf of the people and communities affected by the movement west. To me, that passion is what teaching is all about."

When we teach in the cracks and purposefully choose our texts, we need to consider three key questions. These questions are supportive of and responsive to the characteristics of effective content reading outlined in the introduction.

1. Does this text respond to core concepts of the content?

2. Is this form of text authentic to the subject area?

3. Will students be able to access this text?

Does This Text Respond to Core Concepts of the Content?

The texts we select in the classroom should respond to the core concepts that we want students to understand. Selected texts need to provide opportunities for students to deepen their understanding of concepts by exploring, explaining, demonstrating, or challenging the topic under investigation. If a text contains information that is interesting but tangential; if it provides background information that could be more efficiently addressed through a targeted mini-lecture, slide show, or demonstration; or even if it contains valuable content, but we don't intend to provide opportunities for students to analyze the ideas or apply the information from the text, then the text is likely better set aside in favor of using time more thoughtfully to engage students in more purposeful content reading.

Reading a text takes time, and our time in the classroom is too limited to spend on texts that don't have high instructional value. I have, on more occasions than I'd like to admit, trapped myself into a no-win situation by photo-copying and passing out something that I thought might be a quick, interesting reading on a topic tangentially connected to the unit we were studying. For example, during a geometry unit on triangles, I once distributed an article about the Greek philosopher Pythagoras and suggested that students read it on their own after completing the regular class work. When students, unsurprisingly, resisted doing extra work for which they saw no purpose, I was stuck with two unappealing alternatives: I could take more class time to engage students with this text in a way that would support learning (and thereby attempt to mitigate the by-now all too clear appearance that I didn't really think through what I was doing), or I could cut my losses and tell the students to read the text for home-work, a task that few would complete and almost none would remember when pressed for details during the end-of-unit test.

It is this kind of experience that leads many teachers to give up on reading in the content classroom. If students are so resistant to reading, why don't we just find other ways to access course content? This reaction is understandable, but unnecessary. When texts are purposefully selected to reflect the core con-cepts of the content, such as in the example from Mr. Gonzalez's history class, they provide unique opportunities for students to explore the topic and acquire discipline-based ways of thinking.

Is This Form of Text Authentic to the Subject Area?

A second question to consider when selecting text addresses the authenticity of the material: is it a text that "real" historians, scientists, mathematicians, artists, athletes, or performers would read? Although the content and difficulty of the text may be somewhat different, the genres that students read should reflect the kinds of texts that their academic mentors might encounter. The opportunity to interact with a range of such texts supports the inquiry stance discussed in the introduction and supports students' content literacy development (Brozo & Hargis, 2003). In addition, the chance to read authentic texts positions students to develop a deep understanding of the nature of study in the content area.

In history, for example, if our classrooms are to mirror the field of study, then our students should read primary sources, including newspaper articles, legal documents, personal accounts, and propaganda, to gain a firsthand telling of the past. Secondary sources, written by scholars to characterize or analyze a particu-lar aspect of history, can provide thoughtful insights to help round out students' developing understanding of an event or time period. Tertiary sources, such as textbooks, encyclopedias, dictionaries, and handbooks, can provide helpful information to fill in gaps in students' knowledge base. Taken together, these many forms of text provide students with access to a process of meaning making that is at the core of the study of history. They allow students to engage in an inquiry into the past, construct their own understanding of people and events, interpret actions and reactions, question others' interpretations, and reevaluate their own perceptions (Drake & Nelson, 2009).

Without access to such varied texts, the study of history, however well presented, is reduced to a single, set narrative in which knowledge is objective and stable (Cohen, 1988; Wineburg, 2001). But academics who study the field view history as anything but objective and stable. To them, historical understanding is a human construction, an "imaginative reconstruction of vanished events" (Becker, 1932). And written history is seen as "a dialogue among historians not only about what happened, but about why and how it happened, how it affected other happenings, and how much importance it ought to be assigned" (National Center for History in the Schools, 1996). When primary, secondary, and tertiary documents are thoughtfully used in the history classroom, students are allowed access to this dialogue. And reading takes on a much more significant purpose. It "is not merely a way to learn new information but becomes a way to engage in new kinds of thinking" (Wineburg, 2001).

Each content area has text genres that are unique to that area (see Table 1.1 for examples). The balance between types of documents will vary based on the nature of the content and the topic under investigation. Given time restrictions and content requirements, not all topics can be afforded a range of text exploration. However, over the course of a unit or a semester, it is important to students' content learning and literacy development that they have the opportunity to interact with a variety of genres authentic to the content.

Will Students Be Able to Access This Text?

A third factor to consider when selecting texts for the content-area classroom is the accessibility of the material. Typically, accessibility discussions for content classes have focused around textbook reading levels. Textbook publishers and state or district textbook selection committees use standardized formulas to determine the "readability" of the textbook. The most prominent of these is the Fry Readability Graph (Fry, 1977). Using two variables, sentence length and word length, this graph predicts the difficulty of the reading material, from first grade through college. Sentence length is determined by the number of sentences per one hundred words. Word length is determined by the number of words per one hundred syllables. The more sentences and words in the given selections of text, the easier the material is to read.

TABLE 1.1. Examples of Authentic Content-Specific Text Sources

History	**Primary Source Documents:** These are produced at the time of the event to which they relate. Examples: declarations, laws, treaties, court decisions, speeches, eyewitness accounts, letters, diaries, and inscriptions. **Secondary Source Documents:** These are produced by historians, social scientists, or historical observers. They relate or discuss information originally presented elsewhere. Secondary sources often involve generalization, analysis, synthesis, interpretation, or evaluation of the original information. Examples: books, journal articles, magazine articles, and historical analyses. **Tertiary Source Documents:** These are selections, distillations, summaries, or compilations of primary and/or secondary sources. They are often intended as reference materials. Examples: textbooks, encyclopedias, dictionaries, handbooks, bibliographies, library catalogs, and survey articles.
Science	**Technical Science:** Scientific journal articles, laboratory reports, statements by governing boards and scientific bodies, online data, and background information. **Popular Science:** Magazine articles, newspaper articles, weblogs, trade books, reference texts, and science fiction stories.
Mathematics	**Developing Mathematical Understanding:** Narrative representations of mathematical concepts. These may be found in the form of mathematical theorems or mathematical proofs in journal articles, textbooks, and scientific, engineering, or other trade publications. **Problem Solving:** Narrative descriptions of data sets and problems to be solved. These may take the form of traditional textbook-based word problems or may be more open-ended when problem solving responds to information gathered via media sources such as newspapers or magazines, laboratory notebooks, online simulations, or tracking software.
World Languages	**Literature:** Novels, short stories, poetry, dramatic texts, graphic novels, and picture books. **Expository Text:** Information books, newspaper and magazine articles, editorials and opinion pieces, government documents, letters, and narrative accounts. **Mass Media and Consumer Documents:** Advertisements, websites, propaganda, instruction manuals, signs, and forms.
Visual and Performing Arts	**Original Materials:** Scripts, screenplays, directors' notes, composers' notes, and production notes. **Critical Analysis:** Critical reviews, scholarly analyses, artists' biographies, autobiographies and memoirs, and historical and contemporary texts to provide context for artistic development. **Craft Development:** Manuals, guides, and skill development texts.
Athletics	**Studying the Game:** Manuals, rulebooks, and strategy guides. **Learning from the Competition:** Biographies, autobiographies, newspaper and magazine accounts, and postgame analyses. **Developing Your Game:** Physical fitness and nutrition guides, skill development books, and equipment analyses.

Although such formulas do provide some relevant information, their reliability is limited and they should not be considered as the only determinants when choosing texts (Nelson, 1978; Vacca & Vacca, 2008). As the classroom teacher, you know your students' interests, their strengths, and the potential challenges they may encounter in a reading. Rather than rely on a somewhat arbitrary reading level when selecting texts for your students, take into account the following factors:

1. *Text structure:* Texts that are specifically organized to support comprehension are often called *considerate* texts (Armbruster & Anderson, 1981). Considerate texts may exhibit the following characteristics:

   • New concepts are introduced one at a time.
   • Concrete examples are provided to support abstract concepts.
   • Complex relationships are explicitly stated.
   • Titles, headings, and/or introductory paragraphs preview the major ideas.
   • Photos, charts, or other visual aids support the main ideas or highlight important information.
   • Irrelevant details are avoided

   Texts that do not exhibit the above characteristics are *inconsiderate*. Typically, the more considerate the text, the more accessible it will be for student readers. Be aware, however, that the presence of chapter headings and visuals does not automatically imply that a text is easy to read. If text features are not thoughtfully planned out for their intended audience or if there is just too much material on a page, the features can be distracting and detract from students' ability to comprehend the material.

2. *Writing style:* A text that is written in a familiar tone, uses a narrative approach, and provides clear illustrations is generally more readily understood. Texts written for academic audiences, materials that date from previous centuries, and/or readings that were translated from other languages tend to be more difficult. Legal briefs and opinions, scientific journal articles, and official proclamations are some of the most challenging texts for students to read as they are often heavy on jargon and tend to make use of unfamiliar structures and stylistic devices. Such language and structure is necessary within an academic, legal, or scientific community in order to assert findings more powerfully and avoid potential counterarguments or loopholes. However, for novice historians, scientists, mathematicians, or

artists, the seemingly repetitive and often verbose nature of the documents make them quite difficult to understand.

3. *Language:* There is a direct relationship between the difficulty of the words in a text and the reader's comprehension of that text (M. F. Graves, 1986; Anderson & Freebody, 1981). Counting the number of syllables in words is one indication of the difficulty of language, but it is not enough to fully appreciate comprehension challenges and expectations. Unfamiliar vocabulary can come in words of varying lengths. Words that are specific to a subject or topic, words that require precise definitions in order to be fully understood within the context of the reading, words that have multiple meanings in different subject areas, and words that are generally unfamiliar to students' language use make comprehension more challenging (Nagy, 1988). Obviously, the more unfamiliar words present in a text, the more difficult comprehension becomes. (Note: A more in-depth discussion of the challenges of language can be found in Chapter 4.)

4. *Students' prior knowledge and interest:* Reading is, at its foundation, an interaction between the reader and the text. An analysis of the text can provide us with some indicators of comprehension challenges and possibilities. But to fully appreciate the potential for student understanding, we must consider what they bring to the text. If students are familiar with and interested in a topic, they will be able to understand more complex texts on that topic. Students' prior knowledge provides them with an understanding of appropriate terminology, framing concepts, and relevant information, which can guide their exploration of new readings on the topic. Furthermore, if they are truly interested in a topic, they are more willing to persevere as they work to make meaning of challenging texts.

So what does all this mean when selecting texts? One thing it does *not* mean is that complexity and challenge should be avoided. To the contrary, it is imperative that we support students' reading development and content-knowledge development by engaging them with rigorous texts (Blau, 2003). Furthermore, if we are to use authentic texts that connect to the core concepts of the content, complex texts are unavoidable. We want students to grapple with the ideas, language, and structures of texts as apprentice content experts. However, we need to be careful not to overwhelm students. As curriculum designers, we need to know the strengths and needs of our students and select texts that will meet them in their proximal zone of development (Vygotsky, 1978), where students are challenged but not overwhelmed, and where content reading can enhance content learning.

Preparing Texts

Judicious preparation of texts can have a tremendous impact on students' ability and willingness to engage with challenging readings. Although it may seem like a minor detail to us, appearances matter to students. If a text looks "friendlier" and appears shorter, they are much more likely to give it a try. A bit of time invested up front in text formatting and editing can yield significant benefits when readings are introduced in the classroom.

Format

Wide margins, large font, and clear structure help prevent adolescent readers from becoming overwhelmed by challenging readings. Providing them with space to write and respond to the text improves comprehension and facilitates thoughtful response. Suggestions for making the format supportive of students' reading success include the following:

- *Font size*: Retype text into 14-point font or use the enlarge feature on the photocopier.
- *Margin space*: Include a wide margin around the edge of the text to allow room for students to make notes and monitor their comprehension as they read.
- *Section breaks:* Chunk text into sections and make the section breaks clear on the page. Being able to see that the assignment has an end (or at least a break) helps build students' stamina.
- *Line numbers:* Numbering lines or paragraphs can make it easier for students to ask clarifying questions and help facilitate later discussions.
- *Graphic organizers:* Prepare for targeted text response by cutting and pasting the text into a chart or matrix that allows room for student response. (Ms. Nguyen used this approach with Dr. Jenner's text, shown in Figure 0.2.) Embedding text in a graphic organizer can be particularly helpful if you're planning to have students work closely with specific quotes. Being able to underline or highlight a portion of text and then respond on the same paper (rather than copy quotes onto a separate page) encourages students to focus on meaning making instead of copying.

Length

Assigning students to read a lengthy text, especially if the text is challenging in its language, content, or structure, can lead to frustration for both teacher and students. However, length is an element over which we can exert some control. We may not control the extent of the original document, but we can choose to excerpt particular passages in order to make the text more accessible for our students.

Rather than providing students with the entire US Constitution, pull out those articles, or parts of articles, that relate most directly to the concepts under investigation. Instead of reading Darwin's complete treatise on evolution, select a few key passages that students can examine closely. Thoughtful selection of portions of complex texts such as these can allow students access to important concepts and authentic texts.

Of course, it is necessary to ensure that the text is not manipulated so dramatically that the intended meaning is lost. Be aware of your own bias when editing down a text, and make sure that you are not selecting passages that provide a skewed picture of the text or the author.

When students know that there is only a limited amount to read, they are more willing to dig in to grapple with meaning and analyze significance. The focus is on understanding the reading rather than getting through the reading. As the following example illustrates, shorter texts can lead to greater understanding.

Preparing Texts in the Civics Classroom

Mr. Egan thought that he had trimmed down the text of the Supreme Court decisions enough. His ninth-grade civics class was immersed in a unit on crime and punishment in the United States, with a particular focus on the merit of the death penalty. For this day's lesson, they were examining the Supreme Court's 2004 ruling abolishing the death penalty for minors. Mr. Egan wanted the students to explore the debate within the Court and had pulled portions of Justice Kennedy's majority opinion, as well as portions of the dissenting opinion written by Justice O'Connor. He had been careful to select paragraphs that conveyed the crux of the pro and con arguments. In doing so, he'd trimmed lengthy legal arguments down to just one and one-half pages of single-spaced text (see Figure 1.1).

As students attempted to slog through references to the Eighth Amendment, previous Court decisions, studies by the American Psychological Association, and America's "evolving standard of decency," it quickly became evident that even at fewer than two pages, the excerpt was too dense and too long. Mr. Egan attempted to support comprehension by rushing around the classroom to answer questions, provide definitions, and paraphrase language, but comprehension still suffered. Students were so bogged down in trying to figure out the unfamiliar language, complex sentences, and unknown references that they lost the larger ideas about justice and morality.

The next day brought change. Mr. Egan's students are on a rotating schedule, and each group of

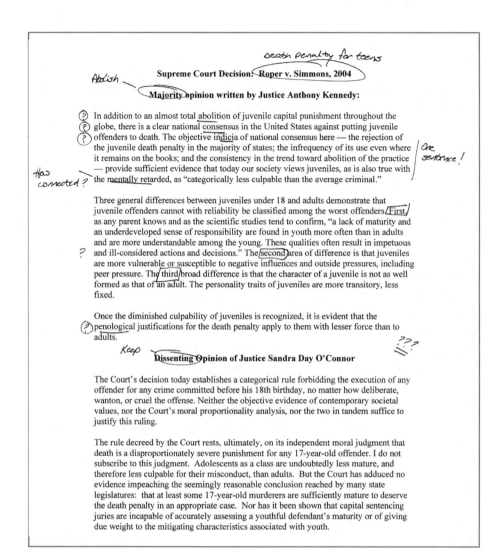

FIGURE 1.1. Mr. Egan gave his first class of students paragraph-length excerpts from Kennedy's and O'Connor's opinions.

students visits his class every other day. Having learned from the previous class, Mr. Egan greeted this second group of students with a much more abbreviated text. Rather than use multiple paragraphs out of each justice's opinions, Mr. Egan had pared down the text to several sentences. Each sentence held the essence of one key argument for that side of the debate (see Figure 1.2). This time around, students worked in groups to dig into each quote. Together they untangled

the language and structure of each sentence in order to paraphrase the justices' arguments. They identified and weighed the merits of the justices' arguments. They compared the opinions and pointed out common themes that had been found in other cases studied in the unit. Mr. Egan wasn't rushing around the classroom frantically this time; instead, he was able to listen in on each group's discussion and ask questions or make comments to deepen their thinking.

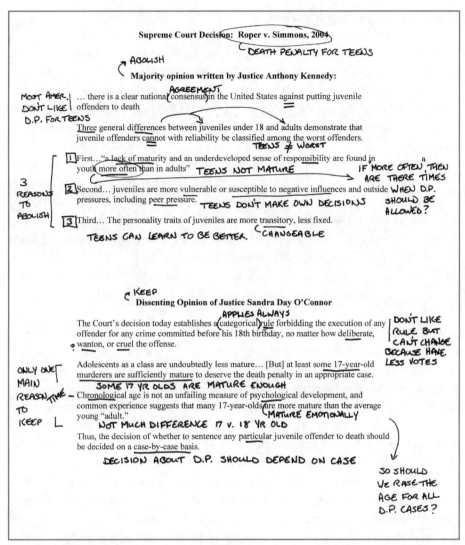

FIGURE 1.2. For his second group of students, Mr. Egan whittled down the Supreme Court opinions to highlight the key parts of the arguments.

Although the students in these two classes were approximately equal in performance on most days, on these days they were decidedly unequal. Later assessments confirmed that shorter text volume allowed for much greater text comprehension. The first day's students had access to longer, more nuanced arguments as penned by the justices. But because the texts were complex and lengthy, students missed both the nuance and the main ideas. The second day's students had access to much less text volume, but thoughtful selection of key quotes and carefully structured text analysis activities allowed students the opportunity to dig in to the excerpts and develop a thoughtful, more nuanced understanding of the ideas themselves.

The Role of the Textbook

Textbooks are an omnipresent fact of life for most content-area teachers. With their glossy covers, encyclopedic coverage, and lengthy list of impressive contributors, they come with an air of authority that can make them seem inerrant. In an era when there is ever-increasing pressure to ensure that students meet all of the content standards, reliance on textbooks can seem appropriate, even necessary.

With so many pressures facing teachers, it would be nice to cede responsibility for content coverage to the textbook and their publishers. However, research on textbooks and their impact on learning cautions against this approach (Barr, 2006; Brozo & Hargis, 2003). Despite all of the money and effort that go into the creation, selection, and purchase of textbooks, they cannot and should not replace the role of the teacher in crafting curriculum.

The "Coverage" Problem

In their efforts to "cover" all the necessary material, textbooks are "long on facts and terms but short on ideas and explanations" (Tyson-Bernstein, 1988, p. 27). This is hardly surprising, given the lengthy standards that textbooks attempt to address, but it is problematic. In crafting textbooks, priority is given to ensuring that all topics are covered. Less importance is placed on the discussion and thoughtful analysis of those topics. As a result, readers often fail to see the connections between topics, understand cause-effect relationships, or recognize the relevance of the textbook topics to their own lives and the world around them.

Furthermore, authoritative listing of facts leaves students with the impression that content learning is all about memorization. Professional academics, when they infrequently wade into the world of K–12 textbook publishing, consistently criticize the materials as far removed from the real work of historians, scientists, mathematicians, engineers, athletes, and artists. Griffen and Marciano (1979) note, "Through their one-dimensionality textbooks shield students from intellectual encounters with their world that would sharpen their critical abilities." When shielded from controversy by the authoritative, seemingly incontrovertible textbook presentation of facts, students fail to "cultivate puzzlement," a practice that Wineburg (2001) notes is at the heart of academic study.

In addition, the coverage of so many topics in textbooks tends to mask the bias that is inherently present in any text. Regardless of how objective any publisher attempts to be, there are values that frame the decisions about what to include, what to leave out, and how to present the material. Revisit any history textbook from fifty years ago and it is immediately evident that the prevailing prejudices of the time caused women and minorities to be largely ignored. Although much progress has been made in this regard, discrepancies continue. Nonmajority perspectives are still often relegated to textboxes and sidebars. And when these histories do make it into the main body of the text, they are often whitewashed to fit the dominant narrative of a patriotic America (Loewen, 1995). Although it would be nearly impossible to include all relevant narratives and perspectives in any one text, the comprehensive nature of a textbook gives the impression that it contains all necessary information and ideas. Without teacher support, students are unlikely to challenge the textbook and consider alternative perspectives or understandings.

The "Interest" Problem

I have yet to meet a student who tells me that he or she enjoys reading a textbook. And looking back at a few of my own textbooks, it is clear that I didn't enjoy reading them either. My mother returned my Advanced Placement (AP) US history book to me a few years ago. For the first few chapters I had underlined or highlighted nearly every sentence—an indication that I was trying to read, but not really comprehending, what the text was saying. And then nothing—no highlights, no underlining, no notes in the margins, no crease in the pages. I'd stopped reading. My teacher had undoubtedly resorted to the same tactics that I and many of my colleagues have resorted to when it is obvious the students aren't reading. She lectured on the material, provided worksheets highlighting the key information, showed movies, and generally created a situation in which it was possible to pass the class without reading the book.

Given a choice, why would students read the textbook? It is often unengaging, uninspiring, and just plain boring. In his impassioned critique of history textbooks, Loewen writes:

> The books are boring. The stories that history textbooks tell are predictable; every problem has already been solved or is about to be solved. Textbooks exclude conflict or real suspense. They leave out anything that might reflect badly on our national character. When they try for drama, they achieve only melodrama, because readers know that everything will turn out fine in the end." Despite setbacks, the United States overcame these challenges," in the words of one textbook. Most authors of history textbooks don't even try for melodrama. Instead, they write in a tone that if heard aloud might be described as "mumbling lecturer." No wonder students lose interest. (1995, p. 13)

Textbooks as a Resource Rather Than The Source

What, then, should we do with textbooks? There are researchers and literacy experts who argue that textbooks should be thrown out altogether (Barr, 2006). They point to the flaws discussed above and say that students would be better off if textbooks were banished altogether and replaced by primary source documents, journals, trade books, and other materials that would provide stronger, more authentic reading opportunities for students. Although I sympathize with the spirit of this argument, I don't think it is realistic or appropriate to ignore textbooks completely.

Rather than frame the textbook discussion as all or nothing, I prefer to think in terms of how best to use textbooks as a resource in the classroom. Textbooks can be an excellent source of information for students and a lifesaver for teachers overwhelmed with too many different preps and not enough time. Some districts mandate their use and many have little funding available for other types of materials. When used judiciously, the textbook can become an excellent classroom resource.

Using the textbook as a resource, rather than as the only source, implies that, at least for some units or lessons, there are multiple texts used in the classroom and that each of those texts receives scrutiny from students. It implies that students are taught to approach texts with a degree of skepticism, recognizing that each brings new information and ideas, but that each is subject to error, bias, omission, and other limitations. Readers gather information and ideas from resources, but ultimately, they construct their own understanding of subject-area concepts.

Using the Textbook as a Resource

Social Studies

In Ms. Beltran's sixth-grade social studies class, students begin each unit with a quick scan through the relevant chapter in the textbook. They spend about fifteen minutes looking through the headings, maps, illustrations, captions, and places in the text where the words are printed in bold. Then together they discuss what they found, completing the first two columns of a K-W-L organizer, by listing what they "Know" (or think they know) and what they "Want" to learn. Although the K-W-L organizer has long been a part of Ms. Beltran's class routine, she has found that the discussions prompted by the organizer have become much richer since she began dedicating a few minutes ahead of time to scanning the text. "Before, when I just had them brainstorm information out of their heads, I got a lot of blank stares and boring questions. I think what works about the chapter scan is that it is the right level of input. They don't feel like there's a monster workload in front of them. They can move around the chapter, read the graphics, focus on the things that are interesting to them, and let their minds wonder. They get a sense of what happened, and the scan prompts them to ask questions about the 'whys' and 'hows' of history."

Science

Ms. Tran's earth science class uses their textbooks as a resource during science labs. During a recent classification lab, for example, students were required to identify various rock samples as igneous, sedimentary, or metamorphic by comparing their observations with the information in their textbook. Although Ms. Tran had broadly introduced the concept of rock classification before the lab began, she decided that students would learn more if they were reading with a purpose—in this case to determine the origins of the rock in front of them—rather than if they simply were reading the chapter on rocks as a class assignment. Working in groups of three, students examined the rocks, recorded their observations, and then referred to the relevant pages in the textbook to determine the classification of their specimens. As students read, they jumped around in the text, moving quickly to the relevant section and relying heavily on skimming and scanning skills to locate the pertinent information. This meant that few students read the entire chapter on rocks from start to finish, but, as Ms. Tran noted, this type of reading is appropriate to the content. "If a geologist or biologist wants to classify something, they're not going to read an entire book on the topic; they're going to look up the charts and descriptions that are most relevant and focus on that."

Math

Mr. Greene's geometry class emphasizes a constructivist approach to student learning. Rather than tell students about a particular concept, Mr. Greene provides opportunities for them to recognize key geometric principles using a launch-explore-summarize lesson protocol. When introducing similar triangles, for example, Mr. Greene gives students protractors, rulers, scissors, and paper and asks them to figure out which of the various triangles photocopied onto the sheet of paper are similar in shape but not size. Students use a variety of approaches to determine similarity. Some cut out the shapes and compare angles by placing one paper triangle on top of another. Others try to compare angles using a protractor. Still others measure the lengths of the sides of

the triangles and use calculators to determine ratios. They compare results and then Mr. Greene guides the students in discussion as they consider potential rules that might apply in identifying similar triangles more generally. It is only after they debate the various ways that angle and side measurements might be used to determine similarity that Mr. Greene instructs them to open their textbooks. Together, they read through the one-page description of similar triangles in the text, stopping every few sentences to draw connections between their hands-on learning and the ideas on the page. Used in this manner, the textbook explanation helps students to solidify their understanding of the concept of similarity, identify alternative methods for determining similarity, and develop the academic language needed to facilitate further discussions of the topic.

History

Ms. Hernandez generally keeps the textbook away from her eleventh-grade US history students. Having been in the classroom for over two decades, she has amassed a wealth of supplementary materials that have become her primary curriculum. But on occasion Ms. Hernandez takes down the texts from where they have been collecting dust and asks students to open to a chapter that describes a time period or event that the class has recently studied. The students are then expected to read the chapter with a critical eye. "What is included?" Ms. Hernandez asks. "How is the information portrayed? What is left out? Where is the emphasis? What is the bias?" The first time she conducts this activity with students, they have a really hard time responding to her questions. But by the end of the year many are experts, carefully pointing out a chapter's strengths and shortcomings. Ms. Hernandez insists that she is not trying to teach her students that the textbooks are bad, just that they are incomplete. "They are going to go off to college and then into the world. They'll be bombarded with all kinds of books and people trying to tell them what to believe. I want them to become confident enough to question authority and to recognize that they can't rely on others to tell them everything they need to know. They have to make up their own minds."

These are only a few examples of effective uses of textbooks in content class-rooms. Textbooks can also be great tools for unit-end or year-end reviews. The primary source documents, video clips, maps, and photos that accompany the teachers' edition of textbooks can be excellent resources for classroom learning. And reading particular chapters to ensure "coverage" can be appropriate when teachers are pressed for time between more in-depth classroom investigations.

Textbooks should not be viewed as the enemy. But nor should they be viewed as the sole authority. As content teachers, we are authorities on our subject area and our students. We need to assert our authority by choosing texts that will best engage our students in content learning. Sometimes this will involve the textbook; sometimes it won't. The key is in considering the purpose for any text's use and carefully structuring students' interaction with the text to promote content learning.

2

Focusing the Reader

What You'll Find in This Chapter

Context and purpose: The chapter begins with a discussion of the role of context and purpose in shaping the reader's understanding of text. Comparative examples from two physics classrooms illustrate the teacher's role in helping students establish a focus for their reading.

Classroom vignettes: Focusing the Reader in the Content Classroom

Characteristics of effective prereading activities: The third section of the chapter highlights the characteristics of effective prereading activities.

Instructional strategies: The third section presents a range of strategies to help focus readers before they engage with texts.

Classroom vignettes: Focusing the Reader in the Drama Classroom, in the Math Classroom, and in the History Classroom

Assessment for *learning:* The final section of the chapter provides a follow-up discussion of how teachers in each of the classroom vignettes assessed students' readiness to engage with texts.

Context and Purpose

Before my first child was born, I was given a collection of parenting books by well-meaning friends. As a conscientious new-mom-to-be, I sat down to try to read through the texts, but found it all a bit overwhelming. The books were designed to answer every question that new parents could possibly have, but not yet having my own child in my arms, most of the material seemed foreign to me. I didn't really have questions about when to introduce solids, nor was I wondering about potty training. And the litany of possible diseases and developmental challenges that infants might experience was simply terrifying. After a few hours of listless efforts at reading, I put the books in the closet. They reemerged only after the baby was born. When I had questions about something my infant was doing (or not doing), I consulted the relevant portion of the texts and found new appreciation for the helpful information and reassuring tone. This time, I had a focus for my reading.

The Role of Context

Our understanding of text greatly depends on the context within which we view the reading. The knowledge that we bring to a reading, the conceptual framework through which we approach a text, and our expectations for why we are reading have significant influence over what we notice when we read. An expert in honeybees, for example, is likely to take away a significantly different impression from a journal article about bee population decline than a lay reader or a doctor specializing in treating people with allergies to bee stings. These individuals would view the article through the lens of their own knowledge and experience and, consequently, would focus on different information and ideas.

Educational psychologists use the term *schema* to describe the internal map within our brains that organizes and stores information. It is the classification structure that allows us to recall particular places or events when we hear a certain song or smell a particular odor. When we receive new information we activate our schema as our brains "look" for connected information or ideas to help us make sense of the incoming data (Jensen, 2005; Sousa, 2001; Sprenger, 1999). Research has shown that readers who approach texts with a strong conceptual framework within which to situate new information and ideas are much more likely to understand, remember, and respond appropriately (Bransford, Brown, & Cocking, 2000). Those who lack an appropriate schema are less likely to understand or be able to focus on the information in the text (Alexander & Murphy, 1998; Sousa, 2001).

In the content classroom, schema activation is often used to refer to the process of providing background information. This is an important element; however, schema activation extends beyond the provision of factual details. Effective schema activation prioritizes the development of a conceptual framework that is responsive to the ideas and concepts that will be explored in the text. It not only provides information that will be relevant in the reading but also helps the reader organize and prioritize that information in order to prepare students to read the particular text at hand. For example, before students read a chapter on the role of alliances in World War II, it may be important for them to locate the nations involved in the Allied and Axis alliances, but it is equally important for students to build an understanding of the concept of an alliance—What is it? How is it formed? Why does it matter? What might cause it to break? Connecting this concept to students' own experiences with bonds of friendship and family alliances can go a long way toward preparing them to understand the geopolitical alliances involved in World War II.

The Importance of Purpose

The purpose we set for reading is a second critical factor in determining how we read and what we come to understand through our reading. Purpose determines what parts of the text we read, how quickly or slowly we read, what information we pay attention to, what we remember, what comprehension strategies we use, and how we respond (Tovani, 2000, 2004). There is a tremendous difference between how we approach the morning newspaper when reading to keep up-to-date on current events, for example, and how we approach a medical text when seeking to learn more about a family member's diagnosis. One is read at our leisure; we skip around to the articles in a newspaper that seem most interesting, and we are content to skim headlines of most articles in order to gain a cursory understanding of what is happening in our communities and the world. The other is read with a sense of urgency, a desire to find specific medical information and master details in order to understand the severity of the diagnosis and ask appropriate questions about treatment options.

When we lack purpose, as I did in my initial reading of the parenting books, we often fail to focus. We skim through material but don't recognize the relative importance of ideas or the connections to larger concepts.

The same applies to reading in content areas. If our students understand that there is a purpose to a reading, they are more likely to engage with the material—to focus on comprehending the text and building an understanding of the information and ideas therein. If they don't have a purpose for reading the text we've set before them, they are likely to allow their eyes to wander through the page without a clear sense of direction. They will retain little information and are unlikely to truly understand the concepts addressed in the reading.

A study by Pichert and Anderson (1977) found that differing purposes had a dramatic impact on text comprehension and information recall. In this study, two groups of readers were provided with the same passage but asked to approach the passage with very different purposes. The passage is a fairly neutral description of two kids going through a house. The readers were divided into two groups: one approached the passage from the perspective of homebuyers, and the other approached the passage from the perspective of burglars. The readers who approached the text as potential homebuyers noticed the description of the new stone siding on the fireplace and the leak in the upstairs ceiling. The prospective burglars, on the other hand, noted where the silver was kept and the distance to the neighbor's house. With different purposes, focus and recall differed dramatically.

Different purposes might also be established for the reading on World War II alliances mentioned earlier. If the reading is embedded in a unit that focuses on the Holocaust, for example, then students might be asked to use the reading to consider how the power dynamics within alliances prevented other nations from responding to early concerns about the persecution of Jews in German-controlled Europe. On the other hand, if the reading is connected to an inquiry into technological developments during wartime, then the students might be expected to use the reading to consider how innovation spreads within and across alliances. In both of these instances, setting a clear purpose, in addition to establishing a context, will help students to engage in the reading and make meaning of the information and ideas found in the text. The context provides a framework to understand the text; the purpose helps readers effectively use the text to further their content learning.

Focusing the Reader in the Content Classroom

In the classroom it is critical that we provide students with both a *context* and a *purpose* to support content reading. They need to develop a conceptual framework for the topic or concept explored in the reading in order to make sense of the new information and ideas they will encounter. They also need to have an explicit purpose that can focus their attention and help them navigate unfamiliar content and text structures.

To illustrate the importance of providing a context and a purpose prior to assigning a content reading, consider the following two classroom examples. Mr. Cole and Ms. Smith both teach eighth-grade physical science. Their classrooms are right next door to each other and they follow the same district-developed pacing guide for their state-adopted textbook. In the sample lessons described next, both are teaching about physical forces. I had been invited to visit these classrooms because both teachers make good use of comprehension strategies during the reading. However, they are dramatically different in their approaches to introducing the topic and focusing their students on the reading.

Force in Mr. Cole's Classroom

The students arrived in Mr. Cole's science class full of the talk and jocularity that usually follows lunch in middle school. They gradually settled into their assigned seats and took out their textbooks. Mr. Cole passed back their notes from the previous day, provided brief feedback on how students could improve their work, and then launched into a preview of this day's lesson. "How many of you have ridden on a roller coaster?" he asked. Many hands around the room went up. Mr. Cole called on a few volunteers who described their favorite coasters and one who provided a vivid description of her mother turning green after riding on a particularly aggressive roller coaster. "Riding on a roller coaster can be a lot of fun," Mr. Cole stated as he worked to prepare his students for the reading. "And it is also a great lesson in physics. When you are riding on the coaster, many different forces are acting on your body. There's gravity pulling you down, momentum pushing you forward, friction keeping you in your seat, and centripetal forces pushing you away from the point of rotation when the roller coaster makes those hairpin twists and turns. We're going to learn more about all of those forces today. Please open your textbooks to Chapter 3 and begin reading. The information is important, so be sure to pay attention. Remember to use the reading comprehension strategies that we've been working on."

With a few sighs, students dutifully opened their texts and began reading. Many did work to apply the reading comprehension strategies Mr. Cole had been teaching. Students outlined key ideas of the chapter by turning headings into questions in their notebooks. They recorded the words in bold and used the text's glossary when they got stuck. But they weren't engaged. After only a few minutes, students began fidget, whisper to their neighbors, and exhibit the kind of behaviors that clearly indicate disinterest. Mr. Cole worked hard to get them back on track, embarrassed that all was not going as well as he had hoped in front of the classroom visitor. "This is important," he reminded students. "You're going to need to know this information." But despite his pleas, most students struggled to maintain focus. They had

been thrown into the text with little knowledge of the concept and no particular purpose. They weren't engaged because they weren't given a reason to engage.

Force in Ms. Smith's Classroom

When students arrived in Ms. Smith's classroom, they were greeted by a video loop projected on the screen at the front of the room. The video, from Wake Forest University's physics department website (http://www.wfu.edu/physics/demolabs/demos/avimov/), showed a professor calmly filling a bucket of water and then swinging the full bucket around in a circle. Despite being upside down as the bucket revolves, the water remains in the bucket. Following the usual classroom routine, Ms. Smith's students took out their science notebooks and recorded a "quick-write" response to the question posted on the white board adjacent to the video screen: "Describe what is happening in the video. Why doesn't the water spill out of the bucket?"

After taking attendance and passing back papers, Ms. Smith opened the floor for students to share their responses. "I wrote that the man is swinging a bucket with water over his head and I think that the water doesn't fall out because it's a trick bucket," one student responded.

"Yeah, I think there must be a sponge or something in the bottom of the bucket to keep the water inside," another student agreed.

A girl at the back of the class countered, "I don't think it's a trick bucket. I think it has something to do with the swinging, like maybe it's going fast enough that the water doesn't have time to fall out."

Ms. Smith listened carefully to student responses, neither agreeing nor disagreeing. Once multiple views had been shared, she took out a bucket to begin her own demonstration. "Take a look at this bucket," she said as she passed it around to several tables near the front of the room. "What do you think? Is there anything special about it? Any tricks that might prevent liquids from coming out?" Students agreed that there weren't any tricks.

"OK, so now, if I put water in the bucket," Ms. Smith began as she filled the bucket with water from the classroom sink, "and then I turn the bucket over, what will happen?" Students unanimously predicted that the water would fall out. "How?" Ms. Smith queried. "Is the water going to just go straight down, or might it go over there?" she wondered, pointing toward the far side of the room. "Or over there? Or behind me?"

"If you just turn it upside down, then it will go straight down, just down," a boy in the middle of the class asserted.

"Yeah, it's going to fall straight down and make a mess," his tablemate grinned.

"Does everyone agree?" Ms. Smith wanted to know. Heads nodded around the room. "Anyone disagree?" No response. "OK, why? What is going to cause this water to fall straight down?"

"Gravity," several students replied in unison.

"Gravity is what makes things fall toward the earth," one elaborated.

"So your prediction is that if I turn this bucket upside down gravity will cause the water to fall down. Let's see if you are correct." Ms. Smith raised the bucket high above the sink and slowly turned it upside down. As predicted, the water poured down directly into the sink.

"It appears that your prediction was correct. Well done!" Ms. Smith said. "OK, now let's try a different one. How about if I fill this same bucket with water and then pull my arms back, turn the bucket to the side, and quickly move the bucket forward." Ms. Smith demonstrated a tossing motion with an empty bucket. "Then what will happen?"

"The water would fly out," a student volunteered. "It would make whoever is standing in front of you really wet," another predicted.

"I like that you said 'standing in front of.' That tells me something about the direction of the water. Tell me more about what direction you think the water will go and why."

"It'll go out, like straight, because that's the direction you're throwing it," one student offered.

"At first it'll go out 'cause that's the way you throw, but then it'll go down 'cause of gravity," another stated, "So it'll be like a curve down."

"I hear what you're saying," Ms. Smith responded, "but I'm not quite sure I understand. You're saying I'm throwing the water, but I haven't actually touched the water. Can you explain your thinking a bit more?"

"Well, you're throwing the bucket," a girl in the back explained. "I mean you're not actually throwing the bucket, you're like making a throwing motion with the bucket and since the water is in the bucket, the bucket is pushing the water forward."

"Nicely stated," Ms. Smith smiled, "So shall we see what happens?" Students giggled nervously, worried that they would soon be the recipients of a face full of water. "Take a look at the screen," Ms. Smith directed as she cued up a video of her tossing water out of the bucket. As predicted, the video showed the water emerging forward out of the bucket and then arcing down toward the ground.

"Looks like your prediction was right again," Ms. Smith observed. "OK, last demonstration. I'm going to fill this same bucket with water and swing it in circles, much like you saw in the first video. What will happen to the water?" Students hesitated. Initially they had been convinced that the video was some sort of trick, but now, after thinking through the other demonstrations, they were less certain.

"I think if you go fast enough it will stay in the bucket, but I don't know why," one admitted.

"I still think it's going to fall out," another stated, "Gravity's gonna pull it down."

"No, I think the side of the bucket is going to keep pushing it around," a boy countered. "It's going to stay in."

Ms. Smith took a few more comments before

stating, "All right, well it looks like we're not coming to consensus, so let's try it and see what happens." She moved to the sink to fill the bucket. "You're not going to actually do it here, are you?" an incredulous student asked.

"Yep," Ms. Smith replied, "we're going to give it a try." Holding the handle of the bucket and keeping her arm straight, Ms. Smith swung the bucket forward, then back, and then around, over her head. The water remained in the bucket as Ms. Smith circled the bucket three times in a smooth revolution from her shoulder before bringing the bucket to a stop in an upright position.

"I knew it," a boy in the front row exclaimed, although he had been cringing only a few seconds earlier, worried that the water would spill out onto him. Ms. Smith smiled as she instructed students to take out their science notebooks. "Make a table with three columns. Label the first 'Observe,' the second 'Predict,' and the third 'Verify.' We've had three demonstrations. For each, I want you to write down what you observed. For example, for the first demonstration I might write, 'Bucket turned upside down, water poured straight down,' in the 'Observe' column." Ms. Smith wrote on the document camera as she spoke. "Then, in the second column, predict *why* the water behaved as it did in each of the demonstrations. For example, for the first demonstration, I could write 'Gravity pulled water down' in the second column." Again, Ms. Smith recorded her notes on the projector. She then asked students to add their observations and predictions to the charts in their notebooks (see sample student chart in Figure 2.1).

"I see lots of good ideas," Ms. Smith noted a few minutes later. "You've done a great job describing some of the forces that acted on the water in the bucket. A force in physics is a cause of an object's motion or change in motion. Now we're going to take a look at Chapter 3 in the textbook. The chapter describes forces, including gravity, momentum, friction, and centripetal forces. As you read, I want you to make connections between the demonstrations you've just observed and the information in the textbook. When you find information on a force that acted on the water in one of the demonstrations, explain that connection in the 'Verify' column of your chart. Many of you will be able to confirm your predictions and learn the scientific terms to describe the forces that you observed. Some of you may find new explanations for the water's behavior. Others may encounter information about additional forces that you hadn't considered. Remember, this is not about being right or wrong, it's about learning more. Just like professional scientists, your job is to look for information and ideas that can help you explain what you've observed." Ms. Smith paused for questions and then asked students to begin reading.

For the next fifteen minutes students remained focused on their work. They carefully moved between the textbook and their charts, recording information in the 'Verify' column to confirm, extend, or refute their predictions. Occasionally students raised their hands to ask a question or whispered an observation to a nearby classmate, but for the most part the room was quiet as students focused on their work. At the end of a period, I asked a student what she thought of the reading. "It was cool," she began, before qualifying her statement. "I mean, the reading was just the usual textbook. But after Ms. Smith throwing the water like that, it was kinda cool to figure out why it happened. I want to go try it on my brother at home."

Although the texts to be explored in these two classrooms were identical, the process of establishing a focus for reading was dramatically different . . . and so were the student responses. In Mr. Cole's classroom, students were well meaning; they tried to read the text, but attention quickly wandered. Their purpose was not clear and, despite good intentions, it was hard to read what was, admittedly, a relatively dry, information-driven textbook. In Ms. Smith's classroom,

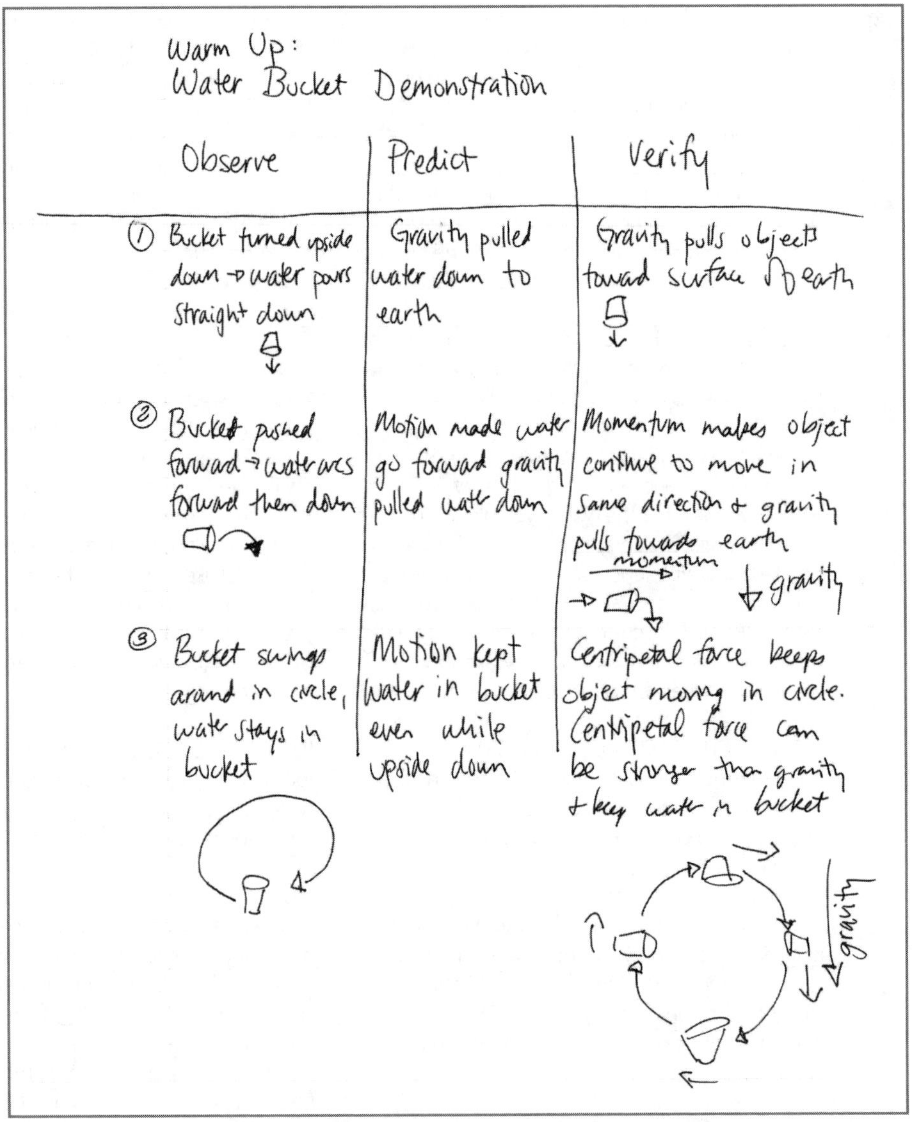

FIGURE 2.1. Ms. Smith's students created charts to document their thinking about the bucket demonstration.

on the other hand, students were able to readily focus on the text. They were able to identify relevant information, make connections to their prior knowledge, and take notes to verify their predictions. These behavioral and performance differences were not due to disparities in students' abilities and attitudes nor accessibility and interest level of the text, but rather to differences in how the teachers had established the reading focus.

Prior to assigning the reading, Mr. Cole had done what many content teachers do—he'd stood up and provided a bit of background. He asked a quick question—"How many of you have ridden on a roller coaster?" He elicited students' responses. He explained that the reading would connect to their experiences. And he told students that the information was important. On the surface, many of these elements are appropriate. Mr. Cole, like most content teachers, instinctively knew that it was important to help students connect to their prior knowledge and to prepare them for the text ahead. But his approach, while well intended, was superficial. It did not adequately contextualize the reading, nor did it prepare students with a clear purpose for engaging with the text. Of course, Mr. Cole is not alone. Many of us have used the "stand up and provide a bit of background" approach. Though research has proven it to be ineffective, it remains timeworn (Beers, 2003). I cringe to remember the number of times that I gave a one-minute summary of the reading and then told students, "Read the chapter for homework. Be prepared to discuss it tomorrow." My students survived, but their reading was far less productive than it might have been. To be truly effective, we need to go beyond simply giving a bit of background and then assigning text—we need to be explicit and focused in communicating to students the context and the purpose for the particular texts that we place before them.

In Ms. Smith's classroom, the context and purpose were much more clearly developed. She began with a series of engaging demonstrations that closely previewed ideas students would encounter in the text. She elicited students' predictions about what would happen in each demonstration. She then required students to describe and then document what they observed in the demonstrations, distinguishing between what they had seen and why they believed it had taken place. She encouraged constructivist debate among her students as they made predictions, described observations, and offered explanations. She allowed students to use familiar language, knowing that their activity-based observations and predictions laid the groundwork for understanding concepts and technical terms that they would later encounter in the text. She previewed students' reading and learning tasks for the lesson and she assigned a very specific purpose for the reading. Taken together, this progression of prereading activities helped students build context and purpose for their reading. They had a preview of the forces that would be described in the text, they had an explicit reading objective, and, perhaps most important, they were motivated for reading by a genuine curiosity to learn more.

Characteristics of Effective Prereading Activities

Not all prereading instruction can or should look exactly like Ms. Smith's approach. (And even the best content teachers can't realistically expect to prepare spot-on prereading activities for every text.) The approach that we choose depends on the text, the students, and the larger instructional purpose. However, there are a number of characteristics of prereading instruction that should exist across classroom settings. Effective prereading activities do the following:

Situate the reading within a larger context. Effective prereading activities provide a context for students' reading. They introduce the conceptual framework through which we want students to view the reading. This context may be in the form of a set of information, a particular perspective, or an essential question (Wiggins & McTighe, 2005). Several questions should be considered when designing prereading activities:

• Why did I choose this text?

• What do I want students to learn from this text?

• How will students apply information and ideas from this text?

• How does this text connect to the larger learning objectives I set for this lesson/unit?

• How does this reading connect to other instructional activities I have planned for this lesson/unit?

Point to an explicit purpose for reading. Effective prereading activities focus students' attention on an explicit purpose for reading the text. They establish a need to know, a reason for accessing the information and ideas in the text. Purposes for reading may include, but are not limited to, the following:

• To investigate differing ideas and perspectives

• To find information relevant to solving a problem

• To compare the merits of alternative solutions

• To gather information to support (or refute) a claim

• To analyze the merits of an experiment, proposal, or strategy

• To identify causal relationships

• To learn about the context of events or the background of individuals

• To understand a concept more fully

- To identify a sequence of events
- To determine the relative importance of information and ideas
- To distinguish fact from rhetoric
- To generate new questions

Engage students' curiosity. In order to learn, students need to pay attention. Although some may be willing to follow along out of a sense of duty, the greatest learning occurs when students are genuinely curious and engaged in the material under investigation (Anderson & Pearson, 1984; Hurst, 2001). Effective prereading activities spark students' curiosity, connect with their sense of fairness and justice, jar their understanding of the order of things, resonate with their own experiences, or present a puzzle that demands to be solved.

Preview the postreading response. Previewing the response that students will engage in after reading helps students focus their attention during reading. Knowing how they will be expected to apply information and ideas from the text helps students prioritize information and respond to ideas as they read. Effective prereading activities preview the activities that students will be participating in after the reading and provide students with an opportunity to give an initial response based on their prior knowledge and experience.

Instructional Strategies

The following are examples of strategies that can be used to establish a focus prior to engaging students in content reading. Strategies should be adapted to fit the classroom setting, the instructional purpose, and the text to be read. Strategies can be particularly effective when layered, providing students with multiple opportunities to grapple with information and ideas.

Demonstrations. Instead of telling students about a physics principle or chemical reaction, show them! As was demonstrated in the vignette from Ms. Smith's classroom, observing what happens when centripetal force counteracts gravity will provoke curiosity and prompt questions that support strategic reading. Use an "Observe, Predict, Verify" chart similar to the one used in Ms. Smith's lesson to focus students' attention on the text. Research has shown that demonstrations are particularly critical in the fields of science and mathematics (Lee, 2000) and, if used purposefully, can lead to higher levels of learning in these content areas (Beasley, 1982).

Visual displays. Photographs, diagrams, maps, video clips, and political cartoons can be great vehicles for building content knowledge and provoking curiosity (Buehl, 2001; Yell & Scheurman, 2004). This is especially true if the visuals show images that don't fit with students' expectations. Photos of "whites only" lunch counters, "colored" drinking fountains, and segregated schools, for example, can provoke curiosity in students who've never experienced this kind of legal discrimination and can provide a focus for investigating the origins of the Civil Rights Movement.

K-W-L. K-W-L charts are designed to help students access their prior knowledge ("What I *Know*"), consider what they want to learn about a topic ("What I *Want* to Know"), and then record what they have learned ("What I *Learned*") once they finish reading (Ogle, 1986). If used on their own, K-W-L charts have a mixed record of success. Students can present false or off-topic information in the "K" column and ask questions for the "W" column that lead in a completely different direction from the intended goals of the unit. However, when grounded by a focusing question, demonstration, sample problem, or set of photographs, as demonstrated in the vignette of Ms. Robinson's drama class that follows, K-W-L charts can provide a good structure for helping students sort out what they know, what they need to now, and how they might go about finding that information.

Anticipation guides. Anticipation guides consist of a series of factual statements to which students must respond either "True" or "False." Statements in the guide preview key concepts of the reading, challenging students to agree, disagree, or question each claim. The best statements are those about which students may have some idea, but not a complete understanding (Yell, Scheurman, & Reynolds, 2004). Examples of statements that might be used prior to a life science unit on plants include "All plants grow from seeds"; "All plants are able to make their own food"; and "Plants are adapted to every environment on earth." An example of an anticipation guide for math is included in the pre-algebra example that follows. Anticipation guides are presented to students prior to reading in order to activate their background knowledge, provoke curiosity, and focus attention toward key concepts in the text. Returning to the anticipation guide after the reading to "correct" prereading responses and discuss new learning serves to strengthen conceptual understanding.

Ethical dilemmas. Grab students' attention with a situation or idea that challenges their beliefs. Pose a thought-provoking question. Ask them to respond to a newspaper article or "What if . . ." scenario that confronts their sense of fairness. Simulate a dilemma and ask them to react. These approaches appeal to the emotional channels of learning and have been shown to promote interest and sustain learning (Muncey, Payne, & White, 1999). Selecting dilemmas that offer parallels to content being studied previews the challenges that decision makers will face and invites students to recognize the complexity of content-based concepts.

Artistic expressions. Bringing art, music, and poetry into other content areas can show interdisciplinary connections, utilize multiple learning modalities, and help frame readings about time periods, events, and phenomena. Wilfred Owen's poem *Dulce Et Decorum Est* provides a haunting image of the terror of war juxtaposed against the title line, "It Is Sweet and Right." This irony is a poignant way to introduce the battlefield experience of World War I.

Focusing the Reader in the Drama Classroom

"Good morning," Ms. Robinson greeted the students in her intermediate drama class. It was first period Monday morning and, as usual, students looked as though they weren't quite awake. "This morning we are going to be starting our unit on historical drama. Before I tell you anything about the play we are going to be working with or the time period when it is set, I want you to do some investigating of your own. I've posted about two dozen photos around the room that relate to the historical setting of the play. Grab your clipboards and go take a look. As you view the photos, write down your impressions. What do you see in the photographs? What do you notice about the subject, the setting, or the tone of the image? Each photo is numbered. As you take notes, record the number of the photo so that you can refer to it during our class discussion. Any questions? Get moving!"

Students lazily dispersed to go view the photos, but as they looked at the images, their apathy dissipated. Ms. Robinson had selected powerful images by Dorothea Lange and other Depression-era photographers documenting the Dust Bowl and the migration west. The photos included images of makeshift tents with dirt-smudged children peering out from inside, a family loaded in a car with trunks and furniture piled on top and bearing the sign "Oregon or bust," an empty farmhouse surrounded by sand and a bit of scrub vegetation, dozens of men in coats and hats standing in line to receive "free coffee and donuts for the unemployed," and the iconic Lange photograph of a mother staring into the distance while her two children bury their heads on her shoulders.

Students were quiet as they viewed the images, recording notes and occasionally talking softly with a peer. Ms. Robinson moved among them, pointing out a detail of a photo here or commenting about her reaction to an image there. Although class time was precious, she allowed students the time they needed to really absorb the images. The production they would be working toward was a stage adaptation of *The Grapes of Wrath* (Steinbeck, 1939). The play, like the book, relies heavily on character development. To be successful in communicating the story to their audience, her student actors would really need to understand and identify with the characters and empathize with the experience they would be portraying on stage. Viewing the rich images in the photos was a significant first step in developing that historical empathy.

"Up until now most of the plays and activities that we've done have been focused on contemporary people and events," Ms. Robinson explained when she pulled the students back together. "But theater isn't just about the present; theater production can be a powerful way to examine the past. Participating in or viewing a historical drama can help people better understand past events and make personal connections with historical figures. As actors, there is an additional responsibility when performing in a historical drama to bring an understanding of the past and an empathy with historical figures to the stage. You need to be able to inhabit the lives of real people living through real historical events. That's a weighty responsibility.

"As you've probably guessed, the play that we are going to be working on focuses on the Great Depression of the 1930s. Today, before we delve into the play, our task is to learn a bit more about that period. So let's talk about the photos that you've just spent time viewing. What did you notice?"

"The people looked so sad," one student commented. "There were lots of children in the photos, and normally, even when things are hard, little kids smile. But none of the kids in these photos were smiling."

"*Everything* looked really sad," another student chimed in. "Maybe it is because the photos were black and white, but the whole scene looked really sad. There didn't seem to be trees or flowers or nice houses or anything that was good. Just a lot of dirt and depression."

"I thought it was interesting that there seemed to be a lot of separation," a girl near the front of the class commented. "The photos with the men in line didn't include any women in line. The photos of the women and children sometimes included men, but often they didn't. And most of the photos included only white people. In the pictures with African Americans, they were separate."

"Yeah, and you know what else?" a boy sitting nearby responded, "In the pictures with the men, it seemed like they were dressed up. I mean they were obviously poor, but they were wearing hats and nice coats. And there was that one woman too who had on like a fur coat. She had dirt on her face and was holding a baby that was all dirty, but she had on a nice coat."

Ms. Robinson let students share their observations without imposing much of a structure at first. She stepped in only to call on students who were ready to share or to ask for clarification or supporting evidence. "What image made you think that they were angry?" she asked a young man who had offered that claim. But after a few minutes, she refocused the conversation to prepare students for the upcoming reading.

"I really like the observations you've made," she praised. "Now, knowing that we're going to be working on a play set in the Depression, I'd like you to consider what you know and what you might need to know about this time period. The play is an adaptation of *The Grapes of Wrath*. It tells the story of one family from Oklahoma and their journey west. Like many of the people in the photos you've just looked at, the family in the play is driven from the farm by drought and economic hardship. They set off toward California in search of a better life, but encounter a lot of hardships along the way. Based on the photos that you've just seen as well as your previous learning about the Great Depression, let's think more closely about what we know and what we might need to know to prepare for roles in this play."

As she was speaking, Ms. Robinson placed a copy of a K-W-L chart on the document camera and then shifted her position to be able to record notes in the first two columns. In the "K" column the class would place information that they knew about the Depression. In the "W" column, the class would ask questions about what they wanted to know. The "L" column would be saved for future use, when students would record what they had learned in response to their questions.

"We know that people were poor," one student volunteered.

"But I don't think they all started off poor," another responded. "Some of them have nice things, cars and coats and stuff."

"I wonder how many people were affected by this," a student questioned. "I mean obviously, it's called the Great Depression, so there are probably lots of people, but most of the photos only have a few people. So is that because the people were spread out or is it because even though it was bad for some people, it was not so bad for others?"

"I had thought that the Depression was just about white people," a young man in the back admitted. "I mean it seems like that's who you see in most of the pictures and stuff. But there were a few pictures with black people. Were they affected by the Depression? I mean, it was during segregation so it seems like they would be pretty hard off anyway. Did this make things worse?"

"I want to know how things got so bad," a young woman wondered. "What caused people to be so poor all of a sudden and what did the government do to try to make things better? And why were they going west? Were things that much better in California?"

As students spoke, Ms. Robinson captured their comments on the K-W-L chart. They had far more questions than answers at this point. But that was OK. The questions were important ones. In order to get inside the characters they would inhabit, students needed to recognize, for example, the mixture of desperation and hope that displaced

Americans felt as they moved off of land they had farmed for generations and headed west. They needed to understand the sense of shame and embarrassment that many men and women experienced when suddenly thrust into poverty. And they needed to be familiar with the scope of the economic difficulties facing the country and understand the limited options that were available to those in need.

After filling not one, but two, K-W-L charts with points of knowledge and questions (Figure 2.2 shows one of them), Ms. Robinson moved to focus students' attention on the reading. "Well done," she began. "You've provided some important pieces of knowledge and I particularly like the questions that you've asked. These are questions that we'll need to address in order to effectively portray the characters in the play and honor their historical reality. Let's take a look at a reading that can, hopefully, provide us with some answers." As she spoke, Ms. Robinson handed out a chapter on the Great Depression from Joy Hakim's excellent series *A History of US* (2003). Written as a narrative of American history, Hakim's work provides an accessible and engaging account that Ms. Robinson knew would answer many of her students' questions. "Now this may not answer everything," she warned, "but that is OK. We'll have other opportunities to learn more through further discussions, some additional research, and a guest speaker in the coming days. For now, your task is to use this reading to answer as many of our questions as you can. The text is photocopied and it is yours to keep. Please feel free to take notes and write on the material as you read. I've numbered our questions on the K-W-L chart so that when you encounter something you think will help answer a question, you can mark that question's number on the paper." Ms. Robinson paused before giving a final direction: "Remember to think like an actor preparing for a part. Your job is to understand the historical events and the people living in this time period so that you can accurately inhabit a character. Get to work."

By layering the photos and the K-W-L chart with an authentic reason to read, Ms. Robinson had successfully focused her students' attention on the text. Although students were not accustomed

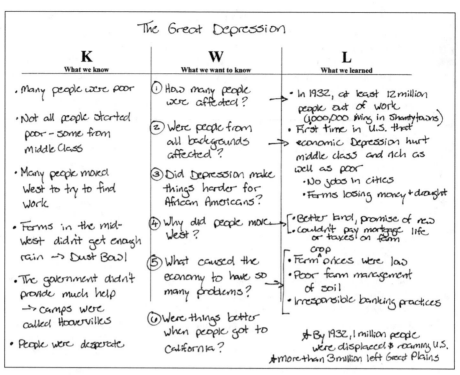

FIGURE 2.2. Ms. Robinson and her drama students used a K-W-L chart to prepare for a play set during the Great Depression.

to reading historical texts in the drama classroom, the prereading activities in this lesson provided both context and purpose for engaging with the text. The photographs helped activate students' prior knowledge about the Great Depression and, perhaps more important, raised many questions about the circumstances and individuals involved. The K-W-L chart provided a structure to focus students' wonderings, helping them to articulate their curiosity as research questions that could be answered by the text. These two strategies, together with the urgency associated with knowing that they would be expected to apply newly attained historical understanding on stage, focused students' attention and guided them toward successful text comprehension and content learning.

Focusing the Reader in the Math Classroom

As students entered Ms. Mendez's pre-algebra classroom, they pulled out their math journals and began to work on the warm-up problem written on the board:

> Every half-hour the cells in Kim's petri dish divide. She begins with one cell in her dish. How many cells will she have after 4 hours?

Some students quickly sketched out a time chart and began to solve the problem. Others stared into space, trying to figure the problem out in their heads. A few whispered quietly to their neighbors asking for clarification. Ms. Mendez finished taking roll and collecting homework and announced, "Time's up! Put down those pencils. Let's hear what your thinking is on this problem.

Turn to a partner, explain your reasoning and then be prepared to share out." Students quickly turned to their neighbor and talked through the problem. Several had gotten stuck on the division question and wondered, "How many does it divide into?" and others had neglected to take the half-hour increments into account, but most seemed to have the general idea. When asked to share out to the whole class, D'Shawn volunteered to go to the board and write up his solution (see Figure 2.3). After hearing his explanation and giving other stu-

dents a chance to ask a few clarifying questions, Ms. Mendez thanked D'Shawn for his leadership and then segued into the body of the lesson.

"Wow!" she commented. "After only four hours we've gone from one cell to 256 cells. That's amazing. Do you know that if we left those cells to continue growing at the same rate, after twelve hours there would be more than 16 million cells in the petri dish? And after twenty-four hours there would be over 280 trillion cells. They probably

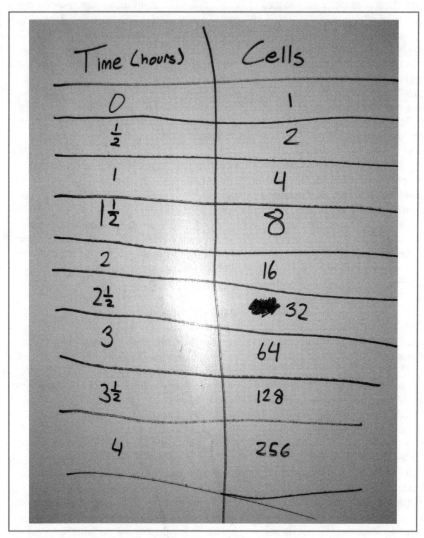

Time (hours)	Cells
0	1
$\frac{1}{2}$	2
1	4
$1\frac{1}{2}$	8
2	16
$2\frac{1}{2}$	32
3	64
$3\frac{1}{2}$	128
4	256

FIGURE 2.3. One student made this chart to solve the warm-up problem at the start of Ms. Mendez's pre-algebra class.

wouldn't fit in the petri dish at that point! This kind of growth can be hard to understand and it also can be hard to represent. All those zeros in billions and trillions can get confusing. So mathematicians and scientists generally don't multiply out all the zeros; instead, they use mathematical shorthand—exponents. They wouldn't say that after four hours there were 256 cells. Instead they would say that there were two to the eighth cells." Ms. Mendez paused to write the notation "2^8" on the board. "The two is the base number; it tells us how many cells are made with each division. The eight is the exponent; it tells us that we are in the eighth cycle of cell division."

"How many of you have heard of exponents before?" Ms. Mendez continued, moving quickly between activities in order to keep her students' attention. She knew that if she spent too long explaining abstract concepts she would lose them. "Wonderful," she exclaimed when most hands in the room went up, "then this will be something of a review." She passed around a prereading anticipation guide that previewed the essential elements of the section of the textbook they would be examining this day (see a student's completed guide in Figure 2.4). The guide contained six mathematical statements that students were to identify as true or false. The statements were grouped under the same headings that could be found in the textbook. "Take a look at each of these statements," Ms. Mendez instructed. "Use your prior knowledge of exponents as well as your mathematical reasoning to decide if each is true or false. Explain your thinking in the space provided. If you don't know the answer, that's OK, this is a preview. Reason it out as well as you can."

Ms. Mendez knew that students would have varying degrees of "correctness" on the anticipation guide, and that was all right. She didn't expect all of her students to be able to answer all of the questions correctly; if they did, then she wouldn't need to teach the lesson. What she did expect, however, was for her students to use this guide to activate their prior knowledge of exponents and to begin to differentiate between what they knew for certain and what they still needed to learn. Success with the guide was measured not by the number of correct answers, but by the degree to which it prepared students to focus on the learning in the coming lesson.

"Time's up," Ms. Mendez announced. "Let's take a look at these questions." She settled onto a stool at the front of the room and placed her own anticipation guide on the document camera. "Question number one says that in the expression two to the third power [2^3], three is the exponent. What do you think, true or false?"

"I say true," responded a boy at the middle table. "The number that is up above is the exponent and the lower number is called the base. Three is up above so it is the exponent."

"OK," Ms. Mendez said, "I like the explanation. Who would like to respond?"

"I agree," a girl at the side of the room commented. "The little number that's up above is called the exponent."

"I think so too," another girl added. "I don't really have a mathematical reason; it's just the definition."

Ms. Mendez allowed several additional students to give their input on this question before bringing discussion to a close. "It sounds like most of you believe that this statement is true," she said, "so I'm going to go ahead and circle 'True' here, and I like Julia's speculation as to the reason—that it's just the definition—so I'll write that in the explanation box. Let's hold on to that prediction for a couple of minutes and look at the second statement before we open our textbooks to confirm. Who'd like to try the second question, four to the zero power equals zero [$4^0 = 0$]? What do you think, true or false?"

The discussion continued as students worked their way through the second statement. Several argued that it was true that a number to the zero power was zero. Others responded that it was false. They weren't sure what it was, but they didn't think it was zero. One young man connected back to the cell division problem. "At the start of the problem, before any divisions happened, there was just one cell," he explained, "so two to

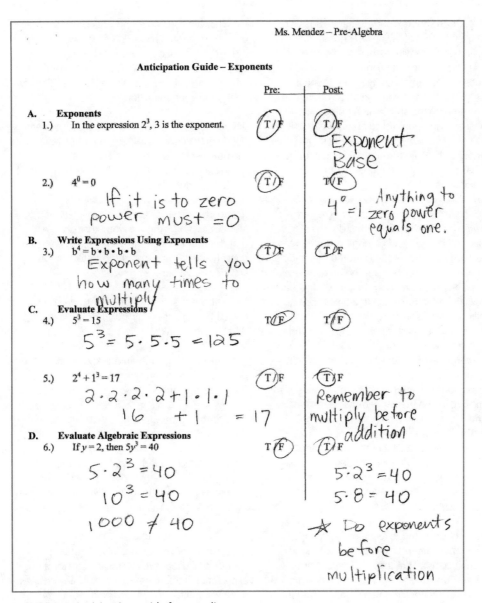

Anticipation Guide – Exponents

Pre: | Post:

A. Exponents
1.) In the expression 2^3, 3 is the exponent.

T / F   T / F

Exponent
Base

2.) $4^0 = 0$

T / F   T / F

If it is to zero
power must = 0

$4^0 = 1$ Anything to
zero power
equals one.

B. Write Expressions Using Exponents
3.) $b^4 = b \cdot b \cdot b \cdot b$

T / F   T / F

Exponent tells you
how many times to
multiply

C. Evaluate Expressions
4.) $5^3 = 15$

T / F   T / F

$5^3 = 5 \cdot 5 \cdot 5 = 125$

5.) $2^4 + 1^3 = 17$

T / F   T / F

$2 \cdot 2 \cdot 2 \cdot 2 + 1 \cdot 1 \cdot 1$
16 + 1 = 17

Remember to
multiply before
addition

D. Evaluate Algebraic Expressions
6.) If $y = 2$, then $5y^3 = 40$

T / F   T / F

$5 \cdot 2^3 = 40$
$10^3 = 40$
$1000 \neq 40$

$5 \cdot 2^3 = 40$
$5 \cdot 8 = 40$
★ Do exponents
before
multiplication

FIGURE 2.4. Anticipation guide for a reading on exponents.

the zero power was equal to one [$2^0 = 1$]. And if two to the zero power is equal to one, then maybe four to the zero power [4^0] is equal to one also." Ms. Mendez asked a few probing questions to try to develop this explanation, but the reasoning proved to be a bit shaky, and, though the student was on the right track, his explanation wasn't clear enough to convince his classmates.

"I like your ideas," Ms. Mendez encouraged, "but it sounds as though we're a bit confused on this one, so for the class prediction, I'm going to make a question mark between 'True' and 'False' and write "Clarification needed" in the explanation box.

"Now we have a focus for the first part of our

reading. Open your textbook to page 180. We're starting a new unit today on factors and fractions, and it begins with a discussion of powers and exponents. The first heading on page 180 is entitled 'Exponents.' Has everyone found it? Good. OK, now I want you to read through that section keeping the anticipation guide in mind. Our first two questions asked about the definition of the term *exponent* and the value of four to the zero power [4^0]. Read through and find information that can help to confirm, clarify, or refute our prereading responses."

Reading math textbooks is not easy. They are filled with lots of information that doesn't always connect in obvious ways. During her earlier years of teaching, Ms. Mendez had ignored the reading in the textbook altogether, relying on her own explanations and using only the problem sets in the text. But after revisiting the work of constructivist theorists such as Vygotsky, Bruner, and Piaget during her master's program, Ms. Mendez realized that when she provided all the information, she was limiting her students' opportunity to build their own understanding. She restructured her classroom to become more inquiry oriented and now relied on the textbook as a source of information against which her students could check their evolving understanding. The anticipation guides provided a focus for the reading, building opportunity for inquiry-based discussion before examining the text, and then for revisiting concepts and checking understanding after reading each section.

"Take your time with the reading," Ms. Mendez reminded her students. "This isn't a race. Good mathematicians read things over several times to check their understanding and clarify their thinking." She paused for a moment to allow students time to read the section through again. "Once you think you've understood the text, revisit the problems from the anticipation guide. Did you learn any information that can help point you toward a 'True' or 'False' response? Compare the statements in the first two prompts to the information in the text and then circle a response and explain your reasoning." She paused again to allow students to complete the postreading portion of the first section of the guide.

"So what did you find for number one?" Ms. Mendez asked the students. "Do you still think that it is true?" Heads nodded around the room. "Why do you think it is true?" she probed, "What new information did you acquire from the reading that confirmed your prediction?"

"It's like someone said before—it's just the definition," one student explained. "The book points to the number that's above the base and says that it's an exponent and that it tells how many times the base is multiplied by itself."

"Does anyone have a different explanation?" Ms. Mendez asked. "Is there anyone that disagrees that this is true?" Students were able to come to consensus fairly easily on this question, so Ms. Mendez moved on.

"How about the second statement? We couldn't decide before as to whether it is true or false. What do you think now?"

"It's false," a young woman quickly asserted. "The book says that any number to the zero power, except zero, is one."

"You sound pretty sure about that," Ms. Mendez responded. "Does everyone agree?"

Heads nodded around the room. "I agree," responded the student who had tried to explain zero powers earlier, "but I don't like their explanation. They just say that it's defined as zero. But there has to be a reason."

"That's a great observation," Ms. Mendez responded. "The book really doesn't provide a good explanation here. Does anyone have any ideas as to why a number to the zero power is one?"

A boy in the front row blurted out, "I know the book says it is one, but I still think it seems like it should be zero, because when you go backward in powers, each time you take away one of the base numbers, like, you subtract them. Two to the first power [2^1] has one less two than two to the second power [2^2], which has one less than two to the third power [2^3]. You take one away each time. So if you take a two away from two to the first power [2^1], then wouldn't you have zero?"

"But it's not adding and subtracting," another student countered. "It's multiplying and dividing. See on the chart here, when the exponent number goes up, you multiply the base. When the exponent goes down, you divide. So if you have two to the first power [2^1] and you take away one of the exponents, then you divide off the two, and two divided by two is one."

The explanation was a bit hard to follow, but it was mathematically sound. Ms. Mendez probed to develop the thinking further, extending students' understanding beyond the text before moving on to the next section of the anticipation guide.

The anticipation guide helped to focus students' mathematical learning by pointing them toward key concepts in the text and asking them to apply those concepts to verify or disprove the statements on the guide. Ms. Mendez's skillful use of this tool created opportunities for students to have conversations about mathematical thinking. The class worked together to construct understanding. The textbook was one voice, but certainly not the only voice, in the discussion.

Focusing the Reader in the History Classroom

As students settled into their chairs and began the warm-up written on the board, Mr. Pereira passed back papers and mentally prepared for the mini-simulation that was about to play out. Only one student, Matt, had been clued in; the rest would be caught off guard by the actions of their normally easygoing and accommodating teacher.

Taking a deep breath, Mr. Pereira went over to Matt's desk and began the simulated interrogation. "Matt, why didn't you come see me yesterday after school?" he demanded. Matt shook his head and muttered something about not knowing that he was supposed to come by. "I stated it very clearly in class yesterday," Mr. Pereira continued. "I told you at the beginning of the period and I reminded you again at the end—you needed to come by to discuss your grade. You all heard me, didn't you?" Mr. Pereira looked out at the class, who by this time had put their pencils down and were wide-eyed with surprise. None of them had heard Mr. Pereira make such a request the day before, but none of them volunteered to correct him.

"Mr. P, I didn't know, honest," Matt responded with his hands up in protest.

Mr. Pereira approached Matt's desk and stood over him, glaring. "You know, that is your problem, you are always trying to find ways to get out of things."

Matt's voice took on an edge, "Are you calling me a liar?" He stood up from the desk and took a step toward Mr. Pereira. "You are the one who is lying. You never said anything and now you are trying to blame me for your problem."

The exchange continued for a few more minutes as the room became more and more tense. The rest of the class remained silent watching the action. A few looked at the observer sitting in the back of the room, with expressions of concern. One edged near the door of the classroom. But no one tried to directly intervene.

After what seemed like forever (but was really less than three minutes), Mr. Pereira brought the simulation to a close and let the class in on the secret—he and Matt weren't really upset with each other. Matt hadn't missed any after-school appointment. And there wasn't going to be a fight. "We're starting a new unit today on America's role in international conflict," Mr. Pereira explained. "We'll be looking at America's role in the Spanish-American War and our actions prior to World War I and World War II, as well as during the Cuban Missile Crisis, the Rwandan genocide, and the conflict in the Balkans. In each case we're going to have to grapple with tough questions about America's decisions: When is intervention appropriate? When should we get involved in conflict? And when should we stand aside?

"What you just participated in was an opportunity to intervene in a conflict. Now, obviously it wasn't quite at the level of a world war, but your response, the moral and ethical dilemmas that you encountered as you listened to my conflict with Matt, are not all that different from the debates that go on at a national scale when the country is debating whether or not to get involved in a conflict.

"I'd like you to take a couple of minutes and think about our little simulation. In your history notebooks, write down number one, a description of what happened, two, a description of your response, three, the reasons why you chose not to get involved in the conflict, and four, events or circumstances that might have led you to get involved." Mr. Pereira listed the four prompts on the board.

After the tension that had built up during the simulation, it was a relief for students to spill their reactions onto paper. Even students who normally wrote very little had a lot to say. While students wrote, Mr. Pereira prepared a chart titled "Reasons For/Against Intervention." He labeled one column on the chart with a plus sign for reasons for intervention and one column with a minus sign for reasons against intervention. After a few moments, Mr. Pereira opened up the floor for discussion, and as students shared out, he skillfully paraphrased descriptions of their behavior in this specific instance into general considerations that could apply more broadly. For example, when a student said that she didn't do anything because she thought if she did she might get in trouble with the teacher and her grade might be lowered, Mr. Pereira responded, "So you were afraid that there might be some payback from me, that you might be hurt later on?" The student nodded and Mr. Pereira wrote "Fear of future retribution" in the "against" column on the chart paper at the front of the room.

Less than fifteen minutes after the class had begun to share, they had listed out a thoughtful range of responses on the chart (see Figure 2.5). Each of these responses directly reflected students' experiences in the brief simulation, but they also addressed the concerns that would be raised again and again as students read primary and secondary source documents specific to the historical case studies Mr. Pereira had mentioned.

"Great work," Mr. Pereira encouraged his students. "You've identified key arguments that work for and against intervention based on your own experience. Now it is time to take a look at what some of the Founders had to say about America's role in international relations. We're going to take a look at excerpts of writings and speeches by Thomas Paine, George Washington, John Adams, and James Monroe. As you read each of these excerpts, I want you to pay attention to the arguments that they make for US intervention or nonintervention. Underline specific arguments, and then next to each, paraphrase the reasoning in your own words. After you've had a chance to examine the readings, we'll look back and see how many of the Founders' arguments parallel the reasons that you've provided based on our classroom simulation."

Establishing the outlines of the arguments for and against intervention through an immediate, relevant scenario provided students in Mr. Pereira's class with the background understanding necessary to recognize similar considerations as they engaged with historical readings. Although the excerpts from Founders' writings and future case study texts would present new information and pose arguments in language grounded in the particulars of the historical context, having a larger framework to understand the major tensions that exist between isolationist and interventionist policies provided a context for the readings. Students were able to focus their purpose and strengthen their comprehension of complex historical texts.

Assessment *for* Learning

We typically don't think about assessment prior to reading. Assessment is more commonly used after a text has been read. However, if we are using assessment

Reasons For/Against Intervention

+	−
• It's the right thing to do	• Fear of getting hurt
• Concern that others will get hurt if I don't get involved	• Fear of future retribution
• Need to support friend/ally	• Risk of alienating friends/allies
• Want to help weak stand up to aggressor	• Not any of my business
• I may need others to help me later on	• Look out for own interests
• If we don't stand up, aggressor may come after us next	• Expectation that higher authority will step in
	• Save resources
	• Hope someone else gets involved

FIGURE 2.5. A prereading exercise in which the class brainstormed pros and cons helped Mr. Pereira's students get ready for a new unit on America's involvement in international conflict.

to support learning, it is critical to assess students' understanding throughout the reading process—before, during, and after students engage with text. Prior to reading, assessment should focus on the same elements that prereading activities are intended to develop: *context* and *purpose*.

Do students have knowledge of *context* that is appropriate for the text? If students have an appropriate conceptual understanding, they will be able to seek and select information from the text, retain that information, and critically respond to ideas in the text (Vacca & Vacca, 2008). If students have no knowledge of a topic, if their conceptual frame contains significant inaccuracies, or if their level of knowledge is insufficient for the intended text, comprehension is likely to be impaired (Alexander & Murphy, 1998; Sousa, 2001). If students' background understanding is inappropriate for the assigned text, it is important to recognize and address this gap before assigning a reading. Prereading assessment of context misunderstandings can help teachers avoid wasting valuable class time and causing frustration for both students and teachers. On the other hand, if prereading assessments reveal greater-than-anticipated knowledge of a concept, it may be appropriate to select a more challenging text, move on to less familiar concepts, or increase the rigor of the learning outcomes expected from students.

In content classrooms it can be particularly critical to assess for misconceptions prior to reading. Proficient content readers are able to recognize misunderstandings and relinquish inappropriate schema as they read. However, less experienced content readers often hold on to their misconceptions and consequently fail to understand the ideas and information contained in the text (Schoenbach, Greenleaf, Cziko, & Hurwitz, 1999).

In addition to considering students' understanding of context, it is equally important to assess students' *purpose* prior to reading. Do they understand why they are reading this text? Do they know what information and ideas they are expected to get out of the text? Do they recognize how they will be expected to analyze or apply knowledge gained from the reading? If students do have a clear understanding of the purpose of their reading, they will be more focused in their engagement with text, comprehension will increase, and content learning will be strengthened (Tovani, 2000, 2004). Without a clear purpose, understanding will diminish and time will be wasted.

Knowing whether or not students understand the context and purpose before reading requires that assessment opportunities be embedded within lessons alongside prereading activities. As can be seen in the examples that follow, prereading strategies such as a K-W-L chart or anticipation guide can double as assessment tools. However, in order for these tools to be effective as assessments, we need to be aware of and responsive to their use in this manner. We can't simply move quickly through a prereading demonstration or a challenging scenario and assume that if we're doing it, students will "get it" and be prepared for the text. Instead, we need to be alert to students' responses, aware of potential trouble spots that crop up, and armed with sufficient knowledge of our content and our students that we can effectively address areas of concern, either on the spot or through more sustained learning opportunities.

Assessment in Ms. Smith's Science Class

Ms. Smith had carefully structured the demonstrations in her physical science class to preview concepts that students would later encounter in the text. The first demonstration, pouring the water straight down out of the bucket, was intended to preview gravitational force. The second, tossing the water horizontally out of the bucket, previewed the idea of momentum while also demonstrating what happens when two forces counteract one another. The third demonstration previewed the idea of centripetal force. As she moved through the demonstrations, Ms. Smith listened to students' observations and predictions to assess whether or not they were recognizing, articulating, and responding to the concepts. To support students' learning, Ms. Smith began discussion with open-ended questions: "What will happen?" "Why?" "What did you notice?" But as she assessed student responses, she asked further questions to clarify and deepen their thinking: "Tell me more about what direction you think the water will go and why." "You're saying I'm throwing the water, but I haven't actually touched the water. Can you explain your thinking a bit more?" These prompts responded to students' comments and focused their attention more closely on the forces demonstrated by the prereading activities. Guiding questions such as these are critical to ensure that fun, attention-grabbing activities, such as tossing water from a bucket, support the larger instructional purpose and help students develop the contextual schema for content reading. In their absence, prereading anticipatory activities risk becoming mere entertainment. The oral discussion in this class as well as students' individual "Observe, Predict, Verify" charts helped Ms. Smith assess and guide students' focus and response to the class demonstrations, thereby ensuring that they were prepared to encounter descriptions of core physics concepts in the reading.

Assessment in Ms. Robinson's Drama Class

Eavesdropping on students' conversations during their viewing of Depression-era photos, Ms. Robinson became aware of significant gaps in students' knowledge. "Why are they moving?" one student whispered to a friend while viewing a photo of a caravan headed west. "I didn't even know they had cars back then," another commented. Students would need answers to these questions before they began their drama production. Fortunately, the informational reading that she had selected assumed little prior knowledge. However, Ms. Robinson knew that comprehension would be stronger if students had a skeletal understanding of events prior to engaging with the text. She also wanted to address some of the misconceptions that students voiced in their initial response to the photos. Although tempted to intervene whenever inappropriate information was aired, Ms. Robinson initially bit her tongue. She knew that if she came across as too authoritarian students would stop sharing their responses. Instead, Ms. Robinson bided her time, allowing students to correct one another initially. Then, during the K-W-L, she provided just enough information to prepare students for the reading. As the one holding the pen, she got to decide what information should go in the "K" section of the chart. When she knew information to be inaccurate or inappropriate, she rephrased the information as a question for the "W" column or provided a quick explanatory correction. "I'm not sure if we can say that the government didn't care," she commented in response to a students' assertion. "Let's make that into a question. How might I rephrase that for the 'W' column?" Thoughtful responses such as this to assessed misconceptions prior to reading helped to ensure that when students did engage with the text they were able to look for and understand appropriate information to support their larger learning purpose.

Assessment in Ms. Mendez's Math Class

As students responded to the true/false prompts on the anticipation guide, Ms. Mendez assessed students' readiness for reading the text. Unlike end-of-lesson evaluations that measure success by the accuracy of the true/false label, Ms. Mendez's assessment process focused more on students' ability to articulate their thinking. She was looking for students to begin to think through the use of exponents and to be able to explain their reasoning. The student who responded, "I think five to the third power equals fifteen [$5^3 = 15$] is true because five to the third power [5^3] means three fives multiplied together and that's fifteen," had a flaw in her mathematical computation, but she was able to begin to reason her way through the mathematical expression. Ms. Mendez recognized that this student had the background and focus necessary to engage with the text, to match her reasoning against the text's explanation, and then, after building additional content knowledge from the reading, to engage in a constructivist discussion with her classmates. On the other hand, the student who responded, "I don't know why b to the fourth power [b^4] equals b dot b dot b dot b, I guess it just does," was missing a key piece of knowledge that the text expected students to have before reading. "Remember that in algebra those dots mean multiply," Ms. Mendez gently responded. "If you think of that expression as b to the fourth power [b^4] equals b times b times b times b, does that make any more sense to you?" Providing information that was needed while not overstepping students' process of constructing their mathematical understanding was a delicate balancing act for Ms. Mendez. It required that she know the material well and understand the text's expectations. A well-designed anticipation guide that provided questions similar to, but not exactly the same as, the prompts in the text helped Ms. Mendez identify potential areas of misunderstanding and step in to clarify where necessary.

Assessment in Mr. Pereira's History Class

As students shared their responses to the in-class intervention simulation, Mr. Pereira listened carefully to their input. In his head, the history teacher had a list of the considerations that supported interventionist and isolationist policies, and he wanted to be sure that these considerations were articulated before students began the unit readings. He wanted to be sure, for example, that students recognized the roles of alliances, self-interest, and fear of retribution. Mr. Pereira had intentionally crafted the simulation to ensure that these considerations were present for students. He had selected a popular student, knowing that Matt had many friends in class who might act as allies and come to his defense. He had intentionally made an issue out of his own mistake (i.e., the fact that he claimed he had asked Matt to see him when he really hadn't), knowing that this would force students to choose between their sense of fairness and their desire to stay out of the line of fire. These were issues that students would see articulated in the readings, and Mr. Pereira wanted to be sure that the prereading simulation adequately prepared them for the ideas they would encounter in the primary source documents. As students shared, Mr. Pereira thoughtfully rephrased their observations, remaining true to the students' intent, but introducing language akin to what they would find in the readings. Where gaps in the share-out existed, Mr. Pereira gently probed to see if he could elicit further considerations from the students. "Did anyone think about going for help?" he queried, knowing that relying on other authorities and alternative influences was often given as reason for nonintervention in global relations. "Who might you have gone to? Why?" he asked. Only when he was satisfied that students had hit the key considerations that would be addressed in the readings did Mr. Pereira introduce the texts. Although students' understanding wasn't yet fully developed, the discussion of the prereading experience suggested they had developed a sufficient schema for understanding the concepts articulated by the Founders.

Not everyone can pull off a simulation like Mr. Pereira or a demonstration like Ms. Smith. It takes a special relationship with a class, for example, to be able to intentionally level a false accusation at a student in front of his peers. However, although we may not all be able to replicate these examples exactly, we all can, and should, craft analogous opportunities to focus students prior to engaging with content texts. With knowledge of both our students and our disciplines, content teachers are uniquely positioned to draw on student interests and experiences and to prepare them to encounter text purposefully. By using strategies like those described in this chapter to build a contextual framework and establish an explicit purpose for reading, teachers can set students up for success and ensure that content reading supports content learning.

3

Supporting Comprehension

What You'll Find in This Chapter

Supporting comprehension in the content classroom: The chapter begins with a discussion of the importance of comprehension and the challenges students encounter as they work to comprehend text. Four approaches to support comprehension in the content classroom are then presented. Discussion of each of these approaches is followed by a list of instructional strategies and a classroom vignette of the approach in action.

Teach Students to Anticipate Text Structure and Content

Classroom vignette: Anticipating Text Structure and Content in the Dance Classroom

Teach Students to Monitor Their Comprehension

Classroom vignette: Monitoring Comprehension in the Math Classroom

Deepen Comprehension through Student-to-Student Talk

Classroom vignette: Using Talk to Support Comprehension in the Humanities Classroom

Capture Comprehension in Writing

Classroom vignette: Writing to Support Comprehension in the Science Classroom

Assessment for *learning:* The final section of the chapter provides a follow-up discussion of how teachers in each of the classroom vignettes assessed students' comprehension of the text.

I listened carefully as Dan read aloud each word of the Preamble to the Declaration of Independence. He sounded out each syllable, had perfect pronunciation, and carefully paused at each comma. But when he finished, he had little understanding of the text's meaning. "So what is this saying?" I asked.

"I don't know," Dan shrugged.

"Why do you think it was written?" I continued.

"I don't know," Dan stated again.

"What do you think the main idea is—the big announcement?"

By this time Dan's patience was wearing thin. "I . . . don't . . . know," he stated firmly, his voice taking on an edge with each word.

I tried to maintain an encouraging attitude. "OK, it's a hard text. Let's read it again and see if we can figure out what it means together."

Dan's face fell. "What do you mean, read it again? I just read it. I don't understand it. I'm done."

In this statement Dan articulated what so many struggling readers in our content classes experience. When faced with unfamiliar text, they try to read the material, their eyes pass over the text, maybe their mouths even sound out the words, but they don't understand the meaning and they don't know how to improve their comprehension.

Tovani (2000) calls this behavior "fake reading." When students fake read, they exhibit the outward signs of good reading, but the cognitive processes that support comprehension don't take place. We've all experienced fake reading at times. Fake reading is what allows us to get halfway through a newspaper article (or a student's paper) only to realize that we've been planning dinner or thinking about last weekend's activities and have no idea what we've just read. Reaction to that realization is what differentiates a proficient reader from a struggling reader. Proficient readers stop, look back to find the place where comprehension was lost, and reread. Struggling readers simply continue on, failing to see reading as an active process and believing that if they don't get it the first time, there's no point in trying again (Beers, 2003).

One of the challenges we have as content teachers is that "fake reading" and "real reading" look an awful lot alike from the outside. Although Dan didn't understand what he was reading, he was nevertheless able to fluently articulate the words and phrases of the Preamble. Many students in our content classes similarly exhibit the outward manifestations of good reading. They open their books, sit quietly, and slide their eyes across the words. Many develop coping strategies to compensate for their lack of comprehension. They fill in as much information as they can by listening to their peers and write down the explanations that the teacher provides. For some, this allows them to "get by"; they may even be able to pick up enough content knowledge to pass the end-of-unit assessment and answer the questions on the course exam. But when students can't read the text, they miss out on essential elements of content learning.

At its foundation, comprehension in content reading is about being able to acquire new information and understand new ideas. If students are unable to read and comprehend content texts, they dramatically limit their ability to access new content material (Moje, 2006). Although students may be able to pick up some information through lectures, discussions, and other classroom activities, they will be not become independent content learners without strategies for content reading comprehension.

In addition, students who cannot comprehend content texts will be limited in their ability to critically engage in content learning. The essence of learning is not simply to take in new facts or understand the ideas of others, but to be able to analyze ideas, evaluate interpretations, and transfer information to new situations (Bransford, Brown, & Cocking, 2000; Wiggins & McTighe, 2005). However, before students are able to analyze and evaluate the ideas of others, they must first understand them. Before students can act as apprentice historians, scientists, mathematicians, and artists, before they can transfer information and apply learning to new situations, they must first comprehend.

It's worth noting that although Dan's example presents the portrait of a reader who struggles with comprehension generally, *all* content learners are likely to struggle with comprehension at some point. The texts that we use in content classes are different from the texts that students encounter in their language arts classes. Content-specific texts have different language, different structures, and different expectations than the narrative readings that students grew up with. We are introducing students to the ways of thinking of our disciplines and, as such, it is natural that they will encounter challenges in comprehension. Indeed, they *should* encounter challenges! If students aren't confronted with challenging new information, ideas, and ways of thinking, then the material they are reading isn't difficult enough (Blau, 2003). As content teachers, part of our job is to provide *all* students with texts that are at an appropriate challenge level, and then to help them access these readings.

Supporting Comprehension in the Content Classroom

There has been a great deal of research into reading comprehension. Many years and many dollars have been spent investigating how to support struggling readers in increasing their understanding of text. Programs such as Reading Recovery and Striving Readers have provided intervention classes. Authors including Richard Allington (2005), Ellin Oliver Keene and Susan Zimmermann (2007), and Cris Tovani (2000, 2004) have written thoughtful, engaging texts about the application of reading support strategies in English language arts (ELA) classrooms. This work has yielded a wealth of material from which content teachers can draw. However, it is important to recognize that the application of reading comprehension strategies and structures in the content classroom will look different from how they appear in a reading support or ELA classroom.

As content teachers, we have two ever-present concerns when approaching discipline-based readings with students. First, we need to ensure that students are able to gain immediate access to content. There is a body of subject-area knowledge we want students to learn, not only to comply with state standards and prepare them for high-stakes tests but also because we are committed to our content areas and want students to leave our classes with an understanding of the discipline. Time in content classes is limited, and when we read texts with students we need to provide the structures and strategies that will allow them to gain access to the information and ideas in the readings in a timely manner.

At the same time, however, we also want to foster long-term, independent content learning. Even under the best of circumstances, students won't be able to learn everything there is to know about our disciplines when they are in our classrooms. We need to equip them with the skills, strategies, and ways of thinking that will allow them to continue to learn after they leave us. Teaching students comprehension strategies, particularly those strategies that are most relevant to texts in our subject areas, is an important component of fostering lifelong content learning.

The balance that content teachers strike between providing immediate access and fostering longer-term comprehension learning varies in each class and with each reading. There are times when it is most appropriate to help students get to text information quickly by telling them exactly where to look and what to expect. There are other times when we want students to work through the comprehension process more thoughtfully, struggle a bit with the text, and become conscious of the strategies that they can use to successfully navigate challenging content material. The balance we strike will depend on our instructional purpose for selecting and teaching the reading.

Being aware of the balance we are selecting is important, but, fortunately, the choice is not a clear-cut either/or. When we provide clear structures, explicit modeling, and repeated opportunities for comprehension strategy application, we are facilitating *both* short-term content access and long-term comprehension development.

The remainder of this chapter describes four research-based, classroom-tested approaches that content teachers can use to support reading comprehension in the classroom. Select strategies and structures within each approach that are most appropriate for your content and your students. Model their use, provide opportunities for guided practice, and, as students begin to take ownership of the strategies, encourage continued application by engaging students in new, more challenging readings. In doing so, you'll be helping students access content material today and facilitating content learning in the future.

Teach Students to Anticipate Text Structure and Content

Each content text comes to the reader as a particular kind of document with a particular structure. Helping students to anticipate the organization of texts can dramatically increase reading comprehension and content learning (Herber, 1978; Vacca & Vacca, 2008). Structures and cueing systems that readers use to make sense of text include the following:

Text features. Titles, headings, subheadings, bold words, italicized print, photos, illustrations, captions, and diagrams are all text features. They are designed to help readers prioritize and visualize the information and ideas in the text itself.

Text structure. Informational texts, such as textbooks, trade books, and magazine articles, are generally built around standard text structures, including description, chronological order, compare and contrast, cause and effect, and problem and solution. Titles and headings can often be used to help students anticipate the structure they will encounter. Signal words, such as those listed in Table 3.1, indicate transitions between events or ideas within the text.

Text genre. Specialized, content-based genres each have their own structural norms and expectations. Content-specific genres include articles from scientific journals, court rulings, artistic reviews, opinion papers, political cartoons, and mathematical proofs. The authors of these documents often expect that readers will have knowledge of the genre and generally do not provide many text features to support comprehension for the uninitiated. Explicit instruction in the norms of the genre can dramatically improve student comprehension.

Before assigning readings in the content classroom, it is appropriate to step back and consider how we might work with the features, structure, and genre of the

TABLE 3.1. Standard Text Structures

	Description	Chronological	Compare-Contrast	Cause-Effect	Problem-Solution
	Standard Text Structures				
Signal Words and Phrases Found within Text Structures	It was	To begin	Similarly	Because	Consider
	She or he	First	In the same way	Since	Take into
	They have	Second	Like	Therefore	account
	At the time	Finally	As	Thus	Resolve
	For example	Then	However	As a result	It is hoped
	In addition	Before	In contrast	If… then	It is expected
	In fact	After	On the other	Consequently	It is anticipated
	For instance	On (date)	hand	So that	Lead to
		At (time)	Although	Accordingly	Result in
			But		

reading to help support students' comprehension. We should ask ourselves questions such as, What do the students need to know in order to successfully navigate this text? How can I best provide them with that knowledge? Sometimes the answers to these questions focus on providing access to content information in text, and the responses can be as simple as informing students that "the author of this article has very strong opinions on the subject, so be careful to look at the facts that he chooses to include," or that "in this theater review, you're going to find a description of the play followed by an analysis of the pros and cons of the performance."

Other times, the responses may focus more on helping students develop their own strategies for the effective use of the features, structures, and genres of the text. This is particularly true for texts or types of text that will be used routinely within your classroom or text genres that are foundational to your content area. For example, a civics teacher who encourages students to read the newspaper every day will find it helpful to nurture independence by teaching students to use headlines and section headings to anticipate the difference between a news article, an investigative feature, and an op-ed piece.

The following are examples of instructional strategies that can be used to help students access texts and develop knowledge of the effective use of features, structure, and genre.

Text previewing. Teach students to preview text features and use the information in headings, illustrations, and boldfaced text to make predictions about the content and organization of the text itself. Previewing features can be an informal oral process or it can involve a more formal written approach. In the vignette that follows, Ms. Doyle previews the text with her students to support comprehension in her dance classroom.

Advance organizers. Provide students with an advance organizer that steps them through the content in the text. Advance organizers may be specific to individual readings, asking students, for example, to identify the four causes and two effects described in an article. Or they may be more general, helping students to recognize the description of a play, performance highlights, acting critique, and critical recommendation that may be expected when reading any theater review.

Text protocols. Develop a protocol of four to six guiding prompts that can be used when approaching texts that are common in your content area. For example, Ms. Keeby, a high school biology teacher, developed the protocol shown in Figure 3.1 to support her students in reading scientific journal articles.

Protocol for Reading Articles from Science Journals

1. **Identify the topic** – Read the title. Look for key words.

2. **Get the "punch line"** – Read the abstract. Look at the first and last sentence to find the "punch line" of the research. What was learned in this study?

3. **Get the context** – Read the introduction and conclusion to figure out why the study matters. How does it fit with and extend what we already know?

4. **Understand the approach** – Look through the figures and tables. You may not understand them at first but examining them now will help you understand the article when you actually read it.

5. **First read** – Reread the abstract and introduction, skim the methods section, read the results and discussion, and study the figures and tables.

6. **Reread** – Read the article a second time. Take notes. Ask questions. Consult the references.

(Protocol adapted from work by Dr. Robert Siegel, Biology Professor, Stanford Univ. http://stanford.edu/~siegelr/readingsci.htm)

FIGURE 3.1. Protocol for reading articles from science journals.

Anticipating Text Structure and Content in the Dance Classroom

Ms. Doyle gathered her beginning dance students together near a portable whiteboard set up at the edge of the dance studio. They were in the midst of a unit on lyric dance and had spent the past couple of days working to design their own choreography to a portion of a Celine Dion song. Ms. Doyle had provided the students with sample steps to include and had modeled the process of choreography by thinking aloud about her own creative process. However, in observing her students at work she noticed that many weren't really responding to the lyrics in the song. For this day's lesson, Ms. Doyle selected an article from *Dance Spirit* magazine that stressed the importance of lyrics and provided some great suggestions to help dancers integrate the lyrics into their choreography. Although she simply could have stated the information herself, Ms. Doyle had found that it could be more powerful when suggestions come from a text. "They need to see that there are other people thinking about these issues," she explained. "That it's not just me. And I want them to become accustomed to taking ideas from a magazine or newspaper and trying them out. Whether it's dance or exercise or cooking, I think it's important for them to be able to transfer and apply techniques to their own experience."

With a range of readers in her class, Ms. Doyle knew that she couldn't just give the students the article and tell them to read. Since the text was rich with photos, illustrations, and other features, she decided to work with students to preview the text. This strategy would help them access the content of the dance article and it would help reinforce a comprehension approach useful in many content-area readings.

Students sprawled on the floor as Ms. Doyle passed out copies of the one-page article "Word Power." "Before you start reading," she announced, "I want you to take a minute and look at the features that are on this page. What kinds of features do you see?" This was an easy question and students were quick to respond: "A title," "Headings," "Pictures," "A box with a separate part of the article in it." Ms. Doyle nodded encourag-ingly, providing more technical terms where appropriate—"Yes, there are *captions* under the photos, good observation"—and asking a prob-ing question or two to get students to recognize features they had missed—"What about this part down here on the right side of the page? Does anyone notice anything about this area?" Students quickly pointed out the title and subtitle, two accompanying photographs with captions, a text box with bullet point suggestions, and two il-lustrations that gave examples of choreographed routines. Satisfied that they had recognized all of the features on the page, Ms. Doyle pushed her students to consider the features more carefully.

Once she was satisfied that students had identi-fied the features on the page, Ms. Doyle encour-aged students to consider the information in the features more carefully. "I want you to go back and look at each of these features more closely. What do you notice about the heading? What ideas or information might you infer from that caption?" She paused and then provided her students with an illustration of this strategy. "For example, when I look at this photo, I notice that it shows a female dancer, that she is dressed in a leotard and tights, that she's barefoot, and that she is positioned in a manner that seems both powerful and graceful—she has her arms and legs extended while balancing on one foot with her head up and eyes forward. These details provide me with clues that might help me predict something about the article. First, her clothing suggests that this article is probably about mod-ern dance rather than tap or ballet. Second, I can infer from the choice of such a powerful position that the article might address something about movement and image."

Ms. Doyle modeled the process of jotting down a few notes about her inferences on her copy of the article and then instructed the students to apply the same strategy to the other features in the text. Working with partners, students discussed the choice of words in the headlines, noticed that the bullet points highlighted specific instructions, and worked to visualize the routines depicted in the illustrations. "Down here the heading is 'Love your lyrics,'" one student commented. "It's almost like a command, like you can't just listen to them, you have to *love* them."

"Do you think it's really possible to love the words in a song?" her partner wondered. "I mean, that seems kind of strong."

"I don't know," the first student responded. "Maybe it means that you have to feel them, like you would feel love. Maybe the article is going to tell us how to do that."

Satisfied that students' conversations indicated they were on the right track, Ms. Doyle played a few bars of music to refocus students' attention. "Good work. I heard lots of nice inferring going on. Now I want you to take a moment before you begin reading and put all of your ideas together. On your paper, write down a one-sentence prediction. Based on what you learned from the features, what do you think will be the main idea of this article?" Several students wrote down their predictions immediately; others paused, chewing on their hair or biting their fingernails while reviewing the features to try to synthesize their thoughts. Ms. Doyle, who had been circulating quietly among the splayed out dancers, quietly commented, "I like the way many of you have used the text features to make predictions. I see some good work. Deena," she said to a student in the middle of the class, "would you share your prediction?"

Deena shyly responded, "Choreography is better if it responds to the ideas in the song."

"Great prediction," Ms. Doyle agreed. "Can you tell me what led you to that prediction?"

Deena's voice gained strength as she explained her thought process. "The photos show dancers who seem like they are really poised and strong. And the headings are about 'love your lyrics' and

'listen to your lyrics' and 'word power', so it seems like it's saying that if you want to be poised and strong and a good dancer like the ones in the photos then you should pay attention to the ideas in the song when you are choreographing your dance."

Ms. Doyle nodded, smiling. "Excellent," she praised. "Who else has a prediction?" Two other students shared their predictions before Ms. Doyle moved to the next stage of the reading activity. "You are absolutely on the right track," she confirmed. "This article is about using the words in songs to strengthen the choreography in your lyric dances. Your job, as you read, is to flesh out that main idea by identifying specific strategies dancers can use to express song lyrics through their dances. At the end of the reading, I'm going to ask you to identify at least three strategies that you've found. And then we're going to think about how we can apply them to our own lyric dances. OK, now get to work."

Previewing the text features provided Ms. Doyle's dance students with a clear direction for this reading and helped prepare them to access, and later apply, the information and ideas in the text. In addition, by providing a clear model and focused questions to guide the process, Ms. Doyle helped equip her students with a comprehension strategy for the long term. Three key questions guided the class's work previewing text features: (1) What features do you notice? (2) What information can you infer from those features? and (3) Based on your inferences, what predictions can you make about the main idea(s) of this text? These questions can be used to facilitate text previewing across multiple texts and multiple content areas. In this lesson, taught fairly early in the year, Ms. Doyle made explicit use of this strategy, actively modeling the process for students. Over time, as students gained more confidence and skill with previewing, she released responsibility for the use of this approach to her students, expecting them to be able to apply the strategy on their own.

Teach Students to Monitor Their Comprehension

Cris Tovani (2000) tells students in her reading support class that good readers have two voices inside their heads. There's the voice that recites the text and the one that interacts with the text. When the first voice pauses at the end of a sentence or paragraph, the second voice works to make meaning from what has just been read. It asks questions, rephrases ideas, makes connections, and draws inferences from the text. This voice is doing the cognitive work of comprehending.

For many students, the second voice shuts down when they encounter challenging content texts. It was shut down when Dan was reading the Preamble to the Declaration of Independence, as we read at the beginning of this chapter. He wasn't monitoring his own comprehension, didn't recognize when meaning broke down, and didn't know how to address confusion.

Helping students to activate this "second voice" is a critical element in supporting content text comprehension. When students actively monitor their comprehension, understanding of text dramatically increases (Hacker, 1997). Also, students who monitor comprehension and recognize when meaning breaks down are much more likely to take steps to repair meaning (Davidson & Sternberg, 1998). Monitoring text meaning won't fix all comprehension challenges; students will still encounter confusion and have questions. But the very fact that they have questions indicates increased understanding. The students I worry about the most are the ones like Dan, who get to the end of a challenging piece of text and have nothing to say about it.

Coaching students to monitor their comprehension requires more than simply telling them to pay attention to the second voice. It involves teaching specific strategies that can be used to focus that second voice as they read. Several strategies are described below. Each can be helpful in providing immediate access to content and, when effectively modeled and regularly implemented, can support long-term independent application. Truly independent content readers have a range of monitoring strategies at their disposal and are able to selectively implement them depending on the situation. When teaching monitoring strategies, I initially require all students to apply the same approach. However, over time, as students gain mastery, I allow greater flexibility and let individual students choose the strategy that works best for them.

Monitoring Strategies

Comprehension scoring. Ask students to score their comprehension on a scale between one and ten. Scoring will help students become more aware of what they do and don't understand and motivate them to re-read parts of the text that are confusing. The power of comprehension scoring was brought home to me at a workshop run by Kylene Beers. She had participants read a poem three times, each time scoring their understanding on a scale between one and ten. My score moved from a three to a nine simply as a result of focusing in on my comprehension and rereading the text.

One-sentence summaries. When content texts are written in an unfamiliar structure or contain unfamiliar language, it can be challenging for readers to make sense of the text at the word and sentence level while simultaneously making meaning at the paragraph or whole-text level. Teach students to chunk the text into sections, stopping at the end of each paragraph or section (or, with a particularly challenging text, each sentence) to record a one-sentence summary. Summaries should be written in students' own words and recorded in the margin or on a sticky note for later clarification or application.

Says/means. In this technique, students select important quotes, information, or ideas from the text to record in the "Says" column of a T-chart. In the "Means" column, they paraphrase their meaning. Monitoring for critical information as they read and then explaining the significance in their own words helps keep students focused on making meaning from text. In her eleventh-grade classroom, Ms. Roberts has set up a Google document template that allows her students to work through Says/Means charts on the class set of laptop computers. Students drag short text selections from an online reading into the Google document and then type a response in the adjacent column (see example, Figure 3.2). With her students reading many of their texts online, Ms. Roberts found the strategy to be particularly useful for maintaining focus and enhancing comprehension.

Selective underlining. When used selectively, underlining and highlighting can be useful strategies to help students determine what is important within a text. Giving students clear guidelines—"Underline the three most important sentences in the text" or "Highlight only the information that shows the effects of global warming"—will help focus their reading and encourage them to reread to clarify confusion and prioritize information. In the math lesson that follows, Mr. Brown uses clear underlining guidelines to help students make sense of word problems.

Quick fixes. When understanding does break down, teach students to use "quick-fix" strategies to strengthen comprehension. Although quick fixes won't work in every situation, they can help students build stamina and

Notes on "The Four Freedoms" Speech to Congress, Franklin D. Roosevelt, 1941

Says	Means
"I use the word 'unprecedented' because at no previous time has American security been as seriously threatened from without as it is today."	U.S. security is more threatened in 1941 than at any time in history.
"Today, thinking of our children and of their children, we oppose enforced isolation for ourselves or for any other part of the Americas."	We need to avoid locking ourselves behind a wall and isolating U.S. from rest of world. It is important for the future.
"I find it unhappily necessary to report that the future and the safety of our country and of our democracy are overwhelmingly involved in events far beyond our borders."	Even though we may not want to, we're going to have to get involved in the war.
"No realistic American can expect from a dictator's peace international generosity, or return of true independence, or world disarmament, or freedom of expression, or freedom of religion -- or even good business. Such a peace would bring no security for us or for our neighbors. Those who would give up essential liberty to purchase a little temporary safety deserve neither liberty nor safety."	We can't make a deal with Hitler or other enemies. They won't honor the treaties and we'll end up without freedom or security.
"In the future days, which we seek to make secure, we look forward to a world founded upon four essential human freedoms. "The first is freedom of speech and expression -- everywhere in the world. "The second is freedom of every person to worship God in his own way -- everywhere in the world. "The third is freedom from want, which, translated into world terms, means economic understandings which will secure to every nation a healthy peacetime life for its inhabitants -- everywhere in the world. "The fourth is freedom from fear, which, translated into world terms, means a world-wide reduction of armaments to such a point and in such a thorough fashion that no nation will be in a position to commit an act of physical aggression against any neighbor -- anywhere in the world."	All countries and people should be able to share the same values. They are 1. Freedom of speech 2. Freedom of religion 3. Freedom from want 4. Freedom from fear
"That is no vision of a distant millennium. It is a definite basis for a kind of world attainable in our own time and generation."	We can make this happen now.

FIGURE 3.2. Ms. Roberts's students used a Says/Means chart to monitor their comprehension of Roosevelt's speech.

work through tough texts (Beers, 2003). Students may have been exposed to these strategies in other classes and previous years, but a reminder is often necessary to help them transfer those skills into the content classroom. Post a chart, model the strategies, and encourage their use by asking guiding questions: "I noticed that everyone had some areas they color coded as being confusing in yesterday's reading. We're going to revisit the reading today. What are some things that you could do to help clarify your comprehension?" Quick fixes include the following:

• Slow down.

• Point to the words as you read.

- Reread a short section.

- Read it aloud.

- Replace an unknown word with a familiar synonym.

- Chunk the text into manageable sections.

- Restate information in your own words.

- Talk with a peer.

- Review your purpose for reading.

- Ask for help.

Monitoring Comprehension in the Math Classroom

Mr. Brown's seventh-grade pre-algebra class began nearly every day with a word problem warm-up. The word problems were designed to reinforce learning from the previous day and support the development of students' academic language. Many of Mr. Brown's students were English language learners and they struggled with making connections between written language and numerical representations. This, to Mr. Brown, was all the more reason to regularly introduce word problems and teach students strategies for making sense of the language. One persistent concern was helping students determine what information was important. Many word problems are written as mini-stories and include interesting but superfluous information. Struggling readers who fail to monitor their comprehension of text often assume that they can simply pull out the numbers, plug the information into a formula, and get the answer. This assumption often leads to misunderstanding and incorrect answers.

As students rushed to make it to their desks before the bell rang, Mr. Brown handed them a half sheet of paper with the following problem and four prompts printed on it:

Ana had some candy to give to her children. She has four children, three girls and one boy. Ana picked out all ten of the strawberry candies to keep for herself. She divided the rest of the fruit-flavored candies evenly between her children. Each child got eight pieces. Her son ate all of his candy right away, while the daughters ate half and saved the rest for later. How many candy pieces did Ana have in the beginning?

1. What is the problem asking?
2. Underline the information that you need to solve the problem.
3. Use the information to write an algebraic expression.
4. Solve.

The same four prompts were written on a chart hanging in the front of the room, along with a few hints (see Figure 3.3). From the very first day of the year, Mr. Brown had modeled the use of these prompts with his students. Initially he thought aloud as he demonstrated his own use of these prompts in solving the problem. Now, four weeks into the course, he continued to guide their learning, but the process was more interactive.

"Good morning," Mr. Brown's voice echoed around the room. Students hurriedly placed backpacks under their chairs, took out pencils, and scribbled their names on top of the warm-up paper. "I like that I see so many of you already beginning to read your warm-up. That is excellent. For those who haven't yet begun, I want you to take a moment and read the problem silently to yourself. This is your first read, so I don't want you to do any underlining yet. On your first read, your job is only one thing. Who can tell me what that is?" Eager to please their much-respected teacher, hands were quickly raised around the room.

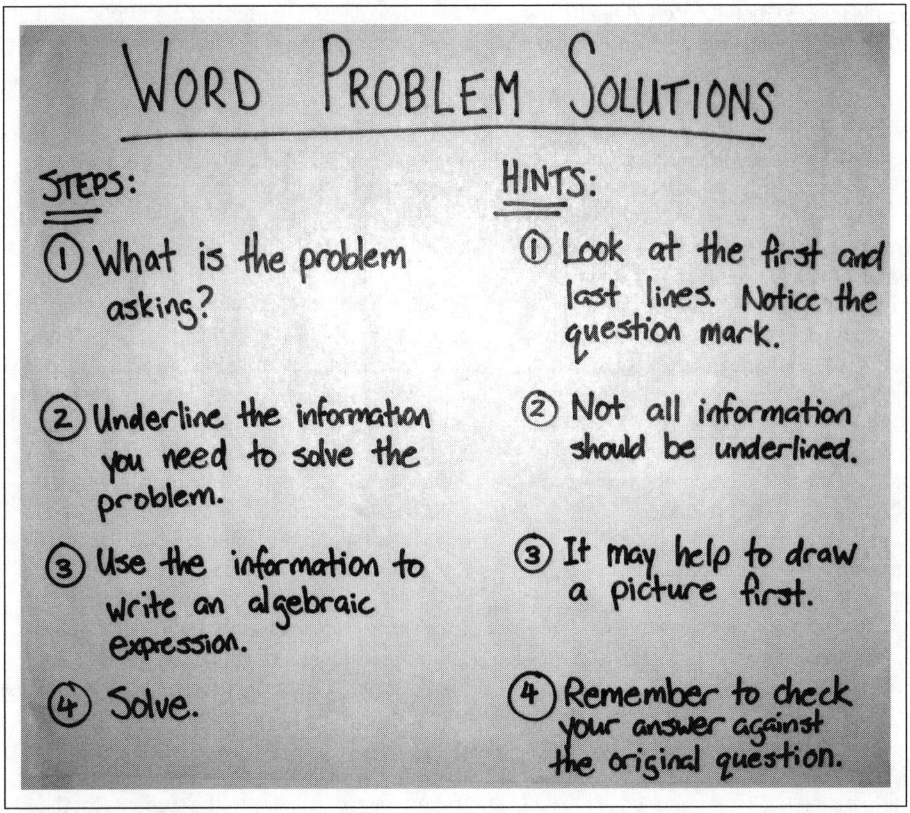

WORD PROBLEM SOLUTIONS

STEPS:

① What is the problem asking?

② Underline the information you need to solve the problem.

③ Use the information to write an algebraic expression.

④ Solve.

HINTS:

① Look at the first and last lines. Notice the question mark.

② Not all information should be underlined.

③ It may help to draw a picture first.

④ Remember to check your answer against the original question.

FIGURE 3.3. Mr. Brown posted the four steps for solving math word problems. Students used these steps throughout the year.

"To figure out what the problem is asking," a girl in the front row volunteered.

"Outstanding," Mr. Brown agreed. "And what are some hints for how we might find that information?" he asked. Eyeballs darted toward the chart hanging in the front of the room.

"You can look at the beginning and end of the problem," one student paraphrased.

Another added, "You can look for a question mark."

Mr. Brown agreed, "Good . . . OK, now do it. Read the problem through to yourself and figure out what the problem is asking. Don't rush. Take your time and reread if you need to. Once you think you know what the problem is asking, write your response next to number one on the bottom of the page."

Mr. Brown had given this same advice and asked these same guiding questions several times before and would ask them several times more in the coming weeks. Mr. Brown knew that the repetition was important. The structures and language of algebraic word problems were unfamiliar to many students, and they needed repeated reminders of the text clues and reading strategies they could use to find relevant information.

After students had written a response at the bottom of their page, Mr. Brown checked to see if they had agreement. "We have to figure out how many pieces of candy Ana had to start with," a student explained. He then focused their attention on the next prompt in the problem-solving process.

"I'm going to read the text aloud this time," Mr. Brown explained. "I want you to follow along and underline only the information that we need to figure out how many pieces of candy Ana has in the beginning. Remember, not all the information should be underlined." Reading the text aloud to the students helped to focus their attention and reduced the difficulty of the task. Struggling readers and English language learners often find it challenging to simultaneously read the words and make sense of their meaning. Mr. Brown wanted the students to focus on selective underlining this time around; his decision to read the text aloud gave all students the ability to do so.

After he finished reading, Mr. Brown instructed students to reread on their own and double-check their work. "If you find more places that need to be underlined, do it. If you find places that don't need to be underlined, erase. That's why we use pencils in math, so that when we get smarter and learn more, we can change our minds. Erasing isn't about a mistake, it's about getting smarter and learning more." Mr. Brown grinned at his students and roved around the room as they reread and revised. He then instructed them to pair up with a partner and compare their choices. A few minutes later, he called the class back together. "OK, what did you decide needed to be underlined?" Line by line the class went through the problem, agreeing for the most part, and disagreeing occasionally, about what information was important in solving the problem.

"The fourth sentence doesn't matter," one boy insisted. "It doesn't matter that she gave them fruit-flavored candies."

"The flavor doesn't matter, but it is important that they were given evenly," another boy countered.

"Yes, but that information is also in the next sentence," the first boy responded. "It says, 'Each child got eight pieces.' We don't need to underline it twice."

Mr. Brown facilitated this discussion at the front of the room, reading each sentence aloud and underlining (and erasing) words and phrases on the document camera in response to student input. He loved the debates and tried to avoid stepping in, preferring to allow the students to come to an agreement on their own. After a few moments, students were able to reach consensus. Though there was some debate over whether "evenly" *needed* to be underlined, in the end they agreed that it was helpful in confirming how the candy was distributed. Mr. Brown went on to guide the students through the process of crafting an algebraic expression and then asked them to solve it using the two-step equation-solving skills they had been learning in recent lessons (see a sample of one student's work in Figure 3.4).

As the year progressed, Mr. Brown released more and more responsibility to the students for the process of using these problem-solving prompts. By the end of the year, he expected to be able to hand them a sheet of paper and stand silently while they conducted the process on their own. The information and complexity of the problems would change over the course of the year as the material changed and students learned more, but the problem-solving approach would remain the same. Repeated practice allowed students to gradually assume ownership of the process. Knowing and being able to use strategies to solve problems was critical in preparing Mr. Brown's students for success in algebra and beyond.

Deepen Comprehension through Student-to-Student Talk

When students have the opportunity to talk about their reading, comprehension increases and retention of information is strengthened (Calwetti, 2004; Marzano, Pickering, & Pollock, 2001). Literacy expert Lucy Calkins describes talk as "a major motor—I could even say *the* major motor—of intellectual development"

Mr. Brown – Pre-Algebra

Word Problem Warm-Up

Ana had some candy to give to her children. She has four children, three girls and one boy. Ana picked out all ten of the strawberry candies to keep for herself. She divided the rest of the fruit-flavored candies evenly between her children. Each child got eight pieces. Her son ate all of his candy right away, while the daughters ate half and saved the rest for later. How many candy pieces did Ana have in the beginning?

1. **What is the problem asking?**

   How many candy pieces Ana has to start.

2. **Underline the information that you need to solve the problem.**
3. **Use the information to write an algebraic expression.**

   4 × 8 + 10

4. **Solve.**

   32 + 10 = 42

   Ana had 42 candy pieces to start.

FIGURE 3.4. An example of one student's use of the protocol for solving word problems.

(2001, p. 226). Research studies across content areas have consistently found that higher levels of learning are directly linked to active construction of knowledge through student-to-student talk (Center on English Learning and Achievement, n.d.; Wolf, Crosson, & Resnick, 2004).

There is a subtle but important difference between readers conceptualizing understanding of text in their head and articulating their thinking to peers. When students talk through their thinking aloud, they test out their conceptual understanding. One of my favorite comments to overhear among students occurs when one is explaining her confusion about a part of a reading, only to interrupt herself with, "Oh. I get it now!" I have those "Aha" moments myself when I'm trying to explain an article about something complex, such as tension in the Middle East, to my own children. In trying to explain it to them, I gain new insights into the topic. The simple act of putting ideas from a text into their own words helps readers construct new knowledge. Simultaneously, listeners deepen their understanding as they work to reconcile their thinking about the text with their peers' representation of that same text. Where differences in comprehension occur, conversation among peers provides the opportunity to clarify and deepen understanding.

Of course, not all talk is meaningful talk. Much of the conversation that occurs in classrooms is more social than academic, and it is tempting to avoid student-to-student talk in an effort to keep the class focused on content. Purposeful talk, or "accountable talk" (Resnick, 1995), is focused and collaborative. It requires that students actively engage with ideas and work to co-construct understanding (Nichols, 2008). As content teachers, part of our job is to structure opportunities for talk that support student comprehension and focus their attention toward the reading purpose. If the reading purpose is to look for relevant information, the talk should help students recognize, prioritize, and conceptualize that information. On the other hand, if the reading purpose is to understand an author's point of view, then talk might help students recognize the author's argument and consider how he or she uses evidence to support that argument.

Instructional Strategies

Think-pair-share. First, provide a focused prompt that encourages students to think. Prompts can be general (e.g., "State the main idea of the text.") or text-specific (e.g., "Why does the author believe the United States should increase the use of nuclear energy?"). Next, ask students to pair with a partner to discuss their response to the prompt. I use a timer during this section to keep the talk focused. Finally, in the whole group, students share ideas and information from the peer conversation. Asking students to share an idea from their partner or a question they discussed together helps to hold students accountable for their conversation. I like to extend the traditional think-pair-share (Lyman, 1987) one step further by asking students to reflect in writing at the end of the share. I use questions such as these to prompt their reflections: What did you think about this topic at first? What new information/ideas did you learn? What do you think now? The writing is another means of holding students accountable for the quality of their talk and helps them to reflect on their learning.

One question, one comment. Instruct each student to generate one question and one comment about a common text to share with a peer. Use this strategy as a quick opportunity to share thinking and clarify confusion in the midst of a text reading or to jump-start a discussion of a particularly challenging text. Teacher and author Kelly Gallagher writes, "This activity never fails to generate an in-depth discussion about the reading assignment and helps those who have struggled with the text to gain meaning they would have otherwise been unable to attain. Even excellent readers learn something new during this conversation" (2004, pp. 48–49).

Active listening. Talking comes naturally to most adolescents; listening is more of a challenge. Teach students sentence stems to use in responding to their peers to increase their ability to listen and respond to each other. This strategy may be used with partner talk, in small groups, or during whole-class discussions. Sample sentence stems include the following:

- "What I am hearing you say is . . ."
- "I agree that . . ."
- "Could you clarify what you mean when you say . . ."
- "I'm not sure I understand . . ."
- "I respect your opinion, but I disagree that . . ."
- "I wonder if you've considered . . ."

Reciprocal teaching. Have students work in pairs to deepen their understanding of a particularly challenging text by focusing in on four reading tasks: (1) summarizing, (2) questioning, (3) clarifying, and (4) predicting (Palinscar & Brown, 1984). Chunk text into short sections and then engage students in a cycle of reciprocal teaching after reading each text. Reciprocal teaching is a strategy that has been around for some time but remains relevant and can be used in a wide range of classrooms. In the humanities example that follows, reciprocal teaching is employed to help high school students grapple with Adam Smith's *Wealth of Nations.* When used regularly, reciprocal teaching has been proven to increase comprehension, reading achievement, and standardized test scores (Rosenshine & Meister, 1994).

Using Talk to Support Comprehension in the Humanities Classroom

Mr. Doherty's tenth-grade class includes students reading at a range of literacy levels, but the humanities teacher doesn't shy away from giving his students challenging material to read and critique. He chooses texts that address issues of social theory and philosophy, readings normally reserved for college students. As he sees it, the class is preparing students for life as adults. He wants to build their stamina and their confidence and equip them with good strategies for abstract thinking.

One strategy that plays a critical role in helping students develop their thinking is student-to-student talk. Before, during, and after a reading, Mr. Doherty provides focused opportunities for academic discourse as students ask questions, build comprehension, and clarify understanding with their peers. Sometimes the talk is short and sweet. A quick think-pair-share, for example, may be used to clarify confusion about a background reading or make predictions about the concepts they'll encounter in a primary text. Other times the talk is much more intense. Frequent Socratic seminars provide students with opportunities to discuss the relevance of an author's ideas and the merits of his or her arguments.

This lesson featured an intermediate step. The text was taken from Adam Smith's *The Wealth of Nations*. Embedded within Mr. Doherty's unit on European industrialization, Smith's writing provided rich material for the class to analyze and debate. But the debate needed to wait. The focus for this lesson was on understanding the material. "There's plenty here to discuss," Mr. Doherty told his students, "and we'll have a chance to dig in to the text during our Socratic seminar next week. But before you begin to analyze and evaluate Smith's ideas, you need to make sure you understand what he has to say. You don't have to agree with his arguments, but you do need to comprehend them."

To support comprehension of this very challenging text, Mr. Doherty did the following: (1) he chunked the text into shorter sections, each only a few lines long (see the sample student paper in Figure 3.5), (2) he previewed challenging vocabulary terms, (3) he introduced focus questions for each section of text (see Figure 3.6), and (4) he provided opportunities for students to talk through their developing comprehension with peers using the reciprocal teaching model.

After first providing time for students to read five lines of the text excerpt on their own, Mr. Doherty encouraged them to reread and try to respond to the focus questions on their own. "These are the questions you'll be discussing with your partner during our reciprocal teaching conversations," he reminded the students. "You don't want to let

Mr. Doherty – World History

Adam Smith, *The Wealth of Nations*, Volume 1, Chapter 2
Of the Principle which gives occasion to the Division of Labour

THIS division of labour, from which so many advantages (are derived) is not
have come =

originally the effect of any human wisdom, which foresees and intends that general
not planned ???

(opulence) to which it gives occasion. It is the necessary, though very slow and gradual
riches

consequence of a certain (propensity) in human nature which has in view no such
tendency

extensive utility; the (propensity) to (truck, barter) and exchange one thing for another.
doesn't see or plan for wealth — tendency — trade

FIGURE 3.5. Mr. Doherty supported his students' comprehension of a challenging text by giving them short chunks to read and respond to.

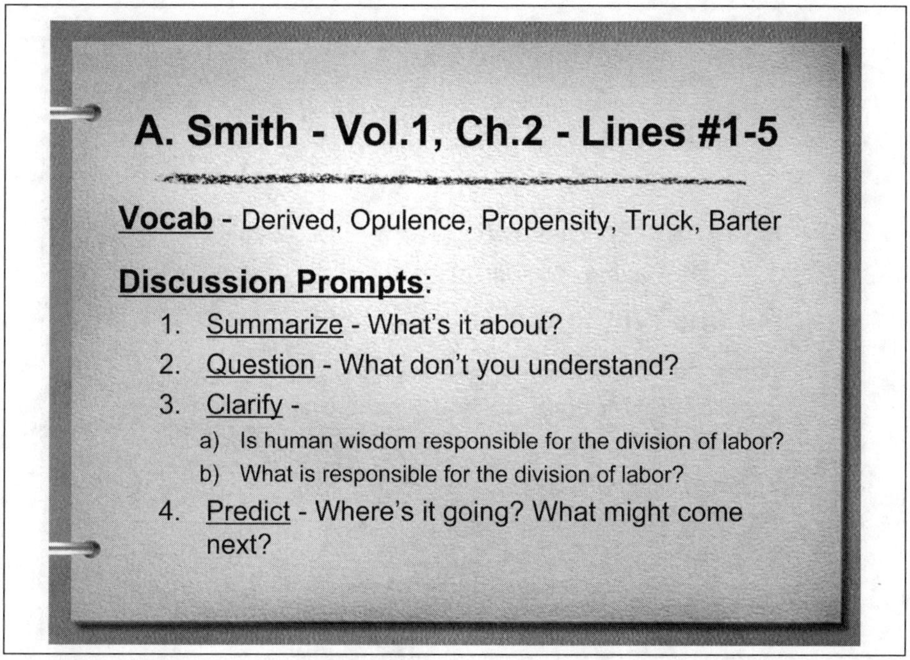

A. Smith - Vol.1, Ch.2 - Lines #1-5

Vocab - Derived, Opulence, Propensity, Truck, Barter

Discussion Prompts:
1. Summarize - What's it about?
2. Question - What don't you understand?
3. Clarify -
   a) Is human wisdom responsible for the division of labor?
   b) What is responsible for the division of labor?
4. Predict - Where's it going? What might come next?

FIGURE 3.6. Students used prompts specific to each chunk of text as a guide to their peer discussions.

your partner down. Write notes in the margins or in your notebook. Be prepared and bring ideas to the conversation to share."

Later in the year, Mr. Doherty's next step would be to move students directly into peer conversations, but when this lesson took place in the early fall, the students had only tried reciprocal teaching a couple of times. It was still a relatively new strategy and some struggled to keep the conversation focused and flowing. Mr. Doherty asked two students who previously demonstrated fluency in reciprocal teaching to be in the "fishbowl" and model the approach for their peers. He reviewed the guidelines for the conversation (see Figure 3.7) and then asked the students who were observing to move their chairs to the periphery of the room. "As you listen to Elena and Brianna talk," Mr. Doherty instructed, "I want you to pay special attention to how they respond to each other. Take note of the questions they ask. Write down the answers they give. We're going to debrief at

the end, and I'm going to expect you to be able to tell me what they did in their conversation."

After an encouraging nod from Mr. Doherty, the two students began their discussion:

BRIANNA: So what do you think the text is about?

ELENA: I think it is about how people started dividing up their responsibilities. What did you think?

BRIANNA: I was confused. I had to read it twice. But I think, yeah, what you said. It tells how the division of labor got started.

ELENA: What part did you not get?

BRIANNA: In the second line, the part about human wisdom, I don't know what he is trying to say here: [Student reads] ". . . is not originally the effect of any human wisdom, which foresees and intends that general opulence to which it gives

Conversation Guidelines

☆ **Connect to the text.**
- Use the line numbers.

☆ **Focus on the questions.**

☆ **Don't be afraid to ask questions.**
- The only "dumb" question is the one that isn't asked.

☆ **Listen carefully.**
- You are responsible for learning from your partner.

FIGURE 3.7. Mr. Doherty provided students with guidelines for their discussions.

occasion." So is he saying that human wisdom helps us with the division of labor or not?

ELENA: I was confused by that part too. But when I read the rest of the line, I figured that he's saying that even though people have wisdom and can foresee things, they didn't plan for the division of labor.

BRIANNA: That was one of our clarify questions. So the answer to 3a is "no"?

ELENA: Yeah, it's "no."

BRIANNA: But wait, we didn't do your question. What don't you understand?

ELENA: I'm wondering if he thinks that the division of labor is a good thing. He says in the first line that it brings lots of advantages, but he seems pretty negative about how we got here.

BRIANNA: I don't know if he's negative about it as much as he's saying that it was just lucky.

We didn't use our wisdom to get here, just our instincts.

The conversation continued in this manner for several more minutes before Mr. Doherty called for time and led the class in a round of applause for the volunteers. "Well done," Mr. Doherty commented. He then turned to the student observers to debrief the lesson. "What did you notice?" he asked. "What did Brianna and Elena do to work together to make sense of Adam Smith?"

"They asked a lot of questions," one student responded. "They'd say what they thought and then they'd ask what the other person thought." Mr. Doherty nodded and recorded the observation on the board.

"They used the questions you gave us," another student observed, "and not just like to start off the conversation. They came back to the question to be like, 'Are you sure we answered it? Are you sure we agree?'"

"I liked how Brianna could show where she was confused, not just like the whole thing, but which lines exactly," a third student commented. "And then I liked how Elena didn't make her feel stupid about it or nothing. She said she was confused too and tried to explain it. That was cool." As Mr. Doherty recorded their observations on the board, he smiled to himself, noticing how similar their comments were to the guidelines he had previously stated. This was an example of the power of "show, not tell." As their teacher, he could have repeated and repeated those guidelines, but when students observe their use in the practice of their peers, they assume much greater authority.

"OK," Mr. Doherty announced. "Now it is your turn." He assigned students to discussion partners and had them pair up to engage in their own reciprocal teaching conversations. They started out using the same five lines that they had already heard modeled in the fishbowl. The now familiar text content allowed students to focus more closely on their contributions to the conversation while deepening their understanding of this very dense text. The pairs then moved on to subsequent chunks of text, repeating the pattern of first reading on their own, then rereading and making notes, talking about the text with their peers using the reciprocal teaching prompts, making more notes to reflect their evolving understanding, and finally sharing out with the whole class to clarify any lingering confusion and develop a consensus understanding.

As I moved among the pairs of students in the class, I was impressed by how focused they were. This was a text I had struggled with as a college sophomore, and these students were high school sophomores. After class I pulled a few students aside and asked what motivated them to stick with such a hard text. One commented on the brevity of the portions of text they were asked to read. Another noted the motivating factor of the upcoming Socratic seminar and their loyalty toward their teacher. And all agreed that the opportunity to talk through the text with their peers was essential. "If I had to read it on my own, I would probably quit," one student admitted, with general agreement from her peers. "That text is really hard and at first you feel kind of dumb for not understanding. But the way Mr. Doherty structures the conversations, it's like it makes it OK. It's like a puzzle that you figure out by talking it through."

Capture Comprehension in Writing

Writing is a powerful way to strengthen and reinforce comprehension. Taking notes or writing a summary in response to a reading helps students to process information, identify main ideas, recognize the relationship between pieces of information, and articulate questions. Research has consistently found that when students capture new learning in writing, their retention of information increases and their understanding of complex concepts is strengthened (see, for example, Faber, Morris, & Lieberman, 2000; Rivard & Straw, 2000).

However, as with the other comprehension supports described in this chapter, it is not simply the strategy, but the *purposeful* use of the strategy, that matters. A colleague recently shared with me an "Aha" moment about the use of writing in history. "I went to a workshop last year where they told me that summaries are good for learning. So I had my kids summarize everything. We summarized chapters in the textbook. We summarized primary source documents. We summarized current events articles. At first it seemed like it was helping;

kids really did seem to be retaining more. But after a few weeks, things slid backward. I asked the kids what was going on and they told me that they were bored. One little girl said that since she knew she was going to have to write a summary after every reading, it made her less interested in actually doing the reading. I think I overdid it."

Summaries can be great tools if we want students to capture an account of what a particular author has to say or a synopsis of an event or phenomenon. When presenting a scientist's findings, for example, or preparing to debate the views of historical figures, summaries can be very useful in helping to synthesize information and ideas coherently and succinctly. But not all situations demand summarization (Wormeli, 2005). Sometimes we are more interested in capturing information that can be used in a cause-effect analysis or understanding chronological events that can be represented on a time line. In these cases it is likely to be more appropriate to engage students in note taking using targeted graphic organizers.

Teacher and author Jim Burke reminds us, "Taking good notes trains students not only to pay attention but *what to pay attention to*" (2002, p. 21, italics added). As teachers, we can help make writing meaningful for students by crafting note-taking opportunities that help to focus students' attention on the information and ideas that are significant in the text. Writing opportunities should respond to the instructional purpose with which we approach the text, helping students to gather the information or understand the concepts that later they will be asked to analyze, evaluate, synthesize, or apply.

Instructional Strategies

- *3-2-1 summaries.* Direct students to summarize relevant information in a series of bullet points (Wormeli, 2005). For example, in a history class investigating British imperialism, a teacher might ask students to identify within a reading *3* regions that were colonized by Britain, *2* benefits that Britain gained from imperialism, and *1* challenge that Britain faced as a result of imperialism.

- *Graphic organizers.* Use charts, matrixes, concept webs, or Venn diagrams to help students capture and organize important text information. Choose structures and headings that focus students' attention toward information they will need to use in future applications. An example of a concept web from a reading for an art history class is seen in Figure 3.8. In the classroom vignette that follows, Ms. Martin's students organize reading information into a matrix that they can apply to observations from their science lab.

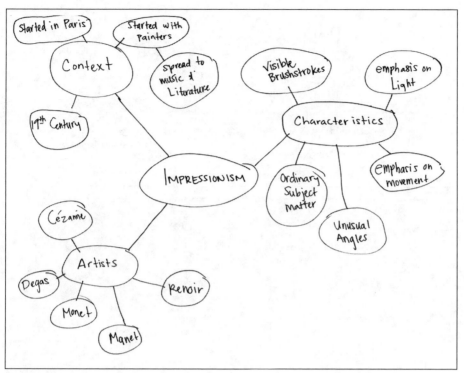

FIGURE 3.8. A concept web, such as this one from an art history class, is one graphic organizer students can use to capture and organize important text information.

- *Something-happened-and-then.* Require students to condense a text description of events down to the basics with this very succinct summarization technique (Wormeli, 2005). An example: "Mt. Pinatubo (something) erupted in June 1991 (happened), releasing 20 million tons of sulfur dioxide into the air (and), temporarily lowering global temperatures (then)."

- *Double entry journals.* Instruct students to divide a notebook page into two columns. Then, they should take notes on important information they find in a reading in the left column and explain why the information matters in the right column. Use a guiding question to focus student readers on the information they will need to apply in future learning activities.

- *Graphic summaries.* Ask students to use pictures, labels, and arrows to represent a description of a system or process, such as blood circulation or the creation of a new law. Figure 3.9 shows a graphic summary of Greek history through an annotated time line. This strategy is great for students who are visual learners.

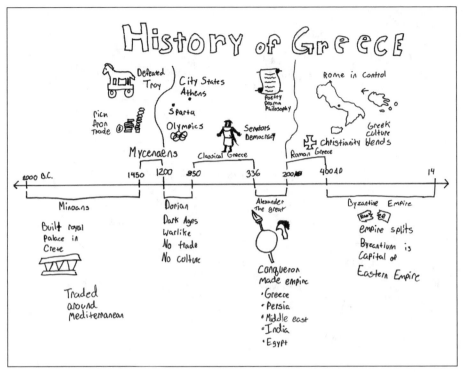

FIGURE 3.9. Graphic summaries such as this one help students demonstrate their comprehension of text information.

- *Cornell notes.* Have students turn chapter and section headings into questions and record them on the left side of a notebook page. They should then read for answers to the questions and record them on the right side of the page (Pauk, 2000). Solidify learning by asking students to craft a summary at the bottom of the page. Figure 3.10 shows an example of Cornell notes from Ms. Heinzeman's algebra class. During the first year that she implemented Cornell notes as a regular feature of the class, both reading and math scores for Ms. Heinzeman's class increased dramatically. Cornell notes are especially appropriate to use with considerate texts when students will need to be aware of all the concepts in the reading for future application.

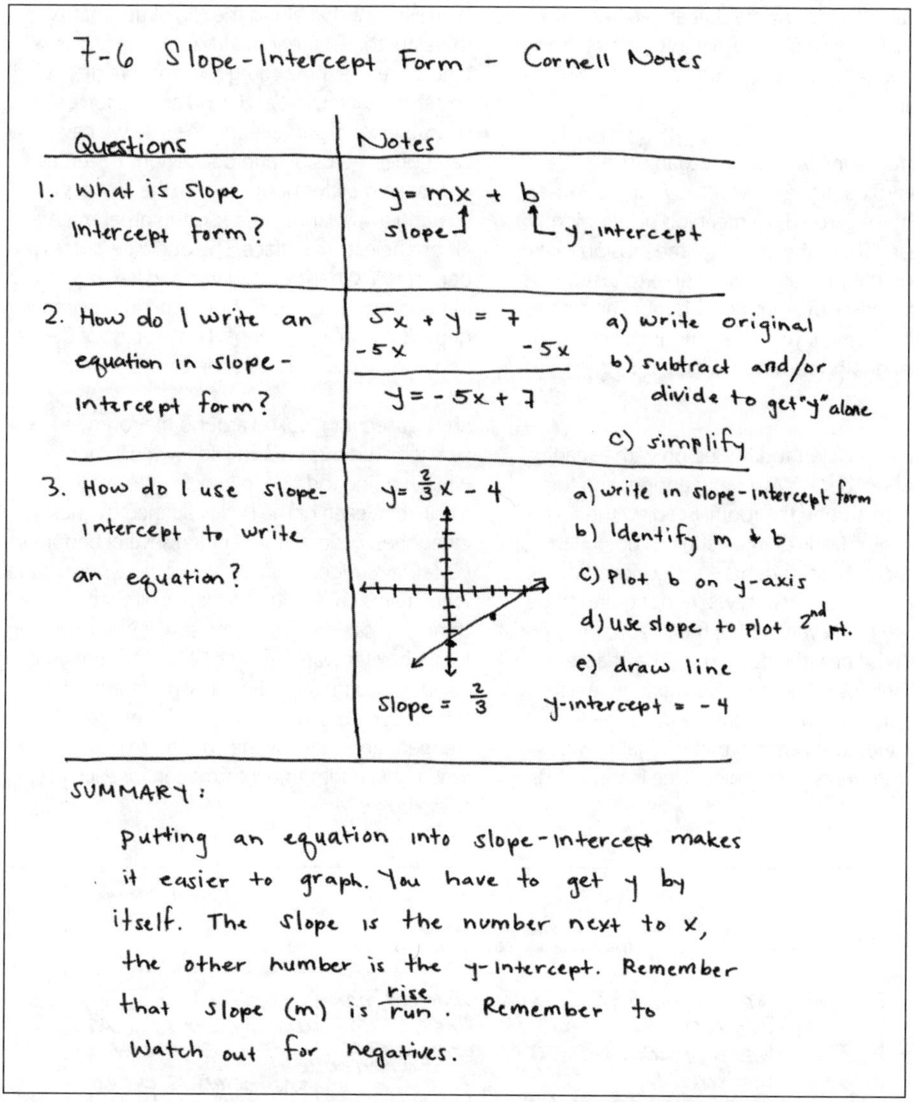

7-6 Slope-Intercept Form — Cornell Notes

Questions	Notes
1. What is slope intercept form?	$y = mx + b$ slope ↑ ↳ y-intercept
2. How do I write an equation in slope-intercept form?	$5x + y = 7$ $-5x \qquad\qquad -5x$ $y = -5x + 7$ a) write original b) subtract and/or divide to get "y" alone c) simplify
3. How do I use slope-intercept to write an equation?	$y = \frac{2}{3}x - 4$ a) write in slope-intercept form b) Identify m + b c) Plot b on y-axis d) use slope to plot 2nd pt. e) draw line Slope = $\frac{2}{3}$ y-intercept = -4

SUMMARY :

Putting an equation into slope-intercept makes it easier to graph. You have to get y by itself. The slope is the number next to x, the other number is the y-intercept. Remember that slope (m) is $\frac{rise}{run}$. Remember to watch out for negatives.

FIGURE 3.10. An example of Cornell notes to support comprehension of a math text.

Writing to Support Comprehension in the Science Classroom

As her ninth-grade earth science students arrived for fourth period, Ms. Martin's computer projected a slide show onto the screen at the front of the room. Images of glacier-carved valleys, hillsides denuded by landslides, and rocks formed in the shape of giant natural arches greeted the students. The class was entering their second day of a unit on erosion. On the previous day Ms.

Martin and her students had worked to define the concept of erosion and had begun to consider the potential forces that shape and reshape the earth. Looking at the same photos that were now projected onto the screen, they had worked with peers to posit hypotheses about the natural forces at work by considering these questions: How had that valley been created? What led the trees to fall down? How did that arch come to exist? Today, they would gather information from their textbook to confirm, refute, or refine their understanding.

"Good afternoon," Ms. Martin began. "Today we are going to continue to work on your erosion lab from yesterday. You did a great job developing hypotheses about the causes of the erosion that you saw in the photos. Now it's time to test out your hypotheses by learning a bit more about the forces and seeing if your predictions match up with what geologists have learned about erosive forces.

"We're going to start today's lesson with a reading from your textbook," Ms. Martin announced to groans from around the room. Reading the textbook was not nearly as interesting as doing lab work as far as most students were concerned. Ms. Miller smiled. "Don't panic, you're not going to be required to read every part of the chapter. You're going to read only the portions of the chapter that will help us gather the information we need to complete our lab." She passed out a reading guide that featured an information matrix with six boxes for students to complete (see Figure 3.11).

"You'll notice that along the top of this matrix there are three categories," Ms. Martin explained. "These are the three categories that we discussed yesterday; water, ice, and wind are the forces responsible for erosion. Along the side we have two categories—erosion and deposition. Yesterday we spoke mostly about erosion, the process of wearing away sand, dirt, rock, and other materials on the earth's surface. The opposite process is deposition. When wind, water, and ice wear away dirt and sand, they don't hold onto it forever; they deposit it in new locations. This process of deposition also helps to reshape the earth's surface."

She paused and looked around the room to make sure the students were still following. "Your job while reading today is to look for information to fill in for each of the boxes defined by these categories. For example, I heard several people yesterday suggest that V-shaped valleys are made when rivers cut through a plateau. If that's something you can confirm in the text, it would belong in the box for water erosion." Ms. Martin paused to demonstrate recording this information on her own matrix on the overhead. "Let's take a moment and preview the chapter to determine where you might find information for each of these boxes."

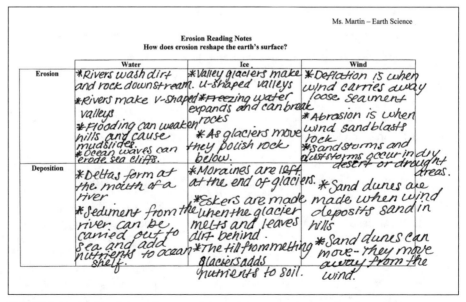

FIGURE 3.11. Ms. Martin's students used a matrix to target their textbook reading.

Together the class opened their textbooks and scanned through the text features to find likely spots for reading. "Ice eroding rock," was quickly identified as a place to look for information for the ice erosion box, and students predicted that "River deposits" would be a good place to look for information for the water deposition box.

"Can we use information from the captions?" a student asked.

"You are encouraged to do so," Ms. Martin responded. "The illustrations and captions can provide great information. And be aware that they don't always match up on the page next to the relevant heading. If you see a picture that you think looks appropriate, don't be afraid to examine it."

After answering a couple more student questions, Ms. Martin concluded her instructions by telling students that they needed to find three pieces of information for each box on the matrix. "You don't need to write complete sentences, but be sure to record enough information so that you can later explain it to a peer. And leave space in your boxes to add more information later on as well. After you're done with your individual readings, I'm going to ask you to compare notes."

As students began to read, Ms. Martin circulated through the room, helping to refocus students where needed and answering questions when students expressed confusion. For the most part, however, students settled into the reading easily. The fact that they didn't have to read everything meant that students felt more ownership and were more willing to engage. This was a different approach than what Ms. Martin had used as a less experienced teacher. Back when she first started teaching, she had seen the textbook as a compilation of required facts. She'd made students read and take notes on everything. But she'd found that they resented the work and resisted the learning. Ms. Martin occasionally still worried that students would miss out on something important, but she knew that she would be able to redirect and provide additional information where needed once she had assessed their work. Besides, this introductory reading and lab were primarily to provide context for the more in-depth lab activity that anchored the unit. In the coming days, students would begin to investigate the process of erosion along local sea cliffs. Learning about erosion more generally provided students with an understanding of the basic process and would help them make connections between what they observed in their own community and what takes place in other regions around the world.

"Two more minutes," Ms. Martin warned her students. They had been working for about twenty minutes to read and take notes on their findings. Nearly every student had been able to fill information into each of the boxes in the matrix. There was something about boxes. If the prompts had been phrased as questions, Ms. Martin knew, several of the students wouldn't have bothered to even try to respond. But for some reason, they were more willing to work to fill in an empty box.

"Good work," Ms. Martin praised. "I really liked the effort that you put into your work today. Reading over your shoulders, I see that you've collected lots of great information. Now I'd like you to have a chance to share that information with your peers. Your job is to get into groups of four. Within your groups you are going to go over what you found in your reading, and for each box I want you to add at least two new pieces of information." Ms. Martin moved to the document camera to demonstrate. "For example, in my box for ice erosion I have written '(1) When water freezes it expands and can crack rocks, (2) Glaciers create U-shaped valleys, and (3) Rocks in glaciers can gouge the rock beneath.' Now I noticed that Juan, you also wrote down that glaciers make U-shaped valleys, but you had more detail in your statement. What else did you add?" Juan quietly explained that it was valley glaciers, rather than continental glaciers, that caused U-shaped valleys. "Absolutely," Ms. Martin agreed, "so that is something I can add. I can write 'Valley' before 'glaciers' to clarify my information. That's one addition; does anyone have another piece of information I can add?"

From the front row, Marisol volunteered, "Glaciers polish the bedrock."

"Excellent," Ms. Martin nodded her head as she added Marisol's information as a fourth point in the ice erosion box on her matrix. "The ice crystals and smaller rocks that are in the glacier act like sandpaper and polish the bedrock, the rock beneath the glacier. Well done."

Ms. Martin encouraged students to record the information she had just shared and then allotted ten minutes for them to share information from the other boxes of their matrixes with peers. This allowed just enough time at the end of the period for the class to return to the photos from the previous day's lab. Students used the information that they had collected on their matrixes to revisit their initial hypotheses. Working in teams, they re-examined photos, decided what new information from their matrixes was relevant, and adjusted their assertions accordingly.

"Yesterday I thought this was a sand dune made by wind erosion," one student, Jena, told her group as they reviewed a photo of a winding ridge in North Dakota. "But now I think it's from ice."

"I don't see ice in the photo," another student, Hector, challenged.

"I don't mean ice today. I mean ice from like the last ice age. The book said that since the climate changed glaciers have retreated," Jena responded.

"Yeah, and you see how it's one long ridge," a third student added, "and there's nothing else around, like no other ridges. It's probably from the glacier's moraine."

"Yeah, I think you're right," Hector agreed. "If you look you can see that there's grass and stuff growing on the ridge. If it was a sand dune, it wouldn't have plants 'cause the wind would have to be able to keep moving the particles."

Conversations such as these helped solidify students' learning. They were able to make immediate connections between what they had read in the text and the photos that were part of their lab. The matrix that had helped focus students' attention during the reading now served as a convenient reference that facilitated conversation and connections. It did what the best note-taking structures are supposed to do: support the application of information from the reading to more authentic, inquiry-based learning activities.

Assessment *for* Learning

Instructional support for reading comprehension in the content classroom can, and often should, simultaneously foster immediate access to content and longer-term comprehension strategy development. Assessment, however, should differentiate these goals. To support students' learning, it is important to know what information and ideas they were able to pick up from the text as well as how successful they were in employing comprehension strategies. When comprehension breaks down, is it because the concepts in the reading were too difficult? Or is it because the text itself was not accessible? When students are able to recognize new information and ideas, is it because the scaffolds provided by the teacher permitted them access? How successful would students be in accessing that information if they were working more independently?

Designing assessments that can answer these questions help us determine next steps in the classroom. If, for example, students successfully demonstrate the use of comprehension strategies but are unable to grasp significant concepts described in a text, we may need to find alternative instructional media or different readings to teach these concepts. On the other hand, if assessments reveal that students are struggling to monitor their comprehension with a difficult text, it may be appropriate to revisit that text or reteach the strategy with a future text.

Each of the teachers whose classrooms are profiled in this chapter used a range of assessments to determine where students achieved success and where comprehension broke down. The following vignettes describe some examples.

Assessment in Ms. Doyle's Dance Class

Ms. Doyle's instruction in text previewing had two purposes. It helped students access the text immediately and it supported students in developing a prereading strategy that they could use in future readings in dance class and other academic classes. Since her instructional purpose was twofold, Ms. Doyle's assessment plan had two foci as well. She assessed students' access to content in real time. Listening in on students' previewing conversations and their predictions allowed Ms. Doyle to determine whether students had enough background to be able to read and understand the text. By confirming their predictions, redirecting conversations that veered off course, and stating a clear and concise reading focus,

Ms. Doyle used these real-time assessments to support student success in reading the article and accessing the content. Later, however, she would use students' written comments to assess their strategy development. Looking over copies of the articles, she observed the inferences students had recorded in the margins as well as the predictions they had written on top. She noted with satisfaction that all students had been able to record at least two inferences and most had crafted an appropriate prediction. This had been a fairly simple text, but student success here indicated a readiness to move on to more challenging material, opening up a wider range of content reading possibilities to Ms. Doyle and her students.

Assessment in Mr. Brown's Math Class

Throughout the warm-up activity, Mr. Brown was constantly assessing his students' comprehension. He roved the classroom looking over shoulders, listening in on peer conversations, and stopping to ask students to share their thinking. "Tell me why you chose to underline this information," he'd routinely prompt students. Or, often as not, "Tell me why you chose not to underline that information." At first, many students assumed that being asked such a question was an indication of an error; previous experience had taught them that math teachers often focus only on what is wrong when providing feedback. However, students gradually came to understand that Mr. Brown was interested in learning about the thinking behind their choices and this, in turn, made

them more thoughtful about their process. These oral assessments provided Mr. Brown with a window into students' comprehension and allowed him to assess whether they had enough understanding of the content of the word problem to be able to find a solution. However, Mr. Brown wasn't content to end the assessment there. He knew that he wouldn't always be around to provide support for students' problem solving, and it was important to determine how well students could apply the process independently. Once each week, Mr. Brown asked students to solve a similar warm-up word problem on their own. They were instructed to use the same process and to show all their work—identify the problem, underline the important information, use the information to write an algebraic expression, and then solve. When Mr. Brown collected these warm-up papers, he was able to gain a much better understanding of students' progress in their ability to read and understand word problems.

This assessment helped him determine which students needed more individual support, which were ready for greater challenges, and how much responsibility he could release to the class to read and respond to problems on their own.

Assessment in Mr. Doherty's Humanities Class

Throughout the reciprocal teaching conversations in his classroom, Mr. Doherty supplemented talk with writing. Before each round of talk, students were required to respond in writing to the prompts from the board. And then after each round of talk, Mr. Doherty required them to capture new understandings in writing as well. "Before you move on to the next section," he would announce, "take two minutes to write down what you learned from your conversation. What do you now understand about the text that you didn't before?" This focused writing captured students' thinking in progress and helped them solidify comprehension of one section of text before moving on to the next. Ten minutes before the end of the period, Mr. Doherty required students to write about their learning once again. "You've been through four different sections of the text today," he would tell students. "Before you leave, you need to write down three things: (1) Look back over your notes and summarize your understanding of the text up to this point. What are the main ideas that Smith is trying to communicate? What evidence does he offer to support his assertions? (2) Tell me one thing that you learned from your conversation that helped you clarify your understanding of the text. How did reciprocal teaching help you with this reading? (3) Tell me what continues to confuse or trouble you about the reading. What do you not

understand?" This final set of writings served three purposes. First, it allowed students the opportunity to synthesize their comprehension of the various pieces of text and recognize the flow of Smith's argument. Second, it encouraged them to think metacognitively about their comprehension process—to recognize how they had made sense of the text and the role that talk had played in their meaning-making process. And third, it provided Mr. Doherty with an excellent set of assessment data. Looking over students' text notes and final reflections, Mr. Doherty was able to get a sense of what information and ideas they understood and where confusion still existed. He was able to identify, for example, that most students understood Smith's main point, but that some stumbled over some of the analogies between the behavior of animals and that of humans. Mr. Doherty would clarify this confusion at the start of class the next day. In addition, Mr. Doherty was able to determine the efficacy of talk in the lesson. He noted that most students self-reported that the conversations helped them significantly and that the before-and-after text notes appeared to support that assertion. But several students didn't appear to gain similar benefits from the reciprocal teaching. Mr. Doherty made note of these names in his plan book, along with a note stating, "Change partners for next recip. teach. Monitor more closely."

Assessment in Ms. Martin's Science Class

After students had gone home for the day, Ms. Martin leafed through their science notebooks. Students had pasted into their notebooks two sets of information that provided her with an excellent assessment of the day's learning. On one page were the matrixes with notes from their

science text. On the facing page were their lab notes. Each set of lab notes included prereading hypotheses and explanations and then postreading assertions and supporting evidence. Looking over their work, Ms. Martin was able to see exactly what students understood and where understanding broke down. Many students had accurately completed both the matrix and the lab notes, indicating success in both reading comprehension and concept understanding. Several, however, showed that they were able to collect information from the reading, having accurately completed the matrix, but that they weren't able to accurately apply this information to the photos. For these students, it was clear that there was a conceptual gap in their understanding and that they would need help making connections between the written descriptions in the text and physical representations. A few other students had big holes in their matrixes, indicating that they hadn't been able to select relevant information from the reading and were struggling with comprehension. These students would need access to the information in the text through other sources to make sure that they didn't fall behind. Ms. Martin made note of these assessments and used them to inform her future planning. She would respond with immediate "quick fixes"—clearing up conceptual confusion with a demonstration at the start of the next day's lesson and providing a "cheat sheet" to students who had struggled to gather relevant information from the reading—and with longer-term strategy instruction designed to develop students' reading comprehension. This dual-pronged approach would support students in gaining access to the content for the short term and help them become more independent readers and learners of science in the long term.

The four approaches described in this chapter all support content reading comprehension. However, as the classroom examples illustrate, it is not necessary to use all four approaches with every reading. Doing so would be cumbersome and overwhelming for both students and teacher. Be selective. Choose strategies that will best fit the particulars of the students, the text, and the discipline. And be strategic. By revisiting a limited range of target strategies regularly over the course of a unit or year, teachers can equip students with the comprehension skills needed to become self-sufficient readers who can independently navigate texts and take ownership of their own content learning.

4

Developing Academic Vocabulary

What You'll Find in This Chapter

Following a discussion of what doesn't and what does work in support-ing academic vocabulary development, Chapter 4 shares suggestions for addressing three tiers of vocabulary instruction. Discussion of each of these tiers is followed by a list of instructional strategies and a classroom example of the strategy in action.

Concept vocabulary (Tier 1): These are the "big idea" words that are founda-tional to building understanding in the discipline.

Classroom vignette: Building Concept Vocabulary Knowledge in the Life Science Classroom

Topic specific vocabulary (Tier 2): These words are the recurring terms that students need to be familiar with in order to engage in meaningful inquiry into content-specific topics.

Classroom vignette: Developing Topic-Specific Vocabulary in the Math Classroom

General academic vocabulary (Tier 3): Having a familiarity with these words that are not discipline specific can significantly increase comprehension of content texts.

Classroom vignette: Developing General Academic Vocabulary in the His-tory Classroom

Assessment for *learning:* Follow-up discussions for each of the classroom vi-gnettes explore how teachers assessed students' vocabulary development.

It should come as no surprise to any of us that decades of research have unequivo-cally shown a direct link between word knowledge and reading comprehension

(Baker, Simmons, & Kame'enui, 1995; Davis, 1968; Farley & Elmore, 1992). It is also not surprising that research has established a strong correlation between content learning and language development (Espin & Foegen, 1996; Flood, Lapp, & Fisher, 2003). What may be surprising, however, is the enormous gap that exists between the language demands of content-area reading and students' vocabulary knowledge. A 1984 study by Nagy and Anderson found that secondary school vocabulary demands facility with up to 88,500 words (a number that has likely only increased in the more than two dozen years since the study was completed). In everyday conversation, most adults use only 5,000 to 10,000 words (Klein, 1988; Trelease, 2006).

Much of the gap between the language demands of secondary academic courses and the vocabulary expectations of everyday speech is the result of the use of technical vocabulary specific to content areas and specialized words that take on new meanings in particular academic contexts (Vacca & Vacca, 2008). Academic success in content areas depends on understanding not just the definition of the term, but also the significance of the term in context. It would be inappropriate, for example, for a student to see the term *revolution* in history class and connect it with the revolution of the earth around the sun. Similarly, it would be inappropriate to see the word *resistance* in physics and equate it with resistance movements of the French Revolution.

Knowing a word means more than simply knowing the definition of the word. Words, especially content-specific words, are often labels for concepts that may take thousands of words to explain (Nagy, 1988). In order to participate in discipline-specific discourse, students need to have more than a general sense of a term; they need to have a nuanced understanding of the word's use in relation to context, its permutations, and its potential implications (Nagy & Scott, 1990). In science, for example, proficient readers need precise definitions of terms. As Gallagher (2007) describes, "Understanding in science is public and shared among all peoples who comprehend a scientific idea or a science process. That is one of the strengths of science. When a scientifically literate person uses a science term or describes a scientific process, others who have an understanding of science gain the same meaning as the speaker" (p. 13). Scientific terms convey concepts that have been "the subject of experimentation, observation, and discovery for centuries, and [their] meaning[s] ha[ve] changed over time as scientists learned more and more precisely articulated the underlying scientific phenomena" (Schoenbach, Greenleaf, Cziko, & Hurwitz, 1999, p. 136).

In order for our students to access content-area readings, increase content learning, and gain the ability to participate in discipline-specific discourse, we need to support them in understanding the language. Support is particularly critical for struggling readers. English language learners (ELLs) as well as native

English speakers who speak non-standard dialects or do not have access to academic discourse in their homes are particularly likely to struggle with the academic language demands of content-area texts. For these students, content learning is even more closely linked to vocabulary knowledge, and systematic instruction is more important (Fitzgerald, García, Jiménez, & Barrera, 2000; August & Shanahan, 2006). This is due largely to what Stanovich (1986) termed the Matthew Effect, after the verse in the biblical book of Matthew that states, "The rich shall get richer and the poor shall get poorer." The reading parallel is that students who are proficient read more, acquire more words, and become more proficient. They are more likely to persevere through challenging texts and work to gradually acquire a deep understanding of content-specific terms. On the other hand, struggling readers avoid reading where possible, skip over terms that are confusing, and tend to become more easily frustrated with challenging texts. "Thus, the gap between proficient and struggling readers grows" (Stahl & Stahl, 2004, p. 61).

What Doesn't Work

Most of us know that teaching content vocabulary is important; what's less clear is what to do about it. Let's begin with time-tested methods that don't work:

- *Weekly word lists.* Assigning a list of words at the beginning of the week that students are to look up, memorize, put into sentences, and then be tested on at the end of the week doesn't work. Drill-and-practice may help students remember words long enough to take the quiz and provide them with passing familiarity such that they vaguely recognize the word when the encounter it later, but this approach does not have a reliable effect on comprehension (Kame'enui, Carnine, & Freschi, 1982; Stahl & Fairbanks, 1986). A key problem to such an approach is that it decontextualizes the words. Without a meaningful context for the word, students are unlikely to remember the definition and often fail to have the depth of knowledge necessary to understand the larger concept (Nagy, 1988).

- *Look it up in the dictionary.* Telling students to "look it up in the dictionary" when they encounter challenging words is similarly ineffective. Although dictionaries and other reference texts are important tools and students should be trained in their use, they are unreliable and unwieldy as a routine response to vocabulary challenges (Ogle, Klemp, & McBride, 2007). Many students will resist taking the time to look up terms, especially given the social stigma that may result from walking across the room to the reference shelf, and will simply skip over the word in their reading, thereby losing comprehension. Others may try to look up the word in a text or online but become confused by the dictionary's multiple definitions, self-referencing terminology, and indirect connections between the dictionary language and the term's usage in the reading (Nagy, 1988).

- *Figure it out from the context.* This is probably the most common response given by teachers to students' questions about vocabulary. The intent is good—we know language demands are so high that we can't teach students all the words they need to know and want to support them in becoming independent readers. And indeed, context is an important element in understanding word usage and will be addressed as a potential strategy later in this chapter. However, as a stand-alone response, "Figure it out from the context" falls short for two reasons: (1) Context clues are often subtle and hard to recognize. Simply telling students to figure it out is not enough; we need to show them how to do so. (2) Not all words can be adequately understood from context. Although readers may be able to pick up a general sense of a word based on how it is situated in a text, context alone is generally not enough to truly understand those words that are essential to the concept or topic being taught (Vacca, Vacca, & Gove, 2000; Baumann, Kame'enui, & Ash, 2003).

What Does Work?

Fortunately, several decades of research into language development have not only told us what doesn't work but also provided us with solid evidence of what does:

- *Access to texts.* The first thing that all researchers agree upon is that time spent reading is the single most important factor in increased word knowledge (Anderson & Nagy, 1991; Baumann, Kame'enui, & Ash, 2003). Nagy states, "Increasing the volume of students' reading is the single most important thing a teacher can do to promote large-scale vocabulary growth" (1988, p. 32). Wide reading—reading a range of forms of materials on a range of topics—has been found to be a major contributor to differences in students' vocabularies (A. E. Cunningham & Stanovich, 1991; Nagy, Anderson, & Herman, 1987). And talking, even talk by discipline experts using high levels of discipline-specific language, is not a substitute for, though it can be an important supplement to, growing vocabulary through reading subject-matter texts (Hayes & Ahrens, 1988).

These findings guide the foundation of this text. The chapters preceding and following this chapter are all about helping students access, understand, and interact with a range of content-specific texts. Doing so will help them learn content concepts and become fluent in the language and discourse of the discipline. If you are exposing students to meaningful opportunities to read content texts, you are doing the most important work that can be done to help grow students' vocabularies.

- *Direct vocabulary instruction.* However, as classroom teachers we all know that sometimes more specific attention to vocabulary is needed. There are students who lose comprehension because they don't understand language in particular texts. And then there are students who lose learning during entire units because they don't understand the larger concepts represented by key terms. How can students understand the founding of the United States if they don't recognize the difference between a democracy and a monarchy? How can they learn algebra if they don't recognize the role of a variable?

  There are times when it is necessary to teach content vocabulary explicitly. Doing so can support reading comprehension *and* content learning (Baumann, Kame'enui, & Ash, 2003; Beck & McKeown, 1991) and is particularly important for ELL students and struggling readers (Goulden, Nation, & Read, 1990). Reading researchers Fisher and Frey explain, "Intentional instruction of vocabulary doesn't stand apart from the content—it is a necessary factor in content mastery" (2008, p. 34).

How then do we go about planning for and providing direct instruction in vocabulary? We know what doesn't work, but what can be done to support students' learning? In preparing for intentional vocabulary instruction, two obvious questions should guide our planning: (1) What words should I teach? and (2) How should I teach these words to students?

The answer to the first question may seem obvious—you teach the words that they don't know. But further consideration makes it clear that the question is a bit more complex. McKeown and Beck (1988) remind us that "word knowledge is not an all or nothing proposition. Words may be known at different levels." Students may have heard the term *friction* before, for example, but may not understand the full scientific meaning of that term. Is it necessary for them to have a full understanding of the term to read a particular text? Well, it depends.

If the text is describing space debris and briefly mentions what happens when natural or man-made items enter earth's atmosphere, it may be enough to know that friction causes heat. On the other hand, if students are going to be asked to solve a physics problem that involves friction, a more focused understanding is necessary. Kame'enui, Carnine, and Freschi (1982) describe three levels of word knowledge: *full concept knowledge, partial concept knowledge,* and *verbal association knowledge.* Although these researchers use these labels to describe student learning, a similar ranking may be used to determine the depth to which we teach vocabulary. I use the designations *concept vocabulary, topic-specific vocabulary,* and *general academic vocabulary* to identify the depth. To decide what level we need to teach to, we can ask ourselves, Do students need to have full concept knowledge of this term? Is partial knowledge more appropriate? Or, is a general association acceptable for purposes of this reading and this unit? Answers to these questions will help determine the strategies we use to approach key vocabulary and unfamiliar terms in texts.

The answer to the second question that should guide our planning, How should I teach these words to students?, is largely dictated by our response to the first question. But there are important principles that guide instruction in any of the three categories outlined above (and discussed in greater depth in the remainder of this chapter). Nagy (1988) notes that to be effective, vocabulary instruction needs to be *integrated, repetitive,* and *meaningful.* Although different researchers use different terms, there is general agreement across the body of research in the field that Nagy's assertions hold true. To be effective, vocabulary instruction needs to be *integrated* into content reading and learning. There needs to be close proximity between direct instruction in vocabulary terms and opportunities to read the terms in print and apply the language in written or oral communication. In addition, repeated exposures are critical for strengthening students' familiarity with terms and helping them understand the complexities and nuances of language. *Repetitive* interaction with terms through multiple readings and application in multiple contexts supports content vocabulary development. And finally, vocabulary instruction needs to be tied to *meaningful* content learning. Just as reading comprehension increases when readers understand the purpose behind the reading, vocabulary understanding and retention will increase if it is tied to meaningful learning opportunities.

These two questions—(1) What words should I teach? and (2) How should I teach these words to students?—are explored in greater depth in the sections that follow. Building on Kame'enui, Carnine, and Freschi's levels (1982) of word knowledge, we'll explore specific strategies for supporting vocabulary development, increasing reading comprehension, and strengthening content learning.

Concept Vocabulary (Tier 1)

There are some words for which students need to have complete concept knowledge. These are the words that are foundational to the discipline, the terms that an educated historian, scientist, mathematician, or artist must understand. These are the terms that we would want students to know long after they have left our classrooms. In history, for example, we want students to remember the meaning of crucial terms such as *revolution, imperialism,* and *migration.* In chemistry, foundational terms include *equilibrium, conservation,* and *thermodynamic,* while in music, *rhythm, tone,* and *genre* are words that students may be expected to continue to use beyond the scope of the class. These are words and phrases that represent more than a simple definition; they are concepts that describe a way of understanding information and ideas within the discipline (D. D. Johnson & Pearson, 1984). For students to gain meaningful understanding of these terms, it is necessary for them to have repeated exposure to them through readings, prereading language development activities, and postreading application opportunities (M. F. Graves & Graves, 1994).

The following activities support language development at the concept level. It is important to note that these activities are most effective when they are layered with reading and writing opportunities and when time is allowed for students to discuss, reflect on, and refine their understanding, as demonstrated by the classroom vignette that follows the strategies.

Instructional Strategies

- *Concept maps.* Concept maps provide a graphic structure for engaging students in thinking about multiple dimensions of a concept. An early concept map, the Frayer Model (see Figure 4.1), asks students to identify the essential characteristics, nonessential characteristics, examples, and nonexamples of a term (Frayer, Fredrick, & Klausmeier, 1969). Variations on this model by Schwartz and Raphael (1985) and J. Allen (1999), among others, extend it to include boxes for properties, comparisons, and personal connections. In the classroom vignette that follows, Mr. Walsh uses a concept map in his science classroom to support students' understanding of the term *ecology.* Concept maps work best when students work collaboratively to think through responses to the categories provided.

- *Concept ladders.* A concept ladder (Gillet & Temple, 1982) is similar to a concept map but may be adapted to more closely focus on specifics of the concept being investigated. Concept ladders generally include six to

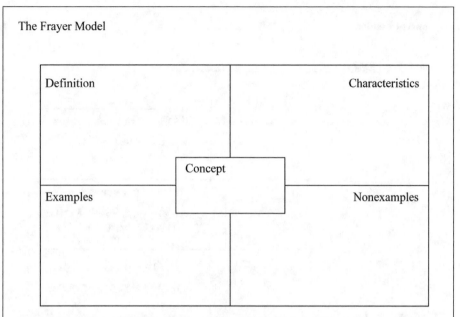

The Frayer Model

Definition	Characteristics

Concept

Examples	Nonexamples

From Frayer, D. A., Fredrick, W. C., & Klausmeier, H. J. (1969). *A schema for testing the level of concept mastery* (Working Paper No. 16). Madison: Wisconsin Research and Development Center for Cognitive Learning. Used with permission.

FIGURE 4.1. The Frayer Model.

ten "steps," with the questions becoming progressively more challenging as they ascend. For a scientific process such as mitosis, questions on the steps might include: What is it? Where does it take place? When does it occur? What are the steps? Why is it important? What might go wrong? What problems could result if something goes wrong? On the other hand, for a historical concept such as genocide, questions on the steps could include: What is it? Where has it taken place? Who is involved? Why does it take place? How does it affect the community? Can it be prevented? Why should I care? (See Figure 4.2.) As with concept maps, concept ladders work best when students work collaboratively to respond to the prompts. Once familiar with the strategy, students can also be involved in generating prompts.

• *Scavenger hunt.* Ask students to seek out examples of a concept from newspaper or magazine articles, photo images, or the Web. As is demonstrated in Mr. Walsh's classroom in the vignette that follows, the articles that students find need not contain the term itself but should be representative of an aspect of the concept. Opportunities to explain the thinking behind

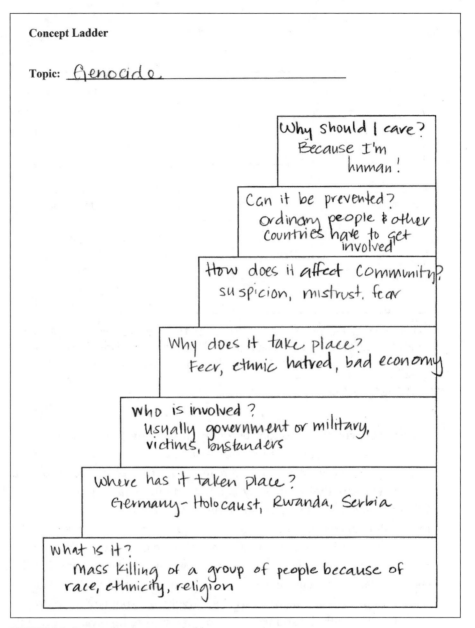

FIGURE 4.2. One student's concept ladder.

their choices in writing and/or discuss with peers the connections they made helps to clarify thinking and provide assessment data that allows the teacher to correct misperceptions.

- *Shades of meaning.* Shades of meaning (Fisher & Frey, 2008) can be used to demonstrate gradations between terms that are related but have important differences in meaning and degree. For example, in an economics class, students might be tempted to substitute the phrase *downturn* for *depression*, but economists would see significant differences between the two. Working collaboratively to arrange terms in progressive order on a set of color chips (Blanchfield, 2001) or a linear array (J. Allen, 1999) can help students recognize the different levels that come between an economic downturn and a depression as they work to define their relative severity and specific characteristics (see Figure 4.3).

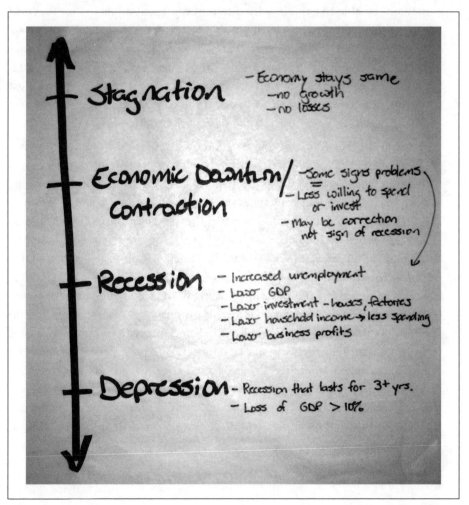

FIGURE 4.3. Students can identify shades of meaning in content vocabulary by creating a linear array like this one.

- *Concrete spellings.* Creating a visual representation of a concept by writing the term in the shape of its meaning is a powerful memory technique and can act as an effective scaffold to comprehension for some students (Beers, 2003; Wormeli, 2005). Have students develop ways to visually represent key terms and then compare the terms. Differences in drawings will prompt discussion of nuances in understanding and will help teachers to identify and address areas of confusion.

- *Analogies.* Making comparisons between terms can help to build and extend conceptual understanding. Students may know, for example, that an *algebraic representation* involves numbers and symbols, whereas a *graphic representation* involves points and lines on the coordinate plane, but they may not be able to explain why different representations matter (beyond getting the right answers in the problem set). Asking students to draw a comparison with another field, such as cooking (a recipe versus the cookies described in the recipe) or architecture (a set of plans versus the actual building), can help to ground an abstract concept. Analogies work best when students are allowed to develop the comparisons themselves and are pushed to explain how the analogy works and where it fails.

- *In my own words.* Many of the preceding vocabulary development activities are designed to be worked through collaboratively, with students and teachers working together to brainstorm responses to various prompts, push each other's ideas further, and construct common understanding. Collaboration and interaction is critical in developing understanding of new concepts, particularly for ELLs and struggling readers (Freeman & Freeman, 2008; Stahl, 1986; Stahl & Vancil, 1986). However, it is also critical for students to have time and space to solidify their own understanding by putting it into writing. Many of the same questions that were described previously in the context of graphic organizers or discussion prompts can be used to guide individual student written responses. These responses can take the form of exit slips, journal prompts, or records in a special section of students' notebooks. History teacher Helena Johnston has students maintain a separate notebook page for each of the key terms in her content area, providing space for them to return to add details, nuances, and further examples and nonexamples as their understanding of the concept evolves.

Building Concept Vocabulary Knowledge in the Life Science Classroom

"I want you to start today by covering up the text on page E–3 and looking just at the pictures," Mr. Walsh said to his life science class after they took their seats. "Take the full four minutes of our warm-up time today to examine those photos, consider what they have in common, and then begin to develop a definition for the term *ecology*. Use the warm-up space in your science notebook to write your thoughts about that definition." Mr. Walsh circulated through the room, conferring with individual students and trying to draw out the thinking behind their responses: "That's interesting. Why did you use the word *study* in your definition?" "Hmm . . . So you didn't use the pictures, you broke the word itself down. Interesting strategy. Can your definition now connect back up to the photos?" A focused share-out revealed that students were all developing in their understanding of the term. Some had connected to an earlier unit on ecosystems; others had drawn connections to things they had heard on the news or what they perceived as the stories behind the photos. Most were on the right track, but Mr. Walsh knew that before he could launch into the substantive readings and labs of this unit, students' understandings needed to be further developed and their misperceptions flushed out.

The class turned next to the textbook definition. With students following along, Mr. Walsh read the two paragraphs in the unit introduction. "Do we have a definition of ecology in here?" he wondered aloud. "Point to the place in the text where you see the definition." Again, most students were able to locate the appropriate lines, but Mr. Walsh was aware that recognizing the textbook definition and "owning" its meaning were two different things. He asked students to discuss the definition with a peer, look up the term in the science dictionaries on their desks, and then write down the definition in their notes using their own words. Again, the class shared out, with Mr. Walsh guiding the discussion to address misperceptions and pushing students to explain the thinking behind their definitions: "Why do we need to in-clude ideas about interaction between organisms and the environment in the definition? Would it be enough just to say 'the study of organisms'?" "Can you think of a more precise term for defining living 'things'?"

Satisfied with the paraphrased definitions, Mr. Walsh moved to application—this is where true understanding, or lack thereof, is often revealed. He passed out copies of *Science News* and *Science Today*, magazines published for middle and high school science classes, and challenged the students to find one article that represented an aspect of ecology. The students were not expected to read the articles thoroughly, but rather to scan the headlines, skim through the text, and determine if the information and ideas in the article were related to the core concept of ecology. As students scanned the articles, the certainty that they had felt when they were reading textbook definitions fell away. They made such comments as, "I'm not sure if this fits. It's an article about tumors on Tasmanian Devils' faces. Maybe it could be related to ecology if the tumors were caused by the environment . . . ?" "In this article humans are helping butterflies to migrate. Can it be about ecology if humans are changing the environment?" The questions students raised provided great opportunities for discussion and built up an understanding of what may or may not fit within the big idea concept of ecology.

Finally, Mr. Walsh placed a concept map graphic organizer (adapted from J. Allen 1999) on the document camera. Using ideas and information they had gathered from their observations of text-book photos, reading of the textbook definition, and review of science magazine articles, students collaborated to create a working definition of ecology and to list out characteristics, examples, and nonexamples (see Figure 4.4). A poster paper version of this concept map was later hung on the classroom wall to be referred to and refined as the unit progressed.

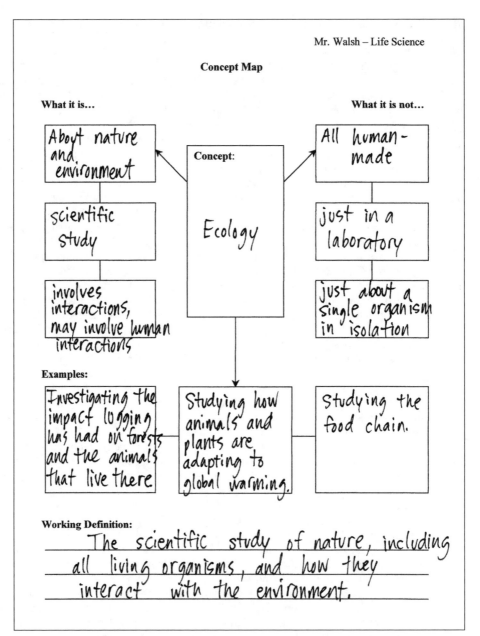

FIGURE 4.4. A student in Mr. Walsh's life science class used a concept map graphic organizer to develop an understanding of the term *ecology*.

In all, Mr. Walsh's class spent just under thirty minutes mapping the concept of ecology. This is not an insignificant amount of time, but packed within that time frame were multiple opportunities to explore the concept through visuals, textbook definitions, article application, and peer discussion. By examining students' writing, conferring with them during their article selection, listening to the reasoning behind their choices, and pushing them to discuss and define the concept with examples and nonexamples, Mr. Walsh was able to identify and correct misconceptions and refine student understanding.

Precision in the use of terminology and core concepts is important in all content areas, but it is especially important in supporting effective communication in science (R. Allen, 2007; J. J. Gallagher, 2007). By layering multiple concept-building activities together, Mr. Walsh provided opportunities for students to build a precise understanding, an understanding that would support the reading and learning activities they would engage in during the subsequent unit on ecology and which would allow them to successfully engage in scientifically appropriate discourse.

Topic-Specific Vocabulary (Tier 2)

A second tier of terms requires partial concept knowledge. These are the vocabulary words that repeatedly arise when discussing a particular content-based topic. When studying the Civil War, for example, students are likely to frequently read, write, and discuss using terms such as *Rebels, Yankees, blockade, casualties,* and *emancipate.* When investigating cell biology, students should be familiar with vocabulary words such as *membrane, nucleus, cytoplasm,* and *chloroplasts.* These are terms that label specific groups of people, places, things, or events. They are less foundational to the discipline as a whole than tier 1 words, but familiarity and facility with their use enables more thoughtful investigation into particular topics. Vocabulary development for words at this level focuses on recognizing and identifying terms and being able to connect those terms with larger concepts or organizational categories.

Instructional Strategies

- *Word sort.* In this activity, students are provided with a list of topic-specific terms that they categorize into groups and then label (Taba, 1967). In a visual arts class, for example, the list might include terms that are used for tools, processes, and materials in various artistic media. Students should work independently or with partners to organize groups of words and then should compare their groupings with peers. When used at the beginning of a unit of study, a word sort can be a great way to assess students' prior knowledge and help students begin to recognize the relationships between terms they will see repeatedly during a unit. When used later in the unit, a word sort can serve to deepen thinking and assess under-standing. The best word sort activities lend themselves to several different categorization possibilities, thus sparking discussion and extending learn-ing. In the math example that follows, Mr. Keller uses a word sort activity to preview vocabulary words for his two-dimensional geometry unit.

- *Word walls.* Having students copy terms into notebooks is a popular strat-egy in content classrooms, but too often students avoid the process of opening their notebooks, flipping to the right page, and scanning through the lines to find the vocabulary information when they encounter a term in their reading or might want to use it in their writing or discussion. Word walls provide a more accessible alternative. Terms that are impor-tant to the topic are written on individual pieces of paper or tag board and posted on the classroom wall. Terms may be organized using an A–Z ap-proach or grouped by another category that is specific to the subject area. Words should be written large enough so that they can be read from across the room; it can be helpful to include a visual representation or some other memory cue alongside the term itself. P. M. Cunningham and Allington (2003) remind us that it is important to "do" a word wall, not just display it. Involving students in deciding what words to post and how to organize them, referring to terms on the wall when modeling reading or writing in the unit, and requiring that students regularly use the words in their own writing and discussions can help to make the word wall an active part of language development.

- *Read-aloud.* Reading aloud to students has been called the "single most im-portant activity for building the knowledge required for eventual success in reading" (Anderson, Heibert, Scott, & Wilkinson, 1985, p. 23). Well-cho-sen read-aloud texts can serve to introduce important vocabulary to stu-dents while at the same time piquing their interest in a topic and building more general background knowledge. Early on in her Civil War unit, for example, Ms. Saavedra reads Patricia Polacco's wonderful book *Pink and Say* (1994) to her fifth-grade students. The book provides a context-rich introduction to words such as *confederate, union, company, musket, buck-board,* and *deserter.* Having the story read aloud to them allows students to focus on word meaning, provides a model of correct pronunciation, and creates opportunities for informal discussion about the events and the language in the text. In addition to picture books (which even older kids like to hear read aloud if they are well written and thoughtfully selected), other sources for vocabulary-building read-alouds include magazine and newspaper articles, excerpts from primary source documents or reports, excerpts from a text or trade book, and quotes from noted experts or important historical figures.

- *Predicting ABCs.* Popularized by J. Allen (2000), this is a simple strategy that can have great effect. Students are given a topic (e.g., "The Renaissance," "Energy Sources," "Triangles") and provided with a simple, one-page handout that contains twelve boxes, each with a pair of letters at the top in A–Z order (see Figure 4.5 for an example of a completed ABC chart for the topic "Natural Disasters"). Students work individually or in pairs to brainstorm as many words as they can that relate to the topic assigned by the teacher and place the terms in the boxes with the corresponding letter at the start of the word. After a designated amount of time (usually two to three minutes), students partner with peers to combine lists and compare and explain terms. This activity focuses students as they connect to their prior knowledge on a topic and introduces new terms and ways of thinking when ideas are shared with peers.

- *Exclusion brainstorming.* In many ways, this activity is the opposite of predicting ABCs, though the goal is the same. For exclusion brainstorming (Blachowicz, 1986), students are presented with a list of words, some of which will be used during a particular reading or unit of study and others

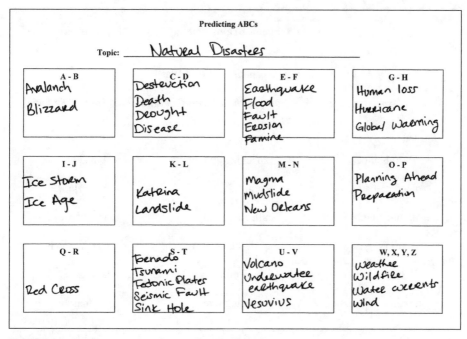

FIGURE 4.5. Students can use the predicting ABCs strategy to brainstorm terms related to a topic under study.

that won't. Students review the list, consider the relevance of each word, and cross out those that they think do not connect with the current topic. (See Figure 4.6 for an exclusion brainstorming list used prior to a unit on World War I.) The process of choosing which words to cross out forces students to pay careful attention to each word, thoughtfully consider its relevance, and seek out more information from peers, texts, and the teacher when they don't know a word's meaning.

- *Size matters.* Some groups of words lend themselves to ordering by size. Terms in the metric system in math, for example, or units of matter in chemistry, can be organized from the smallest unit to the largest. Provide students with a set of index cards and ask them to sort terms from small to large. Make it a contest by setting a time limit and instituting a "yes" or "not yet" response policy when they ask you, "Do we have it right yet?" Having the terms on cards allows for easy movement, enabling students to re-sort if need be. For ordering history terms, try organizing by time period.

- *Visual aids.* Hearing about the meaning of a new term can be helpful. Seeing the visual representation of the term can be even more helpful. Visual

---

Exclusion Brainstorming

Topic: Weapons of World War I

Read and consider each term. Cross out those terms that are not relevant to the topic.

B-20 bomber	machine gun	biplanes
hand grenade	air raid shelters	body armor
atomic bomb	ballistic missile	trench warfare
mustard gas	U-boats	nuclear weapons
bayonet	land mines	howitzers
anti-aircraft guns	battering ram	gas masks

FIGURE 4.6. In this example of an exclusion brainstorming activity, students would cross out terms that are not relevant to the topic of weapons of World War I.

connections spur new learning and increase retention. Engage students in the work of identifying visual representations by providing them with a list of terms and sending them on a scavenger hunt through the textbook to find and label the relevant images. Or stretch their thinking by showing a new image and asking them to apply the terms listed neatly on the illustration in the textbook to a less obvious photo or drawing. Transferring terms such as *xylem, phloem, vein,* and *cuticle* from the textbook graphic to photographs of actual leaves, for example, can help students recognize the relationship between form and function and build understanding of the diversity of plant life.

Developing Topic-Specific Vocabulary in the Math Classroom

Mr. Keller's seventh-grade math class was poised to begin a new unit on two-dimensional geometry. From past experience, Mr. Keller knew that this unit would present both challenges and opportunities. After spending much of the year on abstract algebraic concepts, it was something of a relief to come to a chapter in the text focused on the concrete shapes and measurements. However, the study of geometry brought with it a huge volume of specialized terms. Although his students would likely have been exposed to many of the terms in previous math courses, he knew that most would have only a partial understanding of the words' meanings. The material in this unit would come quickly, and Mr. Keller needed his students to be at ease with the use of content-specific terms. He decided to begin the unit by spending the first half of his block period building students' content vocabularies through a word activity.

"Good afternoon," Mr. Keller's voice boomed around the room.

"Good afternoon," his students responded.

"I am glad to hear such an enthusiastic greeting and to see that you all are looking ready to learn today." Mr. Keller grinned at his students as he removed a student's hat and placed another student's backpack on the back of her chair. "Today we have a word sort challenge. We are starting a new unit with lots of new terms. Your job today is to sort those words into appropriate categories." Mr. Keller directed students' attention to the words at the front of the room. In all there were twenty-eight words listed on the board (see Figure 4.7). This was more than he had assigned in similar activities in the past, but Mr. Keller thought his students could handle the challenge, especially since many of the words were at least somewhat familiar.

"Some of these words probably look easy to you," Mr. Keller continued. "*Circle, triangle, square* . . . Those are words you've known since you were in kindergarten. But other words may be a little less familiar. You may not have heard of a *rhombus* or a *trapezoid* before, and that is OK. This activity is about learning new words and thinking in new ways about familiar words." Mr. Keller moved to the front of the room to point to the steps of the activity written out on the board as he gave oral directions. "You're going to work in teams of four that I assign. First, as a group you need to read through all the terms. Second, you will talk about the terms with your group to make sure everyone knows what they are. Third, use your textbook to look up any terms that you don't know. You can use the index to find the page number in the chapter where the term is explained or the glossary for a quick definition. For the fourth step, you'll discuss how the terms might be organized into groups. I'm not going to tell you the word groups; you need to figure them out for yourselves. You need to have at least two groups, but

Word Sort

Center	Sides	Radius	Rectangle
Parallelogram	Diagonal	Angles	Heptagon
Diameter	Trapezoid	Composite Figure	Circumference
Octagon	Circle	Line Segment	Rhombus
Hexagon	Area	Interior Angle	Polygon
Pi	Altitude	Quadrilateral	Base
Triangle	Vertices	Square	Pentagon

FIGURE 4.7. Mr. Keller asked students to develop categories and sort these geometry terms into them as a way of solidifying their understanding of the concepts.

you may want to have more. Fifth, place each of the terms in one of the groups. If you have a lot of terms that don't fit in the groups you've chosen or a lot that belong in more than one group, you may want to rethink your word groups. And sixth, you'll finalize your lists and label the groups." He paused to answer a few questions and assign students to teams of four before telling the students to get started. "You have twelve minutes," Mr. Keller said. "At the end of that time you need to be prepared to present your groups to the class and defend your choices. Ready, set, go!"

Mr. Keller's clear directions and high expectations propelled students to work. Each group was soon flipping through pages in the math book as they worked to clarify their understanding of terms. "What's the difference between *vertices* and *angles*?" one team wondered, while another debated the meaning of *radius* and *diameter*. Mr. Keller smiled as he heard the heated conversations between students; it was fun to see them so engaged in conversations about math.

"I told you that a rhombus could be a square," one student claimed, pointing at an illustration in the book.

Her partner responded, "Yes, but not every rhombus is a square; a rhombus doesn't have to have all right angles."

As students moved to begin to group terms, Mr. Keller went around the room distributing poster-size sheets of paper for them to use to display their findings. Some teams moved quickly to identify groups, only to discover that their initial categories couldn't accommodate a significant number of the terms. Other teams spent more time debating the groups that they should use. "There should be three groups, one for quadrilaterals, one for polygons, and one for circles," one student argued.

"But quadrilaterals *are* polygons," her team argued back, "so why do they need a separate group?" As they worked, teams frequently referred to their textbook a second, third, or fourth time to clarify their understanding of terms before writing their choices down in marker on the poster paper. Mr. Keller made his way around the room answering questions and posing challenges. "I see you've placed *area* in the polygon group," he commented to one group of students. "Could it be in the circle group as well?"

After the designated twelve minutes plus a three-minute extension requested by students, Mr. Keller called the class back to attention. "I observed some excellent work and heard some great thinking from your teams," he said. "Some of your teams came up with very similar groupings, but others had some unique ideas. We're going to take a few minutes to share out, and as we do, I want you to listen for similarities and differences, not just in the way you organized terms, but also in your understanding of the terms themselves." Mr. Keller called on three different teams to share their findings. He had specifically selected these teams because, while each of their charts was thoughtful and logical, each was unique. One had grouped terms based on their application to polygons or circles (see Figure 4.8). The second group had a column for "Things You Measure" and another for "Names of Shapes." The third group separated listings into three categories: "Shape Names," "Shape Describing Words," and "Area Words."

As each team stood to hold up their poster and share their thinking, Mr. Keller asked questions to encourage a dialogue within the class. "Andre, I noticed that your team placed *circumference* in the "circle" group, while Tomas's team placed *circumference* in their "measurements" group. Is that a conflict?" he probed. Later he wondered, "Is one of these groupings better than another? Can they coexist? Why?" The questions were designed to help students recognize the dimensions and purpose of the various terms they had encountered. By probing about groups, Mr. Keller hoped that not only would students think more closely about terms, but also, later in the unit, when they were studying how to find the area of composite

figures, for example, students would remember and be able to apply the appropriate terms in describing their calculations.

Satisfied with students' learning, Mr. Keller wrapped up the discussion by requesting a round of applause for the teams that presented and by thanking all who participated. "You did a great job with your teams and with the class," he said. "I particularly appreciate the respectful manner in which you debated one another. Challenging discussion supports everyone in learning. Well done!" He then asked students to write up five of the geometry terms in the "math glossary" section they had created on the final twelve sheets of paper in their math notebooks. Students had maintained these alphabetically organized glossaries throughout the year, regularly adding terms in response to their readings and discussions in class. Mr. Keller didn't want the glossary to become so crammed with terms that it was overly laborious and impractical to find definitions, so he asked students to be intentional in their selections. "Choose five terms that were new to you, that you learned something new about, that you thought about differently, or that you think are going to be particularly important during this unit. For each, write the term in the first column, write the meaning in your own words in the middle column, and draw an illustration of the term in the last column."

Working individually, students recorded terms and meanings in their notebooks. This record would serve as an assessment check for Mr. Keller and a resource for students as they progressed through the unit. However, it also had a more immediate purpose. It provided students—both the vocal students who had participated most energetically in the team discussions and the quieter students who had spent much of the discussion observing—an opportunity to reflect on their learning and record their understanding on paper. Doing so helped cement the knowledge they had gained during the earlier conversations and provided each student with individual ownership of the content terms.

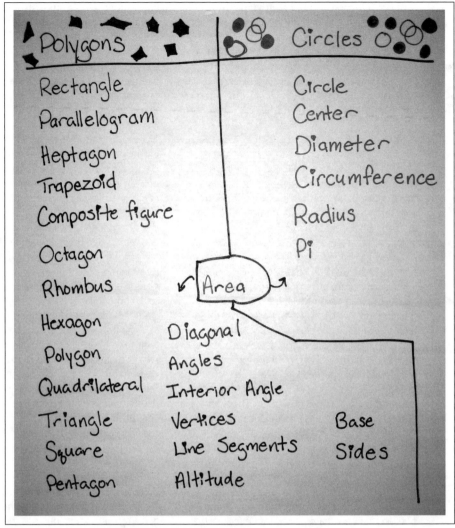

FIGURE 4.8. One group of students in Mr. Keller's class came up with two categories for the geometry terms—polygons and circles.

General Academic Vocabulary (Tier 3)

A final category of vocabulary learning relates to words that are not content specific but nevertheless can pose challenges for reading in content areas. These are the terms that can be found in vocabulary study guides and SAT test-prep books—words such as *divest, illuminate, nettlesome,* or *obsolete.* These are the words that we would like students to know as they develop their academic vocabularies. Their use is not foundational to the discipline nor essential to understanding a particular topic within the discipline. For purposes of content learning, students do not need to have deep knowledge of the words. However, these are the academic vocabulary words that appear in content readings, and being familiar with the words can significantly increase comprehension. Strategies to address these words in content-area classes should focus on providing enough information to increase students' immediate text comprehension and on teaching the skills and strategies that will support their continued learning when they encounter challenging academic language in future readings.

Instructional Strategies

- *Knowledge ratings.* Asking students to rate their understanding of words that are likely to pose comprehension challenges can be a great way to preview vocabulary and assess students' prior knowledge. In this activity, developed by Blachowicz (1986), teachers identify ten to fifteen challenging vocabulary words in a text and list them for students. On their own, students rate each word under headings such as "Know It," "Have Seen/ Heard," or "Not Familiar." Once students have rated words based on their own prior knowledge, engaging in peer-to-peer talk, teacher-led discussion, or use of resources such as glossaries, dictionaries, or the Internet can help move students higher on the rating scale before they encounter the words in text. In the lesson that follows, Ms. Miller uses a knowledge rating activity to prepare her US history students to read Dr. King's "I Have a Dream" speech.

- *Context clues.* Although context alone is not enough to teach the specific meaning of new academic terms, explicit and repeated instruction in the use of context clues can improve students' ability to comprehend text (Buikema & Graves, 1993; Jenkins, Matlock, & Slocum, 1989). Although it would be inappropriate to rely on context clues to make meaning of concept or topic-specific words that are essential to the core focus of content instruction, teaching students to use context clues can help them navigate the general academic language that is found in the texts.

    Vacca and Vacca (2008) note that there are three types of context clues: typographic, syntactic, and semantic. Typographic clues are the easiest to recognize and use. They include footnotes, italics, boldfaced print, parenthetical explanations, textboxes, and glossaries that provide direct definitions of terms. These are most often found in textbooks and trade texts specifically designed for K–12 readers. More challenging are the syntactic and semantic clues that are found embedded within the main text. These clues may include definitions in the same sentence set off by commas, linked synonyms that are part of a descriptive list, contrast or antonym clues introduced by signal words such as *unlike* or *in contrast*, or more subtle "gist clues" that require the reader to infer meaning from the general context of the passage (Beers, 2003).

Teaching students to use these clues requires modeling and repeated practice. It is not enough simply to give students a list of rules or tell them how to use context once or twice. Students need to observe the process by which a fluent content reader uses context clues to make sense of words through explicit modeling. Modeling may take place during a read-aloud or in response to a vocabulary development activity such as "knowledge rating." Take the handful of words that students don't recognize, find them in the text, and then think aloud about the process of making meaning in context. Further support student learning by providing regular opportunities for students to practice using context in low-stakes situations. In his high school classroom, Kelly Gallagher uses a warm-up activity to help students practice using context clues. Once or twice each week he'll write two to three sentences on the board with one word underlined in each. Students copy the sentences into the first column of a three-column chart in their notebook, predict the meaning of the underlined word in the second column, then work with peers to discuss, look up, and record meaning in the third column. He notes, "This exercise takes no more than three minutes and helps students learn that good readers use context to help them when comprehension breaks down" (2004, p. 77).

- *Morphemic analysis.* Teaching students to analyze the parts of words—roots, suffixes, and prefixes—can help to enhance understanding and recall of vocabulary words and improve reading comprehension (White, Sowell, & Yanagihara, 1989; Nagy, Diakidoy, & Anderson, 1993). Although the concept of teaching word parts in a content class may seem overwhelming, investigation into the use of roots and affixes suggests that focused instruction in a relatively small number of word parts can have a significant impact. The twenty most common prefixes, for example, are used in 97 percent of the words with prefixes (White, Sowell, & Yanagihara, 1989).

  A schoolwide (or departmentwide) approach to learning word parts can be most effective. Some schools divide word parts between departments or across grade levels. Magnolia High School in Anaheim, California, for example, uses a 30–15–10 system in which all students are required to know the 30 most common prefixes, 15 most common roots, and 10 most common suffixes (Gallagher, 2004). If such an interdisciplinary collaboration is not an option, identify the most common word parts encountered in content texts at your grade level, create your own list, and focus on those.

As with context clues, teaching students to use structural analysis requires modeling and practice. Stopping to think aloud during a read-aloud, modeling the analysis of a word's structure during a prereading vocabulary development activity, or using a graphic organizer such as "words in context," demonstrated in the following example, to analyze word parts can all be effective at teaching students the process of morphemic analysis. Students' word analysis skills can be developed as they read (e.g., "Scan the text to find one word that is challenging and then demonstrate how you can break it down into word parts to find meaning") or through quick stand-alone activities such as word trees (Beers, 2003). To build a word tree, choose a root word and then build as many branches as possible, each with a new word that includes the root. This type of activity can act as a sponge for those three extra minutes that remain at the end of class while also reinforcing language development.

- *Peer talk.* Peer-to-peer discussions can be great tools for supporting students in overcoming challenging language to recognize the meaning of text. Teacher Becky Gemmell explains that although she might push students in her English class to think more analytically about the meaning of particular words they encounter in literature, in her dance class she is less focused on individual word meaning and more concerned about overall comprehension. "I want them to get the big idea. When I provide structured opportunities for the students to talk to each other as they read the articles, they are able to overcome most vocabulary challenges." Two strategies to structure peer conversations are think-pair-share (Lyman, 1987) and turn-to-your-partner-and. . . . These strategies can be used to support students in focusing on understanding words in context and to develop students' thinking on the nuances of particular terms in the text. In a think-pair-share, you might ask students to find three challenging words in the text, *think* about their meanings, *pair* with a classmate to discuss ideas, and *share* their learning with the whole class. For the turn-to-your-partner-and . . . activity, you might say, "Turn to your partner and brainstorm three *catastrophic* events that might lead to climate change."

- *Keep it simple.* There are some times when, rather than teach the reader new words or strategies, it is necessary to change the reading. There is a direct relationship between the difficulty of the words in a text and the reader's comprehension of that text (M. F. Graves, 1986; Anderson & Freebody, 1981). The exact proportion of challenging words readers can tolerate depends on many factors. It is different for each individual and often for each text (Nagy, 1988). As classroom teachers, we need to be aware of the difficulties posed by the language in our content texts and selective about which texts we choose to use, which we choose to set aside, and which we choose to alter. That last option, altering the text by substituting words, creating our own glossary, or simplifying text structure, can be controversial. However, as history educator Sam Wineburg stated in a recent presentation, "If the house is burning down, don't try to save the curtains" (Wineburg, 2008). If we want students to understand concepts that are foundational to our subject areas and to have access to the kinds of documents that are representative of our disciplines, sometimes it is more appropriate to change the language and provide an approximation of the original.

Developing General Academic Vocabulary in the History Classroom

As her eleventh-grade class filtered into the room, Ms. Miller handed each student a single sheet of paper. On one side was a photocopy of the first eight paragraphs of Martin Luther King Jr.'s "I have a dream" speech. On the other was a list of fifteen challenging vocabulary words that students would encounter as they read the text. The terms were listed in the order they were found in the text, from *fivescore* to *invigorating*.

Ms. Miller loved teaching the "I Have a Dream" speech. It represented an amazing moment in history and it was a masterful speech delivered by a gifted orator. During the previous few days, she had been priming her students for the text by talking with them about civil disobedience and leading them through investigations of the events leading up to the March on Washington. Equipped with an audio version of the speech, Ms. Miller was always tempted just to leap right into the text itself, to simply hope that the emotion and cadence of King's voice would convey the meaning. But experience had taught her that the language of the speech was challenging for many of her students and that if she failed to preteach key vocabulary words, students would lose mean-

ing. They might remember the "I have a dream" refrain, but they would fail to understand the context against which King's dream took shape.

"Take two minutes," Ms. Miller told her students as they settled into their desks, "to rate your knowledge of these words. Each will appear in Dr. King's speech, and you need to be familiar with these terms in order to understand his dream. Don't pretend to know more than you do. Be honest. The ratings are only for you and will not affect your grade." Students quickly placed checks in boxes on a knowledge rating guide (see Figure 4.9) and then, in response to their teacher's direction, shared their ratings in groups of three. Looking over their shoulders, Ms. Miller noticed that most students seemed to have a passing familiarity with the majority of the words, but no one expressed confidence about every term. Several students, including struggling readers and English language learners, had rated many of the words with question marks. Ms. Miller ensured that they were partnered with peers who could provide language support and made a note to herself to check back as the activity progressed. As they collaborated, students made notes in the far right column of the chart, writing down their prediction about each word's meaning or noting a question when the triads couldn't agree on a definition.

When conversations appeared to be wrapping up, Ms. Miller called the group back together. "I heard some great conversations about these words," she praised the class. "Good work! Now, what questions do you still have? What terms are you still feeling 'iffy' about?"

"*Tranquilizing*," one student called out.

"OK," Ms. Miller said. "Any ideas? Who can help Alyssa and her partners with the word *tranquilizing*?"

A student in the back row raised his hand. "Our group thought that it was like calming, since tranquil means calm and a tranquilizer is something you take to calm down."

"Excellent," Ms. Miller agreed. "That's a great definition, Pedro, and I really like how you shared your thought process. So Alyssa, your group and

---

Ms. Miller – U.S. History

Prereading Vocabulary Knowledge Rating

"I Have a Dream" by Martin Luther King Jr.

Word	Know It	Have Seen It	???	Notes
Fivescore			X	SOUNDS like sports??
Momentous		X		Big deal
Manacles			X	man & shackles?
Prosperity	X			$ $ $
Languished		X		Tired, wasted
Exile	X			Sent off, away
Promissory note	X			Like MONEY
Unalienable			X	??
Sacred	X			Holy
Insufficient	X			Not enough
Hallowed		X		Holy
Tranquilizing		X		Peaceful → Calming
Gradualism		X		A little at a time
Legitimate	X			Legal & legit
Invigorating		X		wakes you up

FIGURE 4.9. Ms. Miller's students became familiar with the general academic vocabulary in Dr. King's speech by using a knowledge rating exercise before the reading.

anyone else who is confused about this word can write the word *calming* or a synonym for *calming* in the comment row next to *tranquilizing*. Next?"

The oral give-and-take continued through six or seven more words as students confirmed definitions or cleared up areas of confusion. Ms. Miller deftly guided the process, repeatedly eliciting both questions and answers from students and stepping in only to confirm or redirect when necessary. Since these were text-specific words that represented general academic vocabulary, she was focused primarily on giving her students enough knowledge to be able to get through the reading. They didn't need to know five different dictionary-style definitions of the terms; they just needed enough of an association to make meaning when they encountered the term in the text. This approach allowed Ms. Miller to move her students quickly through the discussion.

As the discussion wound down, two vocabulary words remained in the question mark columns on students' charts. *Fivescore* and *unalienable* were terms that students hadn't been able to figure out on their own. Ms. Miller quickly decided that she would simply tell them the definition for *fivescore*. *Score* was a rarely used term and it was unlikely that they would encounter it often. They needed to know it to get through this reading, but it wasn't all that important that they remember it for future use. "*Score* is an Old English term meaning twenty," she explained. "So *fivescore* is one hundred. You probably heard something similar when you studied President Lincoln back in eighth grade. He used the term *fourscore* in the Gettysburg Address. That's important because Dr. King is drawing parallels with President Lincoln in this speech."

For the term *unalienable*, however, Ms. Miller decided to model the process of using context and morphemic analysis to determine meaning. Ms. Miller walked her students through this process about once each week and had found that regularly working together to think through word meaning as a class helped students to use a similar process during their own reading. *Unalienable* was a term that was a good candidate for this type of a model because it included familiar word

parts and was a term they were likely to encounter again. In addition, a thoughtful understanding of the term was critical to understanding the ideas in Dr. King's text.

Ms. Miller placed a graphic organizer titled Analyzing Words in Context (adapted from J. Allen, 1999) on the document camera and asked students to find the term *unalienable* in line twenty-one of Dr. King's speech. (Before photocopying primary source documents, Ms. Miller numbered each line so that both she and her students could quickly refer to specific portions of the text during both prereading warm-up activities such as this and after-reading discussion and analysis.) One student read aloud the sentence that included the term while Ms. Miller copied a portion of the sentence into the top box of the organizer (see Figure 4.10). She then proceeded to walk students through the organizer. "What parts of this word do you recognize?" she asked. *Un-* was quickly identified as a prefix that meant *not*. They also recognized *alien* but were less sure about its meaning.

"I think of aliens as little green things from Mars," one student said, "but it doesn't seem like that is what Dr. King would be talking about."

Ms. Miller smiled, "OK, let's hold off on that for a moment and think about other words or phrases we might know with these word parts. For example, for *un-*, I think of *unhappy* or *unwilling*, meaning not happy or not willing. Other ideas?" Students shared several *un-* words before Ms. Miller pressed them to consider *alien* again. "In addition to space aliens, when have you heard the word *alien* used as part of a larger word or phrase?"

A student on the edge of the class volunteered, "People talk about illegal aliens."

"Oh, and my uncle's green card says that he is a resident alien," another student said.

Ms. Miller added those terms to the organizer. "So in those cases, what do you think *alien* means?" she asked. A student observed that for both the space reference and immigrant reference, *alien* could mean *different*.

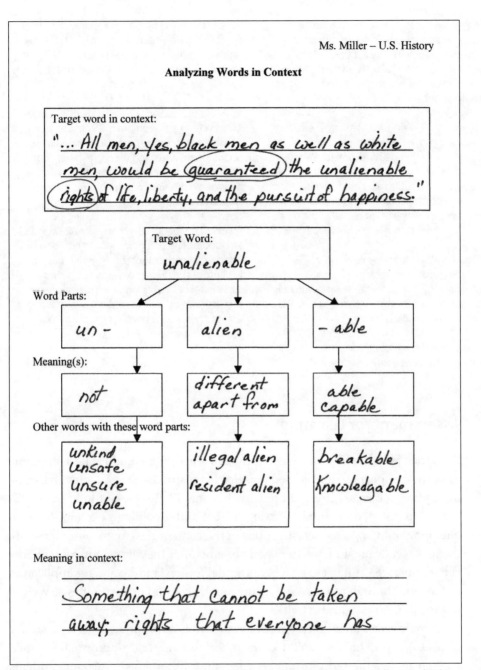

Analyzing Words in Context

Target word in context:

" ... All men, yes, black men as well as white men, would be (guaranteed) the unalienable (rights) of life, liberty, and the pursuit of happiness."

Target Word:

unalienable

Word Parts:

un -

alien

- able

Meaning(s):

not

different apart from

able capable

Other words with these word parts:

unkind
unsafe
unsure
unable

illegal alien
resident alien

breakable
knowledgable

Meaning in context:

Something that cannot be taken away; rights that everyone has

FIGURE 4.10. Because *unalienable* was an unfamiliar term for students, Ms. Miller taught them how to analyze the word's meaning in context using this graphic organizer.

Ms. Miller concurred, "Great observation. *Alien* can stand for something that is different or apart from what we consider to be the accepted norm." She added notes to the organizer and then stepped back to think aloud about how she might put the pieces together.

"In addition to *un-* and *alien*, we have the suffix *-able*, which, conveniently, means 'able.' So if I put *un* and *able* together we have 'not able.' And then I can add the *alien*. So it could be 'not able to be made alien' or 'not able to be made different' or 'not able to be taken apart.' Let's go back to the context and see which of those makes the most sense. Can someone reread the sentence for us?"

As a student read the sentence aloud, Ms. Miller circled the words surrounding *unalienable*. "I didn't notice this the first time we read, but look at the words surrounding our term—*guaranteed* and *rights*. *Unalienable* is the adjective that is describing the rights that are guaranteed. That is a fantastic clue. Now who can help me put it all together? What does *unalienable* mean?"

Several students raised their hands, but it was a quiet English language learner who said, "It means 'something that cannot be taken away.' Unalienable rights are the rights that everyone has that can't be taken away." Perfect.

In all, the prereading vocabulary activities in Ms. Miller's class had taken just under fifteen minutes. The initial knowledge rating and discussion took about ten minutes, and the more in-depth analysis of *unalienable* in context took five. Ms. Miller considered this time well spent. The students were now equipped with the language they needed to engage with a challenging piece of text. And the discussion of *unalienable* provided an opportunity to demonstrate an explicit, but not heavy-handed, model for figuring out words in context. The prereading activities provided support for academic language development, yet they were short and focused enough to ensure that the primary emphasis of the class remained on learning history.

Assessment *for* Learning

Strategies for assessing students' vocabulary learning should reflect the same awareness of purpose that is used for selecting instructional strategies. In assessing *concept vocabulary*, for example, teachers are likely to want to know if students can go beyond simply affixing a label and are able to explain the term and apply it to ongoing investigations in the content classroom. Since these are the ideas we want students to remember long after they leave our content-area classrooms, we want to assess for conceptual understanding and for application of the term through purposeful writing and discussion opportunities as well as authentic, inquiry-based activities.

A more recall-focused assessment approach is appropriate with *topic-specific vocabulary:* Are students able to remember and respond appropriately when they encounter the term in unit readings and discussions? Quizzing students on terms, asking them to label elements of a diagram using appropriate terminology, or using a fill-in-the-blank activity are all quick approaches to assessing students' familiarity with and recall of terms that are specific to an individual unit. These approaches are best used during the early or middle portions of a unit to determine whether students have the vocabulary needed to proceed. By the end of a unit, students should be familiar enough with topic-specific vocabulary such that they are able to use the words in their writing and conversation. Unit-culminating assessment that focuses specifically on vocabulary should be unnecessary; rather, the expectation of appropriate vocabulary use should be embedded in larger conceptual assessments.

In the science, mathematics, history, or art classroom, assessment of *general academic vocabulary* is most effective when it is done in concert with the reading to which it applies. As a history teacher, I was not really concerned if students remembered the meaning of the term *melancholy* at the end of a semester or even a unit. *Melancholy* was a word that, while interesting, was not particular to my content area; history could be understood without knowledge of this term. However, one of my favorite readings on the Black Death used the term *melancholy* in describing the reaction in Europe to the spread of disease. In order to understand the text, students needed to understand the term. Therefore, I taught the term alongside the reading and assessed whether students were able to understand the text. My focus was on text comprehension; assessment of general academic language was a concern only insofar as determining how language knowledge supported or interfered with comprehension.

The following material describes assessments used in the classroom vignettes featured in this chapter.

Recognizing Language Meant to Manipulate Meaning (Tier 4)

In addition to considerations of content vocabulary and academic language, there are times when it is important to consider another aspect of the use of language. Sometimes words are chosen not to clarify meaning, but rather to change or subvert meaning. Think of the advertisement for a "cozy bungalow" that turns out to be a run-down hovel. Helping students recognize language intended to manipulate can be particularly important in disciplines such as history or political science, where authors and orators often choose words that support their own agenda. Linguist George Lakoff (2004), for example, has written compellingly about how politicians have used terms such as *death tax* (versus the less ominous *estate tax*), *family values*, and *big government* to reframe the debate over national social and economic policy.

Strategies that can be used to help students recognize language meant to manipulate meaning can include reading (and designing their own) magazine promotions or newspaper want ads, examining direct-mail political claims, and looking at how advertisers frame ads for different audiences. *History Lessons*, a great book by Lindaman and Ward (2006), provides powerful examples of how history textbooks from around the world portray US history. Examining these examples provides strong evidence demonstrating how language can be manipulated to tell the same story with very different meanings. Teacher and author Kelly Gallagher (2004) teaches about loaded language using euphemisms from his favorite comic, George Carlin, and his book *Brain Droppings* (1997). "Having students play with these euphemisms gives me the opportunity to ask some pointed questions about the use of language: Why would a car dealer selling a used car rather call it a *previously used vehicle*? Why would a military spokesperson use the term *remains pouches* instead of *body bags*? Why do people who are trying to persuade us choose their words carefully? How can carefully chosen language influence us?" (2004, p. 170).

Assessment in Mr. Walsh's Science Class

Mr. Walsh's lesson provided multiple opportunities to assess and develop students' understanding of the concept described by the term *ecology*. Students wrote the definition in their own words, identified potential applications in magazine articles, and discussed their understanding during class development of a concept map. Throughout these activities, Mr. Walsh gently pushed and prodded with his questions to help students move away from inappropriate conceptualization and toward more thoughtful understanding. When a student claimed that an article was connected because it had to do with "a heart, and hearts are living, and ecology is about living things," for example, Mr. Walsh responded, "OK, I see how that relates to biology, which is the study of living things. Is ecology the same as biology?

How might they be different?" Regular monitoring and response during the concept development lesson helped to ensure that by the end of the lesson all students had a fairly clear understanding of what ecology was and wasn't. The real assessment of student learning, however, would come at the end of the unit, when students were asked to apply their learning to an analysis of the impact of pollution on a local estuary. Using data collected by local environmental agencies, students would apply their knowledge of ecology to understanding how water pollution impacts the organisms that call the estuary home. Students' work on this investigation would demonstrate their level of conceptual understanding, not just their knowledge of the definition of a word.

Assessment in Mr. Keller's Math Class

When math teacher Mr. Keller leafed through students' journals at the end of the day, he was pleased to see that nearly all had successfully defined new vocabulary words in their self-selected notebook glossaries. He used sticky notes to flag a couple that needed revisions to remind himself to follow up with these students one-on-one. Mr. Keller continued to assess and develop topic-specific language as the unit progressed. Prior to the lesson on quadrilaterals, for example, Mr. Keller showcased a concept circle (Vacca & Vacca, 2008) for the day's warm-up. He drew a circle with four quadrants on the board and filled in three of those quadrants with the terms *rhombus, square,*

and *trapezoid*. In the fourth quadrant he placed a question mark. Students were required to copy the circle into their notebooks, describe the relationship between the three terms in writing (all are quadrilaterals, meaning that they are closed figures with four sides and four vertices), and fill in an appropriate term in the fourth quadrant (possibilities include *rectangle* or *parallelogram*). This quick warm-up helped to refresh topic-specific terminology in students' minds and allowed Mr. Keller to assess students' readiness to continue with a lesson that would focus on describing, drawing, and determining angle measurements of a range of quadrilaterals.

Assessment in Ms. Miller's History Class

Ms. Miller's focus was on students' ability to understand and respond to the text of Dr. King's speech. Her language preview activity provided her with an initial assessment check and an opportunity to build up students' knowledge of the general vocabulary words they would encounter in the text. It also helped her identify students who were more likely to struggle with the text because of limited academic vocabulary. During

the reading, Ms. Miller worked more closely with these students, checking in more frequently to monitor their comprehension and partnering them with more fluent readers to provide language support. After the reading, Ms. Miller used a 3-2-1 summary (Wormeli, 2005) to check students' understanding. Each student was required to write down *3* of King's main points, identify *2* areas of confusion, and record *1* connection to earlier learning. Ms. Miller collected this assessment as an exit slip as students left the classroom and used the data in the students' responses to plan for the next day's follow-up lesson. Before students' moved on to the second portion of Dr. King's text, she would clarify areas of confusion by rereading and paraphrasing the text, working to ensure that students understood the meaning behind Dr. King's words.

It would be nearly impossible, and certainly impractical, to individually teach the tens of thousands of words that students encounter over the course of their school careers. As teachers with limited time and resources, we must be strategic in choosing what words to teach and how to teach them. By differentiating between concept vocabulary, topic-specific vocabulary, and general academic vocabulary, Mr. Walsh, Mr. Keller, and Ms. Miller were able to craft lessons that responded to the needs of their content and their students. When we are similarly cognizant of the varying vocabulary demands in our classrooms, we position ourselves to help students develop deep knowledge of those words that are foundational to our disciplines, facility with topic-specific vocabulary, and the skills needed to navigate unfamiliar academic language. The differentiated approaches to vocabulary instruction described in this chapter work in concert to equip students with the knowledge and skills needed to read and understand content texts. And the more students read, the more they develop both their content understanding and their vocabularies.

5

Constructing Understanding

What You'll Find in This Chapter

Teaching critical literacy in the content classroom: Chapter 5 begins with a discussion of the importance of teaching critical literacy in the content classroom. It provides an overview of instructional approaches that support students in developing a deep understanding of texts and concepts.

Engaging students in critical literacy: Two facets of critical literacy are highlighted in this section: analyzing texts and applying content learning. Discussion of each of these facets is followed by a list of instructional strategies and a classroom vignette or two showing the strategies in action.

Analyzing texts: This section examines strategies to help students uncover bias in text and become critical consumers of content.

Classroom vignette: Analyzing Text in the Science Classroom

Applying content learning: This section discusses strategies for helping students use the knowledge and ideas gleaned from texts to solve problems, generate new insights, and respond to authentic questions.

Classroom vignettes: Applying Content Learning in Visual Arts and History Classrooms

Authentic outcomes: This section highlights culminating assignments that allow students to articulate and defend their analysis or demonstrate their application in real-world contexts.

Assessment for *learning:* The final section provides follow-up discussions for each of the classroom vignettes and explores how teachers assessed both students' understanding of the content and their development of critical analysis and application skills.

When I initially imagined myself as a history teacher, I envisioned students engaged in thoughtful discussions about the past. I saw myself mediating as they debated the merits of particular arguments or the validity of texts. I assumed that we would be involved in thoughtful inquiry, make connections between past and present, and recognize essential themes of the human experience. In short, I wanted to pass along to students what I found interesting about my discipline. I wanted them to engage in the same sort of inquiry and debate that I had grown to love in college.

Much of that early vision came crashing down when I entered the classroom. There, I encountered students with limited content knowledge, poor reading skills, and general disinterest in learning about history. In addition, I was confronted with content expectations from my district that emphasized "getting through" a tremendous amount of material, the vast majority of which focused on factual knowledge and memorization. The great discussions that I had imagined appeared very much at odds with this reality.

Many content teachers confront similar realities. With middle and high school students struggling to access content reading, state content standards that emphasize large volumes of knowledge, and ever-increasing pressure to pass state content examinations, "coverage" seems to have become the teaching norm. Teachers lecture or assign readings, students take down material, we test their knowledge, and we move on to the next topic.

Lost in the grind of coverage, however, is the "So what?" Why does this material matter? How does it connect to my prior knowledge and beliefs? What can I do with the information and ideas in this text? How do the information and ideas affect me? These are the critical questions of learning. Although demands of coverage may necessitate that we move more quickly through some topics, it is essential that we find time to address "So what?" questions within our content classrooms. If we fail to inquire into the meanings behind the information in texts, then we are deadening our disciplines for both our students and ourselves.

Dewey described understanding as "the result of facts acquiring meaning for the learner" (1933, p. 137). This acquisition of meaning does not come by luck or happenstance but through active engagement with material. Educational psychologist Jerome Bruner observed that "the most characteristic thing about mental life, over and beyond the fact that one apprehends the events of the world around one, is that one constantly goes beyond the information given" (1957, p. 218). To go beyond the information given—to acquire understanding— one must grapple with information, analyze data, synthesize various perspectives, apply knowledge to new settings, reflect on one's own learning, and revise prior conceptions and beliefs. If we want our students to develop understanding of core concepts within our disciplines, we need to provide opportunities for students to go beyond comprehension when engaging with texts. Reading for learning needs to involve application and analysis of the information and ideas they encounter. Literacy expert Sheridan Blau (2003) states that there are really only three questions we need to ask students about text: What does it say? What does it mean? and What does it matter? The first two questions get at literal and inferential levels of comprehension. They need to be addressed and should be supported by strategies such as those discussed in Chapter 4. But the third question is equally important. For students to move beyond seeing texts as discrete collections of information and move toward an understanding of that information as it relates to a larger conceptual framework, they need to address the question "What does it matter?" As content teachers, we need to provide opportunities for students to critically evaluate texts, synthesize information across texts, apply facts and ideas from texts, and make connections between information in the text and prior understandings. Doing so will move students beyond text-based knowledge, which is often quickly forgotten, and toward what Wiggins and McTighe (2005) describe as "enduring understanding"—ownership of the ideas that reside at the heart of the discipline and have value beyond the classroom.

In addition to supporting the development of conceptual understanding, engaging students in the "So what?" questions of content reading also supports the development of habits of mind appropriate to learning and thinking within our disciplines. A historian does not simply read a primary source document and accept the information within it as true. He or she interrogates the document, questioning its veracity, seeking out background on its source, and considering the biases it might represent. Similarly, a scientist is unlikely to read a journal article simply to acquire information. Rather, he or she will examine the methods behind the research and consider how the findings might apply to other areas of investigation. Teaching students to go beyond comprehension of content texts helps them to develop in the ways of thinking of the discipline, positioning them to be able to grow as independent content learners after they have left our classrooms.

Within academic circles, this idea of going beyond comprehension is often referred to as "critical literacy." This approach encourages readers to actively analyze text and uncover underlying meaning or meanings. It builds off of the work of Paulo Freire (1970) who, while teaching literacy in underprivileged communities in Brazil, argued that education should equip individuals to analyze existing structures of power and privilege and work to change those structures to become more egalitarian. Kris Gutiérrez (2001) built upon Freire's critical pedagogy perspective to focus on the power dynamics that exist in language and text. In what she describes as the "discursive politics of knowledge production," she argues that any exchange of language or knowledge necessarily involves issues of power and that readers need to become aware of these power dynamics in order to truly understand text. Norman Fairclough (2001) goes on to assert that the more conscious individuals are of their own literate identities and the social structures within which language and text are produced, the more they are able to exert control over their own lives. Educators with a critical literacy perspective aim to help students recognize the interplay of power between producers of text and consumers of text. These educators ask students to consider the "So what?" questions, to uncover the origins and purposes of text, and to consider the impact that text has on their individual understanding and, more broadly, on the manner in which knowledge is conceptualized.

Beyond developing students' conceptual understanding and introducing them to the habits of mind of our disciplines, there is another, more personal— some might even say more selfish—reason to go beyond comprehension and engage students in critically reading content texts. We need to do so for our identities as educators who are also historians, scientists, mathematicians, or artists. Most of us chose to teach in our content areas because we felt a connection to the discipline that goes beyond knowledge acquisition. I initially became a history teacher because I wanted to engage students in debates about justice and progress, to help them make connections between past and present, and to work together to consider common threads of the human experience. When I later added mathematics to my teaching credential, I was excited about the opportunity to help students grapple with mathematical concepts, to support them in developing logical problem-solving techniques, and to help them draw connections between seemingly abstract mathematical principles and real-world applications.

To remain passionate about my content, I need, and I think most teachers need, opportunities to explore these higher levels of discipline-based thinking with students. Educator Ellin Oliver Keene writes, "I can think of nothing so gratifying in teaching as introducing students to a more intellectual life—a life in which text messaging and iPods play a role, but in which time in class is spent in pursuit of ideas that have intrigued readers and writers, scientists and historians, artists and musicians for generations" (2007, p. 38). Teaching students text comprehension is necessary, but it is only a starting point. If we are to support students' understanding of core subject-area concepts, help develop habits of mind that are representative of the discipline, and remain true to our own role as content experts, we must go beyond comprehension and work toward critical literacy in content-area reading.

Teaching Critical Literacy in the Content Classroom

There are multiple approaches that can be used to support the development of critical literacy in the content classroom. Critical literacy strategies will necessarily vary depending on the subject area, students' strengths and needs, the reading material, and instructional goals. However, across contents and classrooms there are four consistent characteristics that support successful critical engagement with content literacy: multiple opportunities to engage with texts and concepts, social construction of understanding, authentic outcomes, and metacognition.

Multiple Opportunities to Engage with Texts and Concepts

Effectively engaging students in thinking critically about texts requires multiple opportunities to interact with texts and concepts. It is not enough simply to read a text once and assume that students will comprehend the material, be able to consider how to apply the material, and be able to analyze the construction of the text. Instead, students need to be provided with opportunities to engage with the text multiple times as they move from comprehension to application to analysis. "They need both a 'down' draft reading to comprehend the basics and an 'up' draft reading to explore deeper meaning" (K. Gallagher, 2004, p. 80). Literacy expert Kylene Beers reminds us that comprehension is a process and that just closing a book or finishing the first reading of a text "doesn't close off the thinking that shapes our understanding" (2003, p. 139). Getting students to see literacy as a process and engage with texts multiple times can be challenging. Many students come to content reading with a belief that they simply need to "get through" it once and then they can be done. To overcome this resistance, we need to model the behaviors of strong content readers and set clear expectations for the purposes of engaging and reengaging with the material.

In addition to multiple readings of individual texts, content classrooms that promote critical literacy often provide multiple texts about a common topic. Research has shown that the more students read on an individual topic, the more likely they are to move from novice to expert ways of thinking (Alexander, Kulikowich, & Schulze, 1994). Science educator Bonnie Hanson-Grafton describes the need for a "three-hit threshold" in developing concept understanding, explaining that addressing a topic only once or twice is unlikely to lead to real learning (as quoted in R. Allen, 2007). History educators Ogle, Klemp, and McBride similarly argue that "students need to be surrounded by *more* rather than less material on the topics being taught. They need to be enticed into reading and writing in as many ways as possible" (2007, p. 27). Critical understanding comes from the opportunity to review, analyze, and compare texts, to see how different authors explore concepts, and to recognize how texts can be used to promote or deny particular viewpoints or accounts. Critical literacy in the content classroom is best supported by opportunities to engage multiple times with a range of texts on common topics.

Social Construction of Understanding

A second characteristic of content classrooms that effectively engage students in critical literacy is that they provide opportunities for student talk. Learning theorists argue that all knowledge is built through social interactions as individuals collaboratively create shared understandings through discourse and debate (see, for example, Bruner, 1986; Vygotsky, 1978). Within the context of content reading, social interactions provide essential opportunities for students to "try out" their conceptual understandings, evolving analyses, and critical responses. Science education researchers Osborne, Erduran, and Simon note that the opportunity to discuss and defend interpretations of scientific data and phenomena with peers is a critical piece of developing scientific literacy. "Argumentation— the coordination of evidence and theory to support or refute an explanatory conclusion, model, or prediction [Suppe, 1998]—is a critically important epistemic task and discourse process in science" (2004, p. 995). They explain that engaging in argumentation helps students clarify their own thinking, better understand alternative conceptualizations, and become more thoughtful consumers of scientific reports and stories about science reported in the media. History educator Bruce VanSledright (2004) similarly notes the importance of student-to-student talk in supporting critical literacy in history and the social sciences. He argues that the opportunity to share and defend interpretations of texts is at the heart of what historians do and that students need to have similar opportunities.

Authentic Outcomes

Critical literacy in the content areas is most effective when paired with authentic learning outcomes. Donovan, Bransford, and Pellegrino (1999) describe authentic learning as a pedagogical approach that allows students to explore, discuss, and meaningfully construct concepts and relationships in contexts that involve real-world problems that are meaningful to the learner. By its very nature, critical literacy is grounded in authenticity because it works to emulate the real-world work of practitioners within the disciplines. In science class, for example, students can debate the merits of reported findings and build on research conclusions to generate new questions for investigation. In history, students can analyze the validity of primary source documents and synthesize evidence across sources. However, it is important that such activities do not simply become intellectual exercises without relevance for students. Students should not simply follow a protocol or fill out a graphic organizer that supports critical literacy skills in order for us to be able to check off the analysis and application boxes on our "things to teach" lists. Literacy experts Doug Fisher and Nancy Frey, in their book on adolescent literacy, caution, "Perhaps the biggest mistake made with graphic organizers is that they are viewed as an end product, not a tool to lead to something else. . . . When the sole purpose of a graphic organizer becomes filling it out correctly, it is nothing more than a worksheet" (2008, p. 131).

It is useful to think of critical literacy outcomes in two stages: process strategies and authentic outcomes. *Process strategies* are those intermediate activities that are designed to get students thinking about the possible application of information or analysis of a document. Process strategies often will involve protocols and graphic organizers designed to help students critically interact with text. On the other hand, *authentic outcomes* are those real-world learning tasks that require students to transform information and take ownership of ideas. Authentic outcomes may involve students acting upon the questions generated by critically reading a text to design, conduct, and report on their own research. Students might present an argument that synthesizes information across texts to respond to a real-world problem. Or they may demonstrate understanding through creative application of ideas. When students are working toward authentic outcomes and they can see the relevance of the task, intrinsic motivation is increased (Mehlinger, 1995), they engage more thoughtfully in critical literacy activities, and the process of reading and responding to content texts more closely approximates the work of practitioners within the field.

Metacognition

In content classrooms that effectively engage students in critical literacy there are regular opportunities for students to reflect on their learning and self-assess their performance. One of the differences between a novice content reader and an expert content reader is that the expert recognizes gaps in his or her knowledge and seeks a remedy, whereas the novice doesn't know what he doesn't know. A novice reader of history, for example, is likely to develop an initial interpretation based primarily on what is on the page and stick with that interpretation. On the other hand, an expert will more thoughtfully reflect on the process she has used to analyze text, identify holes in her knowledge, consider what questions have not been asked, and revise her interpretation as she searches for a deeper understanding of the issues (Wineburg, 2001). Engaging students in critical literacy in the content classroom means helping them recognize what they don't know, self-assess their progress, and seek out additional information and resources and continue to deepen their interpretation of texts and their understanding of concepts (Bransford, Brown, & Cocking, 2000).

Engaging Students in Critical Literacy

Literacy researchers Peter Freebody and Allan Luke (1990) posit that there are four roles a literate person plays when engaging with text. The first two, code breaker and meaning maker, focus primarily on reading comprehension. Readers in these roles decode text and use their prior knowledge of content and text structure to comprehend the author's meaning. Freebody and Luke's latter two roles, text critic and text user, move beyond text comprehension and into the realm of critical literacy. They require readers to analyze and apply the text, considering not just what the author said, but how it was said and why it might be relevant. Reading content texts in the role of text critic and text user moves students toward deeper understanding of concepts and closer to approximating the learning of content experts.

The remainder of this chapter focuses on strategies designed to engage students in analyzing texts and applying content learning. These two elements of critical literacy are closely linked, and their connections are evident in the classroom vignettes that follow. However, text critic and text user, as defined by Freebody and Luke, are distinct roles, each with unique objectives. To effectively support students in developing the ability to analyze texts and apply content learning, it is important that we understand the specific goals of each and be able to tailor classroom instruction to support those goals.

Analyzing Texts

When readers assume the role of text critic, they seek to uncover the intent, bias, and effect of a text on the text's audience. Text critics question the validity of a text's argument and the evidence used to support the argument. They interrogate the methods used to justify a claim and wonder what information and ideas were not pursued. They analyze the source of the document and participate actively in the creation of its meaning.

Every reading, whether it claims objectivity or not, contains bias, specific points of view, and divergent perspectives (Alvermann, Moon, & Hagood, 1999). Texts make assumptions about who their readers are and what they should think. Authors select language, structures, and information to convey their own beliefs and understandings. No text is neutral. Readers who analyze texts disrupt the noncritical transmission of information and ideas from text to consumer. They seek to consider multiple perspectives, noticing voices and viewpoints of people represented in texts as well as noticing those that are missing or silent (G. Johnson, 1999; Lewison, Flint, & Van Sluys, 2002; McLaughlin & DeVoogd, 2004).

Teaching our students to become critical readers in content classes prepares them to be critical consumers of text within and beyond the classroom. They learn to ask hard questions of authors, producers, and distributors of information. In an information age when so much information is bandied around as "truth," these skills are vital for student success and for the strength of our society as a whole (Wineburg & Martin, 2004).

History educator Sam Wineburg describes the difference between a critical reader and a lay reader as being akin to the difference between a prosecuting attorney and a member of the jury. Critical readers work through texts as if they are prosecuting attorneys; they look for discrepancies, question sources, and delve into conscious and unconscious motives of authors. Lay readers, on the other hand, are like jurors, "patiently listening to testimony and questioning themselves about what they had just heard, but unable to question witnesses directly or subject them to cross examination" (2001, p. 77). Table 5.1 further describes differences in the reading behaviors of lay readers versus critical readers.

I recently had the opportunity to watch as Dr. Wineburg demonstrated these differences at a workshop for history teachers. To begin, he invited a teacher participant to demonstrate her reading process in front of the group. She bravely thought aloud about the one-page text excerpt, reading from the top and pausing regularly to check for understanding, connect to prior knowledge, visualize images in the text, and fix up confusion. She did a beautiful job of comprehending the text. Dr. Wineburg then played a video clip that showed a historian interacting with the same text. Rather than start from the top, the historian began his reading by looking for clues about the origins of the text. He focused on the fact that the text was a diary entry and anticipated the biases and motives he might encounter in the text. He identified the time, place, and setting of the document and began to build a context for the diary entry by drawing out his prior knowledge of the period. When he did read, he did so slowly, pausing to question the veracity of the information and working to corroborate the claims that were being made. At the end of the first reading, he paused to consider the source again. "We all know about diaries," he mused. "The nineteenth? He wrote it that day? Maybe. Or maybe later. Could have been used to cover his

TABLE 5.1. Reading Behavior of Novices versus Critical Readers

Reading Behaviors of Novices versus Critical Readers	
Novice Readers	Critical Readers
• Believe comprehension is main goal of reading	• See comprehension as first step in understanding text
• Are content to read text once	• Revisit text multiple times
• Focus on identifying main ideas	• Analyze logic and consider flaws in author's arguments
• Uncritically accept information and ideas in text as true	• Actively question information and ideas in text to determine sources and credibility
• Focus on literal meaning of words	• Consider word choice and implications
• View the text as objective	• Seek to uncover the bias inherent in text
• Do not consider context of text	• Wonder about author's purpose and intended audience
• Remain unaware of alternative interpretations and perspectives	• Consider alternative interpretations and speculate on differing perspectives
• Are content to read only one source	• Actively seek out additional sources to better understand a topic
• View locus of authority as "the text" (Wineburg, 2001, p. 77)	• Believe locus of authority is "questions . . . formulated about the text" (Wineburg, 2001, p. 77)

backside. Maybe he decided it was better to write to say that he lost control over his men than to have fired the first shot. Might be useful in an inquest." The meaning that the historian derived from the text was significantly different from that of the teacher participant. The difference came not from discrepancies in their background knowledge—the historian was a medievalist and had only limited knowledge of the American Revolution, the time and place in which the diary was situated. Instead, the difference derived from the stances with which the readers approached the document. The teacher participant saw the text as a material to be understood. The historian saw it as an artifact to be interrogated.

Instructional Strategies

- *SOAPSTone.* Originally developed by the College Board, SOAPSTone provides a protocol for analyzing texts. Each letter of the acronym prompts students to analyze a different aspect of the reading. Taken together, the protocol guides students to uncover the source of the text, its intended purpose and audience, and the context within which the text is situated. An example of the use of the SOAPSTone protocol can be found in the history classroom vignette later in this chapter.

Subject(s): Identify the subject and the main idea of the text.

Occasion: Discuss the context of the text. Consider the setting, circumstances, events, and historical or cultural context.

Audience: Identify the intended audience. Discuss why this audience was targeted.

Purpose: Analyze what the author's purpose was for composing the text. Consider both explicit and implicit purposes.

Speaker: Identify the author of the text. Discuss what you know about the author and how his or her experience influences the text.

Tone: Determine the emotional sense of the piece. Consider why this tone was used.

- *Questioning the author (QtA).* Teach students to aggressively interrogate a text using QtA prompts (see Figure 5.1). These prompts are designed to uncover bias, recognize assumptions, identify flaws in logic, and consider alternatives. Though teachers will need to model their use and guide application initially, the prompts are intended to be used by students as they select and adapt the questions to respond to the information and ideas they encounter in a text. Some of the questions will not have straightforward answers, and some will be left unanswered. This is OK. As is demonstrated in Ms. Sanchez's science classroom in the vignette that follows, the point of this strategy is not to get definitive responses to the questions, but to empower students to think critically about text (Beck, McKeown, Hamilton, & Kucan, 1997).

- *New perspectives.* How would you understand the Declaration of Independence if you were reading as a British noble? An indentured servant? A woman? A slave? The interpretation we develop of text has a great deal to do with the perspective through which we view the material. Assign students to take on a new perspective. Have them make notes in the margins as they reread—What do they notice? What's most important to them? What's missing? Compare perspectives to gain new insights on the reading.

- *Socratic seminars.* Socratic seminars are "exploratory intellectual conversations centered on a text" (Lambright, 1995, p. 30). They provide students with opportunities to analyze and respond to challenging readings. In an effective Socratic seminar, students take charge of the conversation as they work collaboratively to uncover the text's meaning, debate its merits, and

Initial questions
- What is the topic?
- What is the author trying to communicate about this topic?
- What information and ideas does the author include?
- What does the author want the reader to understand?

Follow-up questions
- Does the author explain ideas clearly? How do information and ideas connect? What "holes" are there in the author's logic?
- What kind of information is included? Is this information credible? What information is left out?
- What is the author's perspective? Does the author address other perspectives? What other ways might we understand the information and ideas in this text?
- How does this text change what you think about this topic? What led to your change in thinking?

Adapted from Beck, McKeown, Hamilton, & Kucan (1997).

FIGURE 5.1. Questioning-the-author prompts.

consider its relevance. The best Socratic seminars take on high-level texts that involve complex ideas and sophisticated intellectual arguments. Although Socratic seminars can take many forms, effective discussions tend to have the following characteristics:

- Questions that guide discussion are open ended. They focus on analyzing the text, evaluating evidence, and critiquing the validity of arguments.

- The teacher acts as facilitator, stepping in to redirect conversation when needed, but mostly allowing students to respond directly to their peers.

- Students support their claims using direct text evidence. Students come to the discussion having already read, analyzed, and annotated text in preparation for the discussion.

- Respectful disagreement is encouraged. Discussing differences of opinion is part of the meaning-making process. However, disagreement needs to remain respectful. Teaching students to use phrases such as "I hear what you are saying, but . . ." "I wonder if you've considered . . ." and "I disagree because . . ." can help to support constructive academic discourse.

It is worth noting that before students can have a successful Socratic seminar, they need to have strong text comprehension. Even fluent readers will struggle to move directly to a Socratic seminar if they haven't first had an opportunity to think through and digest the meaning of a text. Engaging students in reciprocal teaching prior to a Socratic seminar, such as was demonstrated by Mr. Doherty in Chapter 3, is a great approach to supporting student learning and preparing them to engage in high-level discussions about complex texts.

Analyzing Text in the Science Classroom

"City Proposes Toilet-to-Tap Water Reclamation Program." When Ms. Sanchez first saw this headline blaring out from the front of her local newspaper, she knew that she had to share it with her chemistry class. They were in the middle of a unit on chemical solutions, and this article provided a perfect context for connecting students' textbook knowledge of chemical bonds, solvents, and distillations with a real-world problem. Equally important, it provided an opportunity for students to critically evaluate the media's portrayal of science. "Science plays such a huge role in our society," Ms. Sanchez said, explaining to me that she regularly brought in science-related news articles for her high school students to read. "But unfortunately, the way we hear about science in the newspapers and on TV is often not accurate. People in the media and political groups manipulate reports to suit their own interests. Not all of my students will go on to become scientists, but I want all of them to be able to be smart consumers of science. I want them to know how to read a news article about food safety or listen to an argument about evolution and ask thoughtful questions. They need to be smart about what they think and not just be swayed by the loudest voices."

Ms. Sanchez enlarged the headline and placed it on the document camera to greet her students on a Monday morning. As they settled into their seats, she instructed her students to take a moment to think about what the headline meant. "Headlines can be confusing," she reminded her students. "There's a lot of information packed into a few words."

"I think it means that the city is trying to find a way to get more water," one student volunteered.

"Yeah, I heard about this on the radio. They want to recycle the water that we already use," another explained.

"Eew!" a girl in the corner shrieked. "I don't want to drink someone else's pee!" Ms. Sanchez grinned. She had gotten their attention!

"I agree," Ms Sanchez said. "It is kind of a gross concept. At first I didn't like the idea either. But if you think about it, all water is recycled. Nature recycles water through evaporation and precipitation. We drink water that comes down the Colorado River and has been used and recycled by people who live upstream. So the question isn't really, 'Is it OK to drink recycled water?' We do that already. The question is, 'Can the water reclamation process adequately purify the water?'" Students were skeptical, but they listened. Although the reclamation concept initially seemed unbelievable, several admitted that their teacher had some good points.

"In a couple of minutes, we're going to take a look at the article that accompanies this headline. As you read, I want you to put on your critical reading hats. Use your knowledge of science to make connections and ask hard questions. Point out where the logic is flawed and look for author bias. This was in our local newspaper. It's a real issue responding to a real concern about not having enough water in this city. Thousands of people are going to read this article. Will they get an accurate representation of the science involved? Is there enough information here for them to be able to develop informed opinions?

"Let's start by taking a critical look at this headline," Ms. Sanchez said as she moved to the document camera and reread the headline aloud. "'City proposes toilet-to-tap water reclamation program.' OK, well, I have some questions right away. I want to know who came up with this name 'Toilet-to-Tap.'" She circled the phrase on the projector and wrote "Source?" next to it. "That doesn't seem like a name that would accompany the proposal. Is that something that the newspaper chose, or some other critic? I also want to know what water is being reclaimed. Is this sewage or storm drain runoff? What happens to that water now? I think

we currently treat wastewater. How will this process be different?" She recorded these questions on the projector as well. "Some of these questions I'll likely be able to answer as I read further, but others are probably not going to be answered. Those are the questions that are sometimes most important. They help us understand what is really going on.

"Now it's your turn," Ms. Sanchez said as she passed out photocopies of the news article. I want you to read through the text once to understand what it says and then a second time to question the author. If you have trouble thinking of questions, remember to use our critical questioning guide." She pointed to a chart that hung near the board at the front of the classroom (see Figure 5.2).

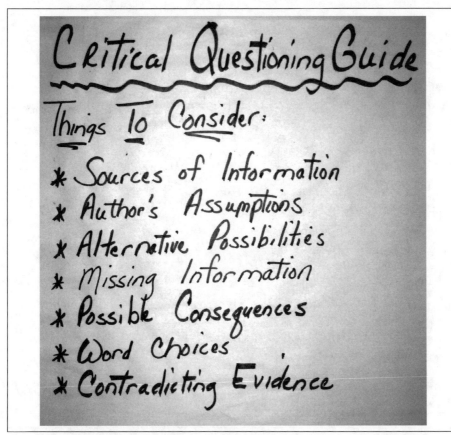

FIGURE 5.2. Ms. Sanchez posted this critical questioning guide to support students when they analyzed a newspaper article.

Students responded readily. They were engaged by the issue and, as teenagers, always appreciated the opportunity to be critics of perceived authority. They recorded notes in the margins of the article as they read. "Not true!" wrote one student next to a critic's claim that water could not be purified. "Distillation or chromatography purify water," noted another. Students questioned sources of information—"Is this guy really a chemist???" "How much of this is written by the marketing department?" They quibbled with word choices—"Water is a *solvent*, not a *solute*." "How do you know it will be *grossly* inefficient?" They pointed out flaws in arguments—"Chlorine can be removed before water is consumed." "Not all pollutants will bond with added chemicals." And they looked for missing details—"Is this being done anywhere in the world?" "How much energy will this take?"

As students completed their readings and began to talk about their findings, Ms. Sanchez passed out a three-column chart intended to help guide their conversations (see sample, Figure 5.3). Students worked in groups to complete the chart, drawing on their responses to the reading and frequently referencing their chemistry textbook. Several went online to review the schematic image of the treatment proposal and search out additional information from other sources.

Ms. Sanchez – Chemical Solutions

Analyzing Text

What's included?	What's missing?	What's inaccurate?
✻ Statements by mayor & other critics ✻ Very brief (1 sentence) explanation of proposal ✻ Lots of concerns —Time (7–9 yrs.) —cost ($800 million $4.5 billion) —Health (do say that we already have contaminants) ✻ Description of need Big population desert environment	✻ Statements in support of proposal —esp. from scientists ✻ Details — How will this process work? How does it compare to other solutions? ✻ History — Has this been tried anywhere else? (Denver, Namibia)	→ Makes it sound like everyone is against it —is this true? ✻ Name "Toilet-to-Tap" is misleading —really should be "Water Reclamation" ✻ Solvent v. solute v. solution ✻ Flocculation ≠ Filtration

FIGURE 5.3. Students used this three-column chart to support their discussions about the newspaper article.

"So what do you think?" Ms. Sanchez called out as students wrapped up their conversations. "What are the biases of this article? Does it treat science accurately and fairly?"

"I think it's all about politics," a young woman in the back of the class responded. "There's some good information about science in here, but a lot of the people they quote aren't even scientists. They're just average people who are grossed out by the idea. By the time the scientists start explaining the process, the article is more than halfway over."

"I agree," a young man said. "It's hard to really understand the process based on what they explain. They say some stuff about clumping together particles and filtering and treating biological waste with chlorine, but it wasn't enough to really understand. We went online to look it up and the plans are much more extensive than they seem in the article."

Several more students commented, most agreeing that the newspaper article was missing important information and appeared to be biased against the water reclamation proposal. "I mean, the headline says it all," a student at the front explained. "They make it sound like the city is just going to hook up a pipe between people's toilets and the drinking water. You have to really read far into the article to find out that the process isn't like that at all."

On the following day, Ms. Sanchez would introduce a lab to students to explore the process of water purification. They would each be given a solution (though not one that included biohazards) and asked to use their knowledge of chemistry to separate out the component parts. Before they left the newspaper article, however, Ms. Sanchez had one final assignment related to the text. "For homework tonight, I want you to write a letter to the editor of the paper," she instructed. "Tell them what you think of this article. Was it fair? Did it accurately represent the science? Tell them what was appropriate. Point out what is missing or inaccurate. Use evidence from the text to support your claims. And mind your language—we're going to be sending these in!" Students groaned as they packed up their bags to leave, but the letters they turned in the next day revealed that they had taken the assignment seriously. In thoughtful language, students critiqued the news article, many taking the editor to task for prioritizing sensationalism over science. "Your article had lots of reaction, but not enough information," wrote one student. "You may not like the water reclamation idea, but newspapers are supposed to inform us about proposals, not bias readers against them," wrote another. Ms. Sanchez smiled as she read through the students' work. "They're starting to get it," she said. "When we first started reading news stories about science, they just accepted what the author said. But now that they have more content knowledge and a little more confidence, they are starting to think for themselves."

Applying Content Learning

When readers take on the role of text user, they seek to answer the question, "What do I do with this text?" (Freebody & Luke, 1990). This is the "So what?" question of reading and, in many ways, returns us to the need for setting a purpose and establishing a context that was addressed in Chapter 2. Real-world content readers do not read text solely for the purpose of identifying information. We read text in anticipation of being able to *use* the information and ideas we find. Text users transfer information and ideas to new settings and new applications. They extend information to ask new questions and form new ideas. They synthesize information across texts to build their own interpretations of events, people, ideas, and phenomena.

Real expertise derives not from how much information is known, but from how well it can be used. Curriculum design experts Grant Wiggins and Jay McTighe explain, "To be truly able requires the ability to transfer what we have learned to new and sometimes confusing settings. The ability to transfer our knowledge and skill effectively involves the capacity to take what we know and use it creatively, flexibly, fluently, in different settings or problems, on our own" (2005, p. 40). Content experts are able to selectively use information, apply skills, and adapt ideas to solve problems, generate new insights, and respond to authentic questions within their disciplines.

Teaching our students to use information and apply skills from their readings helps them to approximate the work of content experts and supports deeper understanding of the material. The more students work with information, manipulate data, respond to ideas, and apply skills, the more ownership they have over the content. They begin to see patterns emerge and construct conceptual frameworks to make sense of the material. Recognizing these "big ideas" supports retention of new knowledge and prepares students to more effectively engage in future learning (Bransford, Brown, & Cocking, 2000).

The following instructional strategies suggest intermediate steps in working toward application. They are designed to help students begin to synthesize information across readings and apply learning to new settings. These are process strategies that help to prepare students for working toward more authentic outcomes.

Instructional Strategies

- *Critical thinking guides.* There are many graphic organizers out there that facilitate application of information and ideas. Select organizers that support the instructional focus of the unit and then use them to help students synthesize information across readings. For example, a Venn diagram can work beautifully to help pull information from different texts to compare and contrast artistic movements. On the other hand, a flowchart may help students understand relationships between viruses and their host organisms. At the application stage, graphic organizers shouldn't be used to simply record the ideas of others, but should help students arrive at their own conceptualizations as they work to identify patterns and connections across texts. An example of the use of a pro–con guide can be found in the history class vignette that follows. Samples of a range of graphic organizers that may be used as application guides can be found in Figure 5.4.

- *Read it–try it.* Sometimes the best learning opportunities are the most direct. After a reading that describes a procedure or practice, have students

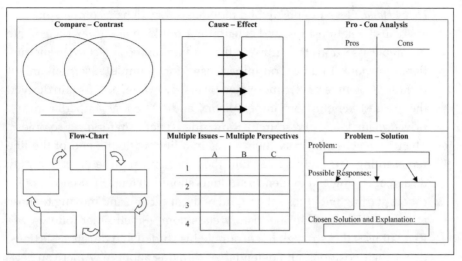

FIGURE 5.4. Critical thinking guides.

try it out through a series of quick, informal learning opportunities. After reading about microscopes, for example, students should have the opportunity to experiment with adjusting the focus, changing the magnification, and making a slide. Opportunities to check back with the reading as tasks become progressively more challenging help prepare students for more formal application. In the classroom vignette that follows, Mr. Costa provides a wonderful series of read it–try it activities to support his art students in developing an understanding of color schemes.

• *Learning logs.* Informal written reflection in a journal or learning log can help students to respond to readings, think about their application, and deepen their conceptual framework. I find learning logs to be most helpful when we are engaged in a unit framed around an inquiry focus, project-based approach, or "essential question" (Wiggins & McTighe, 2005). As students progress through the unit, read new texts, and encounter new information, they record their evolving understanding in the log. Logs can also be a place to raise questions, collect data, and try out initial conclusions. Thoughtfully designed writing prompts can help guide student response. In a unit investigating immigration policy, for example, I might ask students to consider how the information they learned in the latest reading on Chinese immigration compares to an earlier reading on Irish immigration. Responses need not be limited to writing; students can also draw visual representations, design political cartoons, or create a graphic representation.

- *Here I stand.* Get students up and moving as they debate comparisons, assess causal relationships, and extend their thinking about texts. Generate debatable assertions that draw on the readings and connect to the instructional purpose. In a unit on imperialism, for example, assertions might include "Colonizers were motivated primarily by greed," "Britain derived the greatest benefit from imperialism," and "Although imperialism deprived many lands of resources, it provided a net gain for most colonies." Then have students array themselves in a line, with one end of the line representing "strongly agree" and the other end representing "strongly disagree." Using text evidence, students should defend their choice of location, starting with those at one end of the spectrum and moving to those at the opposite end. In the history classroom vignette that follows, Mr. Kendall uses this strategy to encourage his students to debate assertions, define their positions, and defend their thinking about the American decision to bomb Hiroshima and Nagasaki at the end of World War II.

Applying Content Learning in the Visual Arts Classroom

"How many of you have ever painted a room in your house?" Mr. Costa asked his introduction to drawing and painting class. Many of the students raised their hands. "What colors did you choose and why?"

"We used white for our living room," a boy said. "My mom says it goes with everything."

"I used lavender in my room," a girl said. "I wanted it to look good with my purple pillows."

"We painted our kitchen green, because the counters are yellow and my mom said that we couldn't have the whole room be yellow; that would be too bright," another student shared. Mr. Costa listened carefully to students' responses and then segued into his introduction of the lesson.

"The colors you chose and the reasons you chose them relate to color theory," he explained. "You may not have known it, but you were following certain color schemes in your selections. For example, when you chose lavender paint to go with your purple pillows, Jannelle, you were following a monochromatic color scheme. And Sondra, when your mom decided to paint the kitchen green to

coordinate with the yellow tiles, she was using an analogous color scheme. Today we're going to learn about four color schemes that artists and designers use to inform their color choices: monochromatic, analogous, complementary, and neutral. We're going to start with a reading and then you're going to try out the schemes."

Mr. Costa passed out a two-page reading that provided information about each of the four color schemes. Although the text was relatively easy to read, with large font size, plenty of room in the margins, and considerate text features, it lacked the one thing that would have been most helpful—color. Rather than see this as a deficit, however, Mr. Costa made it into an application opportunity. "Read the text one section at a time," he instructed. "After you finish each section, pause for a moment and think about an application: What might an example of this color scheme look like? Then, use colored pencils from the supply boxes at your tables to create an example or two. For instance, in the section on monochromatic color schemes, you'll learn they consist of two or more different shades of a single color. So I might then choose a purple and a lavender, like Jannelle's room, and color those next to each other in the margin. Or I could choose a pink and a red, a dark blue and a light blue . . . You get the idea. Do that with each of the four schemes and then we'll check in to see if your applications match the descriptions in the text."

Ten minutes later, the once black-and-white texts were colorfully illustrated. Mr. Costa conducted a brief share-out, clarified a few areas of confusion, and quickly moved on to the next application. "I've placed a series of magazine photos on your desks," he explained. "They're all from design magazines and show pictures of rooms or clothing with different color schemes. Take a look, identify the colors, and label the scheme."

"A white couch and tan walls," a student observed. "This one's neutral."

"I think this pink and purple dress is analogous," another suggested. "Because pink is a shade of red and red and purple are next to each other on the color wheel."

"Eew! An orange and blue bathroom," a girl in the middle of the room exclaimed. "It's complementary, I know, but it's also ugly!"

Mr. Costa flipped the lights off and on to gain students' attention. "Once you have identified the color scheme in your photo, I want you to take a minute to look back at the text. The reading suggests that each scheme evokes different emotions or feelings. Find the section on your scheme. Reread it to find the information about emotions. Then take a look back at the photo. Do you think the ideas fit? Does the color scheme create those feelings? If so, why? If not, why not?"

"I guess so, yeah," a student holding a photo of a living room with light blue and green furnishings said to others at her table. "It says that analogous color schemes are found in nature and this room reminds me of the ocean. I'm not sure if I'd call it bright and cheery though. Maybe if there were brighter shades instead of pastels."

"I think there's just too much color," decided the girl with the photo of the blue and orange bathroom. "I agree with what it says in the text, that complementary colors are vibrant but can be tricky in large doses. This is definitely too large a dose. Maybe if they had some white or beige to break it up it would be OK."

As students shared their observations, Mr. Costa was pleased to hear them begin to move from labeling to utilizing. They were beginning to see how shades and quantities could be adjusted to create a more pleasing feeling or a more evocative image. The next application would extend this shift in students' thinking.

"OK, next step," Mr. Costa announced. "On the board I've written a dozen different adjectives. There's everything from *cheerful* to *bold* to *authoritative*. You are going to choose one adjective. Then you're going to design a color scheme to represent that adjective. This time, I want you to use tempura paints and create a spectrum by mixing the colors you choose. For example, if I wanted to make a spectrum of color that is soothing, I would probably want to choose a monochromatic color scheme. And I might use a color that generally seems soothing as well, like green. On my palette I would get green paint and white paint and try out various combinations by mixing the green and white in different proportions. Then, on the paper, I'd create a spectrum with a light green on one end building up to a darker green on the other." Mr. Costa demonstrated with his own paper and paints before getting the students started on theirs.

By building a series of targeted, short application opportunities, Mr. Costa deepened students' understanding of the concepts presented in the reading and helped them begin to take ownership of the concepts for their own use. In coming lessons they would apply the principles of color theory to their own work, beginning by creating masks that represented some aspect of themselves. By trying out the ideas of color schemes through a series of quick, low-risk activities, Mr. Costa was laying the groundwork for more authentic applications in the future.

Applying Content Learning in the History Classroom

Was the United States justified in dropping the atomic bomb on Hiroshima and Nagasaki? This question, prominently displayed on the board at the front of Mr. Kendall's eleventh-grade US history classroom, had focused classroom learning for the previous four days. During that time, students had read primary source documents by eyewitnesses to the destruction, analyzed secondary accounts that described the context of the War in the Pacific by

August 1945, dissected President Truman's writings on his decision, and reviewed present-day historical analyses that examined the impact of the use of the atomic bomb and speculated on how the war might have ended differently had it not been used. For each reading, students had analyzed its source, considered its context, and worked to identify its biases using the SOAPSTone protocol (see example, Figure 5.5).

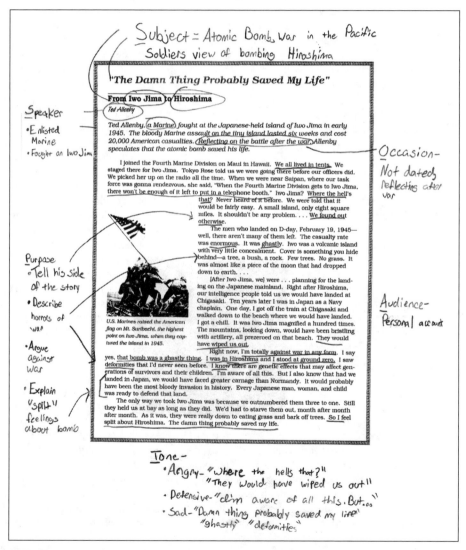

FIGURE 5.5. A student used the SOAPSTone protocol to analyze a reading on the atomic bomb.

As they worked through the texts, Mr. Kendall had encouraged peer discussion as well as individual reflection in learning logs. "What new information have you learned?" he'd ask. "How does this new information connect with what you already know? How was your understanding of the bombing changed?" Students had arrived in class with a wide range of preconceptions of war and the use of force. Several had family members who were deployed in the military, and others had parents who were children of the '60s and had been taught that violence is never justified. Mr. Kendall intentionally crafted his lessons to push students to consider alternative perspectives. He chose texts and asked questions that moved them back and forth in their responses to the unit question. After a reading describing the horrors of radiation poisoning, for example, Mr. Kendall presented an account of the atrocities American POWs faced at the hands of the Japanese. He wanted students to recognize the complexity of the issues involved, to see the past not in terms of black and white, but in shades of gray.

For this day's lesson, Mr. Kendall placed a line of bright blue masking tape down the center of the classroom. He made ten hatch marks along the line and posted a sign stating "1–Strongly agree" at one end of the line and another sign stating "10–Strongly disagree" at the other. During the lesson students would choose places along the line in response to statements posted on the overhead. The statements were provocative and multidimensional. They were designed to push students to synthesize information from a range of sources, consider multiple perspectives, and begin to develop their own interpretations.

As the bell rang announcing the beginning of third period and the last student slipped into the classroom, Mr. Kendall explained the guidelines for the "here I stand" activity and then turned on the projector to reveal this statement: "President Truman had no other real alternative. He was forced to order the use of the atomic bomb." At first, no one moved. Students stared at the screen, unsure of how to respond. "Look at the statement carefully," Mr. Kendall said. "Consider the language that has been used. Think back over our readings. And then move to a place on the line that repre-

sents your response to this statement." Students began to move into place. Some strode forward confidently, asserting their position along the line. Others were more cautious, uncomfortable assigning themselves to a number.

Once students were in place, Mr. Kendall directed them to discuss their choices. "Talk with your neighbors. Tell them why you chose to stand where you did and ask about their reasoning. Use evidence from our texts to justify your decision. After you chat, think, 'Am I in the right place?' If you need to move, go ahead. You aren't glued to your position." The room filled with talk and nervous laughter as students shared the reasons behind their choices. After a few minutes of peer-to-peer talk with students who had made similar choices, Mr. Kendall asked volunteers to share the reasons behind their position.

"We chose eights and nines because we feel that Truman did have other choices," a young woman standing near the "Strongly disagree" end of the spectrum proclaimed on behalf of those standing nearby. "He knew that the Japanese army was weak and that Japanese leaders had been talking about surrender. The Russians had agreed to enter the war against Japan on August 8, just two days after the bomb was dropped on Hiroshima. The war in Europe was over and soldiers and resources could be redeployed. He wasn't forced to use the bomb."

Mr. Kendall looked expectantly at students near the other end of the line.

"OK, what you said as your first argument, right there, that's one reason why he did have to drop the bomb," a young man standing at the third hatch mark declared. "You said that Truman knew that the Japanese leaders were discussing surrender. And that's true, but the transcripts we read of intercepted codes showed that they'd been talking about surrender for over a year and they still hadn't done it. If they hadn't surrendered yet, why would Truman think that they would have surrendered anytime soon? He had a tired nation that was ready for the war to end. Over 400,000 Americans had died already. Secretary of State Byrnes was telling him that if they launched a conventional invasion of Japan a million people would die. He had to drop the bomb."

"He didn't *have to*," responded a young woman near the center of the spectrum. "Look, I see the arguments on both sides, and in general, I think I lean more toward the idea that he was justified in using it. But the statement says he was 'forced to,' and I just don't think that is true. He had options. He was getting advice on both sides. He *chose* to use the bomb. I don't think it was a bad choice, but it was a choice."

Mr. Kendall invited several more students to respond before asking, "Anyone want to change places? Why? What made you change your mind?" Nearly a dozen students shifted their positions along the spectrum. "I had thought I was more toward agree because I think the political conditions were forcing Truman's hand," said a young man who chose to move from a seven to a four. "But Kelsey's argument about how he did the bombing made me rethink my position. He could have done a test and issued an ultimatum or he could have followed General Marshall's advice and warned the Japanese so that the civilians could escape. But he didn't. I also was really persuaded by Tony's argument that it wasn't strategically necessary to bomb both Hiroshima *and* Nagasaki."

During the class period the students responded to three more statements about the use of the atomic bomb. For each statement, students continued the pattern of placing themselves on the line, justifying their position with text evidence, and then reconsidering their place in response to the arguments of their peers. Mr. Kendall encouraged students to respond to one another, push one another's thinking, and reflect on their own learning. He was less concerned about a student's choice of placement along the line than he was about the student's ability to substantiate their thinking and their openness to hearing alternative perspectives.

At the end of the lesson, students built on the arguments and evidence from the "here I stand" activity to begin crafting a pro–con analysis chart in response to the original question, Was the United States justified in dropping the atomic bomb on Hiroshima and Nagasaki? (See Figure 5.6 for a student sample.) These charts would serve as outlines for their upcoming analytical essays on the same topic. In their essays, students would position themselves as historians, articulating their interpretations and defending their analyses. Having the opportunity to try out analyses and experiment with the use of evidence to support arguments during the "here I stand" activity helped students develop a deeper understanding of the material and prepared them to apply their learning to a context authentic to the discipline.

Authentic Outcomes

Culminating assignments that allow students to articulate and defend an analysis or demonstrate an application of learning in real-world contexts help to cement learning and provide a sense of authenticity and legitimacy to classroom activities. Theorists Lewison, Flint, and Van Sluys (2002) remind us that a key element of critical literacy is taking action and promoting social justice. Culminating assignments, such as those described in the following vignettes, allow students to demonstrate their analysis and application of text in a manner that can resonate with a larger audience and may help to facilitate increased awareness and promote change. In addition, the process of engaging in an assignment that requires a more polished, audience-ready response and often involves revision pushes students to deepen their understanding of content and take owner-

Was the U.S. Justified in dropping the bomb on Hiroshima and Nagasaki?

Yes	No

• Japan had proven its willingness to fight us to the death on Iwo Jima & Okinawa. If U.S. had to invade mainland Japan it was estimated 50,000 - 250,000 U.S. lives lost (Truman)	• Top military commanders believed bomb not necessary
	  -Eisenhower — Japan already
	  -MacArthur — "beaten back"
	  - Leahy — & weakened
	  -Nimitz

• American people ready for war to end. War fatigue War in Europe ended 5/7/45 400,000 Americans dead	• Soviets declared war on Japan 2 days after Hiroshima & 1 day before Nagasaki = Extra troops
• Fire bombing of Tokyo had killed 100,000 but Japan still refused to surrender under U.S. conditions	• Warning to Japan was vague "prompt and utter destruction"
• New moral climate = The Blitz firebombing of Dresden, make it morally OK to destroy "Any nation that had the bomb would have used it."	• U.S. intelligence knew that Japanese officials were considering surrender [but had been considering for 1+ yrs.]
• Need to impress Soviets - Seen as next global threat	• Bomb was used on civilian population more than 200,000 killed plus many sickened by radiation poisoning
	• Use led to fear from world + stockpiling of nuclear weapons during Cold War.

FIGURE 5.6. Mr. Kendall's students developed pro–con analysis charts and used them as outlines when drafting their essays.

ship of their ideas. The work is akin to what literacy educator Donald Murray (1980) articulated in his description of the writing process. He explained that writers engage in a process of exploration and clarification as they move from drafting through revision to publication. The more writers work to clarify their meaning for their audience, the deeper their own understanding becomes.

Several of the classroom descriptions earlier in this chapter included suggestions for authentic outcomes that build on the critical analysis or application activities. In Ms. Sanchez's science class, for example, students were instructed to write a letter to the editor critiquing the content and tone of the newspaper article on water reclamation. In Mr. Costa's art class, students would apply their newfound knowledge of color theory to their own original artwork and designs. And in Mr. Kendall's history class, students would use their enhanced understanding of the pros and cons of the decision to drop the atomic bomb on Hiroshima and Nagasaki to craft thoughtful essays to be published in the online class journal. Additional authentic outcome possibilities include, but are not limited to, the following.

- *Real-world solutions.* Apply students' learning toward solving real-world problems. For example, have them use principles of probability to create "mathematically correct" carnival games for a nearby elementary school, apply their understanding of physics to design a footbridge from recycled materials, or use their knowledge of art and culture to design a mural for a local community center. Share solutions with an authentic audience through oral, written, and/or multimedia presentations. The process of developing a proposal and preparing for a presentation encourages students to critically and creatively apply content knowledge.

- *Analytical argument.* Teach students to respond to the big ideas or core issues addressed in a unit by making and supporting a claim. Students may argue, for example, that the South was justified in declaring independence before the Civil War or that individual freedoms should trump community security. Effective argument requires that students synthesize information across a range of texts, apply evidence strategically to support their claim, and anticipate and refute counterarguments. Arguments may be presented as a traditional essay, in the form of a persuasive letter, as part of a class debate, or through a media presentation.

- *Creative "re"presentations.* Extend students' learning by having them present information to a new audience in a new format. They could design a website that explains genetic mutations to expectant parents, draw a political cartoon that captures historical tensions between the three branches of government, create an animation that shows the relationship between area and perimeter in geometry, or create a picture book for children that describes the origins of jazz. The process of sharing information with a new audience in a new and creative format pushes students to consider the core principles of a topic of study and select information from their readings that will best illustrate these ideas for their audience.

- *How-to analysis guide.* Students can share their insights on the process of text analysis by crafting a how-to guide for peers. Guides may include sample documents, guiding questions, model analyses, and an explanation of the importance of analyzing content texts. The crafting of such a guide requires that students thoughtfully reflect on their own process and consider the rationale behind critical literacy.

- *Letter to the editor.* Have students explain their analysis of text directly to the author or editor. In a letter to the editor, students use text evidence to critique the author's argument, their presentation of information, and their data sources. Sending the responses to the addressee empowers students to realize that critique is not simply an academic exercise and that they have a voice in the meaning-making dialogue.

- *Research proposal.* The more we know about a topic, the more we realize we have to learn. Support students' continued learning by having them craft research proposals to pursue questions prompted by content readings. Proposals should incorporate an explanation of the question, a literature review explaining what is already known about the subject, a description of procedures that may be used to carry out the research, and a discussion of anticipated outcomes. Using a research proposal as a culminating activity may initially seem contradictory. After all, school research projects are often situated at the beginning of a unit of study or independently from whole-class learning activities. However, content experts rarely begin their own research until they have studied a topic in depth. Generating research questions and developing proposals at the end of a unit helps students synthesize what they have already learned, identify areas that require additional research, and consider methods through which they may extend their understanding.

Assessment *for* Learning

The goals of critical literacy instruction are (1) to deepen content knowledge and develop conceptual understanding and (2) to support students in developing the analytical and application-focused habits of mind appropriate to the discipline. Assessment of student learning should respond to both of these goals. We need to design assessments and examine student work to assess their understanding of the content: Are they able to use a range of factual information? Are connections between pieces of information relevant? Do statements reflect an appropriate understanding of the big ideas within the lesson or unit? At the same time, we also need to use assessments to determine students' development of critical analysis and application skills: Are students able to question the text? Are they able to identify the biases of the author? Can they synthesize information across texts? Can they apply information and ideas to new settings?

In many ways, these two assessment objectives are bound tightly together. If I look at a student's flowchart describing cause–effect relationships in the lead-up to the Revolutionary War, for example, I'm going to find data revealing students' knowledge of content as well as evidence of their ability to apply information from the readings to the critical thinking guide (the flowchart). However, a closer look may reveal subtle distinctions in understanding. For example, if the student is able to accurately explain the cause–effect relationships in the samples provided by the teacher, but cannot identify pre–Revolutionary War examples of his own, it may indicate a limited understanding of the concepts being studied. If this is the case, it may be necessary to reteach material within this unit prior to moving on. On the other hand, if the flowchart contains a great deal of appropriate content information, but the student is unable to make predictions about the impact of events on the conduct of the war, it may indicate that there is a weakness in his understanding of cause–effect relationships. This may be something that needs to be addressed within this unit, or it may be something that could be addressed in future content investigations. Being aware of the dual objectives connected to analyzing and applying content readings helps us design, examine, and respond to assessments effectively.

Assessments used in the classroom examples featured in this chapter are described in the following vignettes.

Assessment in Ms. Sanchez's Science Class

To effectively assess student response to the "toilet-to-tap" article, Ms. Sanchez collected both her students' letters to the editor and the photocopies of the article that students had marked with questions and comments. Taken together, these samples of student learning revealed information about her students' ability to connect textbook science learning to real-world examples, their analytical reading skills, and their ability to synthesize their analysis into a coherent argument in the form of a letter. Overall, Ms. Sanchez was pleased with what she saw. Students were able to ask a range of critical questions as they read, pointing out everything from flawed logic to missing information to biased word choices. Most had been able to synthesize observations from the critical reading activity to craft thoughtful letters to the editor, albeit with some grammar and spelling concerns. Many had made important connections between information in the science article and their developing understanding of solutions. However, the connections were not always consistent. One student who picked up on the newspaper's misuse of the terms *solvent* and *solute*, for example, completely missed a similar error in confusing the terms *molarity* and *molality*. Ms. Sanchez wasn't able to tell, simply by looking at the students' responses to the news article, if this was a gap in concept knowledge or just an oversight. But as she looked through students' work, she made a few notes to herself of terms and concepts to reinforce in upcoming lessons.

Assessment in Mr. Costa's Visual Arts Class

The multiple try-it opportunities to apply concepts from the reading on color schemes provided multiple assessments of student understanding. As students used colored pencils to illustrate the text, discussed the color schemes of the design photos, and then mixed paints for the color spectra, Mr. Costa was able to immediately assess and respond to their application efforts. When a student inappropriately used royal blue and turquoise to illustrate the monochromatic color scheme, for example, Mr. Costa was able to easily catch and correct the mistake. "Tell me about the color scheme you are illustrating here," he inquired. After the student explained that it was monochromatic because it was two shades of blue, Mr. Costa gently corrected the misunderstanding by saying, "It sounds like you have the right idea, but let's think a little more about the colors you've chosen. Remember, shades, or tints, are when we add white or black to the original color to lighten or darken it. Could I get turquoise just by adding white to the royal blue? Probably not. I'd have to add some green or yellow. What you've created is more of an analogous color scheme, which is when the two colors are next to each other on the color wheel." Quick assessments such as this helped correct misperceptions and support students as they applied information from the text to progressively more challenging tasks.

Assessment in Mr. Kendall's History Class

Throughout the "here I stand" activity on the use of the atomic bomb, students in Mr. Kendall's class assessed and responded to one another. They were quick to point out flaws in the arguments of peers standing on the other end of the spectrum and readily provided missing content knowledge to support the ideas of those standing nearby. Mr. Kendall spent most of his time during this activity listening. He stepped in a few times when misinformation was repeated and once when the tone of the discussion became disrespectful, but mostly he let the students talk. As he listened, he took a few notes on his clipboard. He wrote down particularly important insights that students shared but that may not have been noticed by the group; he would reinforce these ideas in later lessons. And he made note of students who seemed confused or unable to appreciate arguments from those with different perspectives. When he collected students' pro–con charts later on, he paid particular attention to the papers of those students who appeared to have struggled or who remained silent during the discussion. The charts helped him to assess if students had limited content understanding, if they struggled to connect evidence with argument, or if they might have difficulty recognizing and articulating views that were different from their own. This was important knowledge to have before students moved on to their analytical essays. Addressing gaps in understanding now would help to make the outcome activity more meaningful for students and more enjoyable to read for their teacher.

With so many pressing demands on teachers, addressing the "So what?" of content reading can seem like a luxury. Between coverage mandates, increased class sizes, limited student literacy skills, and the always-looming standardized tests, it may appear almost impossible to carve out the time to engage students in critically responding to content readings. However, if we fail to go beyond comprehension and ask students to consider why the text matters, then it is reasonable to wonder why we bothered to assign the reading in the first place. After all, if what we really want is straightforward knowledge of facts and figures, there are many easier ways to attain that objective.

As the classroom vignettes in this chapter illustrate, there is much to be gained when we engage students in analyzing texts and applying their learning. They are able to construct understanding of core concepts and develop habits of mind appropriate to the discipline. They grapple with big ideas and explore an intellectual discourse that approximates the "experts." And they see relevance in the content and recognize application that goes beyond the walls of the classroom. Plus, it's just fun. It's electric to be in the classroom while students vociferously debate the justification of the bombing of Hiroshima and Nagasaki or express collective outrage at the inaccuracies in media coverage of the "toilet-to-tap" proposal. Those are the moments when academic passion sparkles. Obviously, it takes much to build toward those moments and, with so many competing demands on time and resources, it may not be possible to engage students in considering the "So what?" as often as we would like. However, if our goal is to construct true content understanding, then it is essential that we carve out deliberate opportunities for students to go beyond comprehension and critically engage with texts.

Postscript

Putting It All Together

A t its heart, teaching and learning are about the relationship between the student, the teacher, and the content. Although this book contains many research-grounded, classroom-tested ideas about instructional strategies that can be useful before, during, and after reading, good instructional strategies are not enough to ensure student learning.

To be successful in using content reading to support content learning, we have to know our content areas. We need to understand the core concepts, the forms of communication, and the ways of thinking within the discipline. In order to plan instruction around the big ideas of a concept, we need to know what those big ideas are and how we can help students connect with them. Teachers who are successful in doing so don't rely solely on college courses taken years earlier or on the score from a No Child Left Behind (2002) mandated standardized test. Effective teachers actively invest in increasing their content knowledge. They stay abreast of developments in their field by reading journals, taking college courses, and engaging in well-crafted professional learning opportunities. Research has shown that some of the best professional development is discipline based (Birman, Desimone, Porter, & Garet, 2000; Cohen & Hill, 1998; Kennedy, 1998). Rather than simply talking about how to teach problem solving in mathematics or inquiry in science, professional development that engages teachers in doing this work deepens understanding and provides inspiration that can be taken back to the K–12 classroom. Students respond when we are passionate about our subjects. We need to nurture our content knowledge so that we can share our expertise and our passion for history, science, mathematics, and the arts with our students.

Successful content reading also requires that we know our students. We need to recognize their strengths and weaknesses, their background knowledge, their talents, and their interests. Doing so allows us to tailor our lessons to both engage and challenge. We can choose readings and design activities that push students to think in new ways and consider new ideas. We can organize learning opportunities that differentiate to meet the needs of all learners in the classroom. We can, in the words of education researcher Lee Shulman, "think [our] way from the subject matter as understood by the teacher into the minds and motivations of the learners" (1987, p. 17). In addition, getting to know our students and forming relationships with them as individuals promotes a culture of caring within the classroom (Noddings, 1984, 1992). Research has shown that it is a sense of caring, more than any particular lesson design, text selection, or pedagogical approach, that encourages students, particularly students from underrepresented backgrounds, to be willing to take risks and engage in learning in the classroom (Ogbu, 2002; Valenzuela, 1999). Students who believe that their teacher cares about them are significantly more likely to learn. Getting to know our students allows us to show that we care through direct interaction and allows us to craft lessons that demonstrate care by responding to the individual strengths and needs of the learners in our classrooms.

Finally, successful content reading for content learning requires that we know ourselves. Not all texts, lessons, or strategies work for all teachers. We need to challenge ourselves to go out of our comfort zone and try new approaches at times, but we also need to be reflective and thoughtful in determining what new ideas to keep and what to set aside. And we need to cut ourselves some slack. Teaching for understanding; crafting authentic, discipline-based lessons; choosing texts and strategies that fit the needs of individual students and respond to the core concepts of the content . . . It's a lot. It takes time and attention to teach in this manner and, quite frankly, it is hard to do every day. Rather than go for all or nothing, choose focused opportunities to engage students in the kinds of content reading that are addressed in this text. Dig "postholes" (Brown, 1996; Scheurman, 2008) where you use authentic texts to go in-depth with critical topics in your discipline. Don't feel that it is failing if all instruction is not authentic all of the time. Ultimately, teaching is not about our performance; it is about student learning. If we can provide them with even a few opportunities to dig into content readings, debate key ideas, and investigate core concepts, then we are providing students with an understanding of our disciplines, and we are planting the seeds for growing that understanding through lifelong reading and learning.

Works Cited

Alexander, P. A., Kulikowich, J. M., & Schulze, S. K. (1994). How subject-matter knowledge affects recall and interest. *American Educational Research Journal, 31,* 313–337.

Alexander, P. A., & Murphy, P. K. (1998). The research base for APA's learner-centered principles. In N. M. Lambert & B. L. McCombs (Eds.), *Issues in school reform: A sampler of psychological perspectives on learner-centered schools* (pp. 25–60). Washington DC: American Psychological Association.

Allen, J. (1995). *It's never too late: Leading adolescents to lifelong literacy.* Portsmouth, NH: Heinemann.

Allen, J. (1999). *Words, words, words: Teaching vocabulary in grades 4–12.* York, ME: Stenhouse.

Allen, J. (2000). *Yellow brick roads: Shared and guided paths to independent reading 4–12.* Portland, ME: Stenhouse.

Allen, R. (2007). *The essentials of science, Grades 7–12: Effective curriculum, instruction, and assessment.* Alexandria, VA: Association for Supervision and Curriculum Development.

Allington, R. L. (2005). *What really matters for struggling readers: Designing research-based programs* (2nd ed.). Boston: Allyn and Bacon.

Alvermann, D. E., Moon, J. S., & Hagood, M. C. (1999). *Popular culture in the classroom: Teaching and researching critical media literacy.* Newark, DE: International Reading Association and Chicago: National Reading Conference.

Anderson, R. C., & Freebody, P. (1981). Vocabulary knowledge. In J. T. Guthrie (Ed.), *Comprehension and teaching: Research perspectives* (pp. 77–117). Newark, DE: International Reading Association.

Anderson, R. C., Hiebert, E. H., Scott, J. A., & Wilkinson, I. A. G. (1985). *Becoming a nation of readers: The report of the Commission on Reading.* Washington, DC: National Institute of Education.

Anderson, R. C., & Nagy, W. E. (1991). Word meanings. In R. Barr, M. L. Kamil, P. Monsenthal, & P. D. Pearson (Eds.), *Handbook of reading research* (Vol. 2, pp. 690–724). New York: Longman.

Anderson, R. C., & Pearson, P. D. (1984). A schema-theoretic view of basic processes in reading comprehension. In P. D. Pearson, R. Barr, M. L. Kamil, & P. Mosenthal (Eds.), *Handbook of reading research* (pp. 255–291). New York: Longman.

Armbruster, B. B., & Anderson, T. H. (1981). *Content area textbooks* (Reading Education Report No. 23). Champaign, IL: Center for the Study of Reading and Cambridge, MA: Bolt, Beranek, and Newman.

Atwell, N. (1998). *In the middle: New understandings about writing, reading, and learning* (2nd ed.). Portsmouth, NH: Boynton/Cook-Heinemann.

August, D., & Shanahan, T. (Eds.). (2006). *Developing literacy in second-language learners: Report of the National Literacy Panel on Language-Minority Children and Youth.* Mahwah, NJ: Erlbaum.

Baker, S. K., Simmons, D. C., & Kame'enui, E. J. (1995). *Vocabulary acquisition: Curricular and instructional implications for diverse learners* (Technical Report No. 14). Eugene, OR: National Center to Improve the Tools for Educators.

Barr, B. C. (2006). Textbooks help us miss the point of education. *English Leadership Quarterly, 28*(3), 2–4.

Baumann, J. F., Kame'enui, E. J., & Ash, G. (2003). Research on vocabulary instruction: Voltaire Redux. In J. Flood, D. Lapp, J. R. Squire, & J. M. Jensen (Eds.), *Handbook of research on teaching the English language arts* (2nd ed., pp. 752–785). Mahwah, NJ: Erlbaum.

Beasley, W. (1982). Teacher demonstrations: The effect on student task involvement. *Journal of Chemical Education, 59,* 789–790.

Beck, I. L., & McKeown, M. G. (1991). Conditions of vocabulary acquisition. In R. Barr, M. L. Kamil, P. Monsenthal, & P. D. Pearson (Eds.), *Handbook of reading research* (Vol. 2, pp. 789–814). New York: Longman.

Beck, I. L., McKeown, M. G., Hamilton, R. L., & Kucan, L. (1997). *Questioning the author: An approach for enhancing student engagement with text.* Newark, DE: International Reading Association.

Becker, C. (1932). What is evidence? The relativist view. *American Historical Review, 37,* 3–23.

Beers, K. (2003). *When kids can't read, what teachers can do: A guide for teachers 6–12.* Portsmouth, NH: Heinemann.

Birman, B., Desimone, L., Porter, A. C., & Garet, M. (2000). Designing professional development that works. *Educational Leadership, 57*(8), 28–33.

Blachowicz, C. L. Z. (1986). Making connections: Alternatives to the vocabulary notebook. *Journal of Reading, 29,* 643–649.

Blanchfield, C. (Ed.). (2001). *Creative vocabulary: Strategies for teaching vocabulary in grades K–12* (2nd ed.). Fresno, CA: San Joaquin Valley Writing Project.

Blau, S. D. (2003). *The literature workshop: Teaching texts and their readers.* Portsmouth, NH: Boynton/Cook.

Bolak, K., Bialach, D., & Dunphy, M. (2005). Standards-based, thematic units integrate the arts and energize students and teachers. *Middle School Journal, 36*(5), 9–19.

Bransford, J. D., Brown, A. L., & Cocking, R. R. (Eds.). (2000). *How people learn: Brain, mind, experience, and school.* Washington, DC: National Academy Press.

Brooks, J. G., & Brooks, M. G. (1999). *In search of understanding: The case for constructivist classrooms.* Alexandria, VA: Association for Supervision and Curriculum Development.

Brown, R. H. (1996). Learning how to learn: The Amherst project and history education in the schools. *Social Studies, 87,* 267–273.

Brozo, W. G., & Hargis, C. H. (2003). Taking seriously the idea of reform: One high school's efforts to make reading more responsive to all students. *Journal of Adolescent and Adult Literacy, 47,* 14–23.

Bruner, J. (1957). *Beyond the information given: Studies in the psychology of knowing.* J. Anglin (Ed.). New York: W. W. Norton.

Bruner, J. (1966). *Toward a theory of instruction.* Cambridge, MA: Harvard University Press.

Bruner, J. (1986). *Actual minds, possible worlds.* Cambridge, MA: Harvard University Press.

Buehl, D. (2001). *Classroom strategies for interactive learning* (2nd ed.). Newark, DE: International Reading Association.

Buikema, J. L., & Graves, M. F. (1993). Teaching students to use context clues to infer word meanings. *Journal of Reading, 36,* 450–457.

Burke, J. (2002). Making notes, making meaning. *Voices from the Middle, 9*(4), 15–21.

Calkins, L. M. (2001). *The art of teaching reading.* New York: Longman.

Calweti, G. (2004). *Handbook of research on improving student achievement* (3rd ed.). Arlington, VA: Educational Research Service.

Carlin, G. (1997). *Brain droppings.* New York: Hyperion.

Center on English Learning and Achievement (n.d.). Raising the level of student engagement in higher order talk and writing. Retrieved September 15, 2009, from http://cela.albany.edu/research/partnerb3.htm

Cohen, D. K. (1988). Teaching practice: Plus que ça change. . . . In P. W. Jackson (Ed.), *Contributing to educational change: Perspectives on research and practice* (pp. 27–84). Berkeley, CA: McCutchan.

Cohen, D. K., & Hill, H. C. (1998). *Instructional policy and classroom performance: The mathematics reform in California* (CPRE Research Report No. 39). Philadelphia: Consortium for Policy Research in Education.

Cunningham, A. E., & Stanovich, K. E. (1991). Tracking the unique effects of print exposure in children: Associations with vocabulary, general knowledge, and spelling. *Journal of Educational Psychology, 83,* 264–274.

Cunningham, P. M., & Allington, R. L. (2003). *Classrooms that work: They can all read and write* (3rd ed.). Boston: Allyn and Bacon.

Davidson, J. E., & Sternberg, R. J. (1998). Smart problem solving: How metacognition helps. In D. J. Hacker, J. Dunloski, & A. C. Graesser (Eds.), *Metacognition in educational theory and practice* (pp. 47–68). Mahwah, NJ: Erlbaum.

Davis, F. B. (1968). Research in comprehension in reading. *Reading Research Quarterly, 3*, 499–545.

Deci, E. L. (with Flaste, R.). (1996). *Why we do what we do: Understanding self-motivation.* New York: Penguin.

Dewey, J. (1933). *How we think: A restatement of the relation of reflective thinking to the educative process.* Boston: Heath.

Donovan, M. S., Bransford, J. D., & Pellegrino, J. W. (Eds.). (1999). *How people learn: Bridging research and practice.* Washington, DC: National Academy Press.

Drake, F. D., & Nelson, L. R. (2009). *Engagement in teaching history: Theory and practices for middle and secondary teachers* (2nd ed.). Upper Saddle River, NJ: Merrill.

Espin, C. A., & Foegen, A. (1996). Validity of general outcome measures for predicting secondary students' performance on content-area tasks. *Exceptional Children, 62*, 497–514.

Faber, J. E., Morris, J. D., & Lieberman, M. G. (2000). The effect of note taking on ninth grade students' comprehension. *Reading Psychology, 21*, 257–270.

Fairclough, N. (2001). *Language and power* (2nd ed.). New York: Longman.

Farley, M. J., & Elmore, P. B. (1992). The relationship of reading comprehension to critical thinking skills, cognitive ability, and vocabulary for a sample of underachieving college freshmen. *Educational and Psychological Measurement, 52*, 921–931.

Fisher, D., & Frey, N. (2008). *Improving adolescent literacy: Content area strategies at work.* Upper Saddle River, NJ: Pearson.

Fisher, D., & Ivey, G. (2005). Literacy and language as learning in content-area classes: A departure from "Every teacher is a teacher of reading." *Action in Teacher Education, 27*(2), 3–11.

Fitzgerald, J., García, G. E., Jiménez, R. T., & Barrera, R. (2000). How will bilingual/ESL programs in literacy change in the next millennium? *Reading Research Quarterly, 35*, 520–523.

Flood, J., Lapp, D., & Fisher, D. (2003). Reading comprehension instruction. In J. Flood, D. Lapp, J. R. Squire, & J. M. Jensen, (Eds.), *Handbook of research on teaching the English language arts* (pp. 931–941). Mahwah, NJ: Erlbaum.

Flowers, N., Mertens, S. B., & Mulhall, P. F. (1999). The impact of teaming: Five research-based outcomes. *Middle School Journal, 31*(2), 57–60.

Frayer, D. A. Fredrick, W. C., & Klausmeier, H. J. (1969). *A schema for testing the level of cognitive mastery.* Madison: Wisconsin Research and Development Center for Cognitive Learning.

Freebody, P., & Luke, A. (1990). Literacy programs: Debates and demands in cultural context. *Prospect: Australian Journal of TESOL, 5*(7), 7–16.

Freeman, Y. S., & Freeman, D. E. (2008). *Academic language for English language learners and struggling readers: How to help students succeed across content areas.* Portsmouth, NH: Heinemann.

Freire, P. (1970). *Pedagogy of the oppressed.* New York: Continuum.

Fry, E. B. (1977). *Elementary reading instruction.* New York: McGraw-Hill.

Gallagher, J. J. (2007). *Teaching science for understanding: A practical guide for middle and high school teachers.* Upper Saddle River, NJ: Prentice Hall.

Gallagher, K. (2004). *Deeper reading: Comprehending challenging texts, 4–12.* Portland, ME: Stenhouse.

Gillet, J. W., & Temple, C. (1982). *Understanding reading problems: Assessment and instruction.* Boston: Little, Brown.

Goulden, R., Nation, P., & Read, J. (1990). How large can a receptive vocabulary be? *Applied Linguistics, 11,* 341–363.

Grant, S. G. (2003). *History lessons: Teaching, learning, and testing in US high school classrooms.* Mahwah, NJ: Lawrence Erlbaum.

Graves, D. H. (2003). *Writing: Teachers and children at work* (20th anniversary ed.). Portsmouth, NH: Heinemann.

Graves, M. F. (1986). Vocabulary learning and instruction. In E. Z. Rothkopf & L. C. Ehri (Eds.), *Review of Research in Education* (Vol. 13, pp. 49–89). Washington, DC: American Educational Research Association.

Graves, M. F., & Graves, B. B. (1994). *Scaffolding reading experiences: Designs for student success.* Norwood, MA: Christopher Gordon.

Griffen, W. L., & Marciano, J. (1979). *Teaching the Vietnam War: A critical examination of school texts and an interpretive comparative history utilizing the Pentagon Papers and other documents.* Montclair, NJ: Allanheld, Osmun.

Gutiérrez, K. D. (2001). What's new in the English language arts: Challenging policies and practices, ¿y que? *Language Arts, 78,* 564–569.

Hacker, D. J. (1997). Comprehension monitoring of written discourse across early-to-middle adolescence. *Reading and Writing: An Interdisciplinary Journal, 9,* 207–240.

Hakim, J. (2003). *A history of US: Book 9. War, peace, and all that jazz, 1918–1945* (3rd ed.). New York: Oxford University Press.

Hayes, D. P., & Ahrens, M. G. (1988). Vocabulary simplification for children: A special case of "motherese." *Journal of Child Language, 15,* 395–410.

Herber, H. L. (1978). *Teaching reading in content areas* (2nd ed.). Englewood Cliffs, NJ: Prentice Hall.

Hurst, B. (2001). ABCs of content area lesson planning: Attention, basics, and comprehension. *Journal of Adolescent and Adult Literacy, 44,* 692–693.

Jenkins, J. R., Matlock, B., & Slocum, T. A. (1989). Two approaches to vocabulary instruction: The teaching of individual word meanings and practice in deriving meaning from context. *Reading Research Quarterly, 24,* 215–235.

Jenner, E. (1798). *An inquiry into the causes and effects of the variolae vaccinae.* Retrieved August 18, 2009, from http://www.gutenberg.org/etext/29414

Jensen, E. (2005). *Teaching with the brain in mind* (2nd ed.). Alexandria, VA: Association for Supervision and Curriculum Development.

Johnson, D. D., & Pearson, P. D. (1984). *Teaching reading vocabulary* (2nd ed.). New York: Holt, Rinehart, and Winston.

Johnson, G. (1999). Multiple readings of a picture book. *Australian Journal of Language and Literacy, 22*(3), 176–191.

Kame'enui, E. J., Carnine, D., & Freschi, R. (1982). Effects of text construction and instructional procedures for teaching word meanings on comprehension and recall. *Reading Research Quarterly, 17,* 367–388.

Keene, E. O., & Zimmermann, S. (2007). *Mosaic of thought: The power of comprehension strategy instruction* (2nd ed.). Portsmouth, NH: Heinemann.

Kennedy, M. (1998). *Form and substance in inservice teacher education* (Research Monograph No. 13). Arlington, VA: National Science Foundation.

Klein, M. L. (1988). *Teaching reading comprehension and vocabulary: A guide for teachers.* Englewood Cliffs, NJ: Prentice Hall.

Lakoff, G. (2004). *Don't think of an elephant! Know your values and frame the debate: The essential guide for progressives.* White River Jct., VT: Chelsea Green.

Lambright, L. L. (1995). Creating a dialogue: Socratic seminars and educational reform. *Community College Journal, 65*(4), 30–40.

Leahy, S., Lyon, C., Thompson, M., & Wiliam, D. (2005). Classroom assessment: Minute by minute, day by day. *Educational Leadership, 63*(3), 18–24.

Lee, C. (2000). Modelling in the mathematics classroom. *Mathematics Teaching, 171,* 28–31.

Lesley, M. (2004/2005). Looking for critical literacy with postbaccalaureate content area literacy students. *Journal of Adolescent and Adult Literacy, 48,* 320–334.

Lewison, M., Flint, A. S., & Van Sluys, K. (2002). Taking on critical literacy: The journey of newcomers and novices. *Language Arts, 79,* 382–392.

Lindaman, D. & Ward, K. (2006). *History lessons: How textbooks from around the world portray US history.* New York: New Press.

Loewen, J. W. (1995). *Lies my teacher told me: Everything your American history textbook got wrong.* New York: Simon and Schuster.

Lyman, F. (1987). Think-pair-share: An expanding teaching technique. *MAA-CIE Cooperative News, 1,* 1–2.

Markham, T., Larmer, J., & Ravitz, J. (2003). *Project based learning handbook* (2nd ed.). Novato, CA: Buck Institute for Education.

Martin, D., Wineburg, S., Rosenzweig, R., & Leon, S. (2008). Historicalthinkingmatters. org: Using the Web to teach historical thinking. *Social Education, 72*(3), 140–143.

Marzano, R. J., Pickering, D. J., & Pollock, J. E. (2001). *Classroom instruction that works: Research-based strategies for increasing student achievement.* Alexandria, VA: Association for Supervision and Curriculum Development.

McKeown, M. G., & Beck, I. L. (1988). Learning vocabulary: Different ways for different goals. *Remedial and Special Education, 9,* 42–46.

McLaughlin, M., & DeVoogd, G. L., (2004). *Critical literacy: Enhancing students' comprehension of text.* New York: Scholastic.

Mehlinger, H. D. (1995). *School reform in the information age.* Bloomington: Center for Excellence in Education, Indiana University.

Meier, D. (2002). *The power of their ideas: Lessons for America from a small school in Harlem.* Boston: Beacon.

Moje, E. B. (2006, March). *Integrating literacy into the secondary school content areas: An enduring problem in enduring institutions.* Paper presented at the University of Michigan Adolescent Literacy Symposium, Ann Arbor, MI.

Muncey, D. E., Payne, J., & White, N. S. (1999). Making curriculum and instructional reform happen: A case study. *Peabody Journal of Education, 74,* 68–110.

Murray, D. M. (1980). Writing as process: How writing finds its own meaning. In T. R. Donavan & B. W. McClelland (Eds.), *Eight approaches to teaching composition* (pp. 3–20). Urbana, IL: National Council of Teachers of English.

Murray, D. M. (2003). *A writer teaches writing* (Rev. 2nd ed.). Florence, KY: Cengage Learning.

Nagy, W. E. (1988). *Teaching vocabulary to improve reading comprehension.* Newark, DE: International Reading Association.

Nagy, W. E., & Anderson, R. C. (1984). How many words are there in printed school English? *Reading Research Quarterly, 19*(3), 303–330.

Nagy, W. E., Anderson, R. C., & Herman, P. A. (1987). Learning word meanings from context during normal reading. *American Educational Research Journal, 24,* 237–270.

Nagy, W. E., Diakidoy, I.-A. N., & Anderson, R. C. (1993). The acquisition of morphology: Learning the contribution of suffixes to the meanings of derivatives. *Journal of Reading Behavior, 25,* 155–170.

Nagy, W. E., & Scott, J. A. (1990). Word schemas: Expectations about the form and meaning of new words. *Cognition and Instruction, 7*(2), 105–127.

National Center for History in the Schools. (1996). *National standards for history, basic edition.* Los Angeles: Author.

Nelson, J. (1978). Readability: Some cautions for the content area teacher. *Journal of Reading, 21*(7), 620–625.

Nichols, M. (2008). *Talking about text: Guiding students to increase comprehension through purposeful talk.* Huntington Beach, CA: Shell Education.

Nichols, M. (2009). *Expanding comprehension with multigenre text sets.* New York: Scholastic.

No Child Left Behind Act of 2001, Pub. L. No. 107-110, 115 Stat. 1425 (2002). Retrieved from http://www2.ed.gov/policy/elsec/leg/esea02/107-110.pdf

Noddings, N. (1984). *Caring, a feminine approach to ethics and moral education.* Berkeley: University of California Press.

Noddings, N. (1992). *The challenge to care in schools: An alternative approach to education.* New York: Teachers College Press.

O'Brien, D. G., Stewart, R. A., & Moje, E. B. (1995). Why content literacy is difficult to infuse into the secondary school: Complexities of curriculum, pedagogy, and school culture. *Reading Research Quarterly, 30,* 442–463.

Ogbu, J. U. (2002). Black-American students and the academic achievement gap: What else you need to know. *Journal of Thought, 37*(4), 9–33.

Ogle, D. (1986). K-W-L: A teaching model that develops active reading of expository text. *Reading Teacher, 39,* 564–570.

Ogle, D., Klemp, R., & McBride, B. (2007). *Building literacy in social studies: Strategies for improving comprehension and critical thinking.* Alexandria, VA: Association for Supervision and Curriculum Development.

Osborne, J., Erduran, S., & Simon, S. (2004). Enhancing the quality of argumentation in school science. *Journal of Research in Science Teaching, 41,* 994–1020.

Palincsar, A. S., & Brown, A. L. (1984). Reciprocal teaching of comprehension-fostering and comprehension monitoring activities. *Cognition and Instruction, 1*(2), 117–175.

Pauk, W. (2000). *How to study in college* (7th ed.). Boston: Houghton Mifflin.

Piaget, J. (1971). *Biology and knowledge: An essay on the relations between organic regulations and cognitive processes.* Chicago: University of Chicago Press.

Pichert, J. W., & Anderson, R. C. (1977). Taking different perspectives on a story. *Journal of Educational Psychology, 69,* 309–315.

Polacco, P. (1994). *Pink and Say.* New York: Philomel Books.

Resnick, L. B. (1995). From aptitude to effort: A new foundation for our schools. *Daedalus, 124*(4), 55–62.

Rivard, L. P., & Straw, S. B. (2000). The effect of talk and writing on learning science: An exploratory study. *Science Education, 84*(5), 566–593.

Rosenshine, B, & Meister, C. (1994). Reciprocal teaching: A review of the research. *Review of Educational Research, 64,* 479–530.

Scheurman, G. (2008). Poetry and postholes: Making history instruction deeper and more personal. *Social Education, 72*(7), 350–353.

Schoenbach, R., Greenleaf, C., Cziko, C., & Hurwitz, L. (1999). *Reading for understanding: A guide to improving reading in middle and high school classrooms.* San Francisco: Jossey-Bass.

Schwartz, R. M., & Raphael, T. E. (1985). Concept of definition: A key to improving students' vocabulary. *The Reading Teacher, 39*(2), 198–205.

Short, K., Schroeder, J., Kauffman, G., & Kaser, S. (2005). Thoughts from the editors. *Language Arts, 82*, 167.

Shulman, L. S. (1987). Knowledge and teaching: Foundations of the new reform. *Harvard Educational Review, 57*(1), 1–22.

Siegel, R. (n.d.). Reading scientific papers. Retrieved from http://stanford.edu/~siegelr/readingsci.htm

Sizer, T. R. (2004). *Horace's compromise: The dilemma of the American high school.* Boston: Mariner Books.

Smith, A. (1776). *The wealth of nations.* London: Strahan and Cadell.

Sousa, D. A. (2001). *How the brain learns: A classroom teacher's guide* (2nd ed.). Thousand Oaks, CA: Corwin Press.

Sprenger, M. (1999). *Learning and memory: The brain in action.* Alexandria, VA: Association for Supervision and Curriculum Development.

Stahl, S. A. (1986). Three principals of effective vocabulary instruction. *Journal of Reading, 29*, 662–668.

Stahl, S. A., & Fairbanks, M. M. (1986). The effects of vocabulary instruction: A model-based meta-analysis. *Review of Educational Research, 56*, 72–110.

Stahl, S. A., & Stahl, K. A. D. (2004). Word wizards all! Teaching word meanings in preschool and primary education. In J. F. Baumann & E. J. Kame'enui (Eds.), *Vocabulary instruction: Research to practice* (pp. 59–78). New York: Guilford Press.

Stahl, S. A., & Vancil, S. J. (1986). Discussion is what makes semantic maps work in vocabulary instruction. *Reading Teacher, 40*, 62–67.

Stanovich, K. E. (1986). Matthew effects in reading: Some consequences of individual differences in the acquisition of literacy. *Reading Research Quarterly, 21*, 360–407.

Steinbeck, J. (1939). *The grapes of wrath.* New York: Viking Press.

Suppe, F. (1998). The structure of a scientific paper. *Philosophy of Science, 65*, 381–405.

Taba, H. (1967). *Teacher's handbook for elementary social studies.* Reading, MA: Addison-Wesley.

Thomas, J. W. (2000). *A review of research on project-based learning.* San Rafael, CA: The Autodesk Foundation.

Tovani, C. (2000). *I read it, but I don't get it: Comprehension strategies for adolescent readers.* Portland, ME: Stenhouse.

Tovani, C. (2004). *Do I really have to teach reading?* Portland, ME: Stenhouse.

Trelease, J. (2006). *The read-aloud handbook* (6th ed.). New York: Penguin.

Tyson-Bernstein, H. (1988). *A conspiracy of good intentions: America's textbook fiasco.* Washington, DC: Council for Basic Education.

Vacca, J. A., Vacca, R. T., & Gove, M. K. (2000). *Reading and learning to read* (4th ed.). New York: Longman.

Vacca, R. T., & Vacca, J. L. (2008) *Content area reading: Literacy and learning across the curriculum* (9th ed.). Boston: Pearson.

Valenzuela, A. (1999). *Subtractive schooling: U.S.-Mexican youth and the politics of caring.* Albany: State University of New York Press.

VanSledright, B. A. (2004). What does it mean to think historically and how do you teach it? *Social Education, 68*(3), 230–233.

Vygotsky, L. S. (1962). *Thought and language.* Cambridge, MA: MIT Press.

Vygotsky, L. S. (1978). *Mind in society: The development of higher psychological processes.* Cambridge, MA: Harvard University Press.

White, T. G., Sowell, J., & Yanagihara, A. (1989). Teaching elementary students to use word-part clues. *Reading Teacher, 42*, 302–308.

Wiggins, G., & McTighe, J. (2005). *Understanding by design* (2nd ed.). Alexandria, VA: Association for Supervision and Curriculum Development.

Wineburg, S. (2001). *Historical thinking and other unnatural acts: Charting the future of teaching the past.* Philadelphia: Temple University Press.

Wineburg, S. (2008, October). *Historical thinking and literacy strategies.* Workshop for middle and high school teachers sponsored by the San Diego Unified School District and the San Diego County Office of Education. San Diego, CA.

Wineburg, S., & Martin, D. (2004). Reading and rewriting history. *Educational Leadership, 62*(1), 42–45.

Wolf, M. K., Crosson, A. C., & Resnick, L. B. (2004). Classroom talk for rigorous reading comprehension instruction. *Reading Psychology, 26*, 27–53.

Wormeli, R. (2005). *Summarization in any subject: Fifty techniques to improve student learning.* Alexandria, VA: Association for Supervision and Curriculum Development.

Yell, M. M., & Scheurman, G. (with Reynolds, K.). (2004). *A link to the past: Engaging students in the study of history* (NCSS Bulletin 102). Silver Spring, MD: National Council for the Social Studies.

Yell, M. M., Scheurman, G., & Reynolds, K. (2004). The anticipation guide: Motivating students to find out about history. *Social Education, 68*(5), 361.

Index

reciprocal teaching, 63, 64–67, 76
vocabulary and, 88
See also talk, student-to-student
compare–contrast guides, *127*
complex texts and length, 11
comprehension
anticipating text structure and
content, 50–54
assessment *for* learning, 74–77
fake reading, 47–48
immediate access vs. long-term
comprehension, 48–49
importance of, 48
monitoring, 54–60
purpose, impact of, 21–22
student-to-student talk, 60–67
writing for, 67–74
comprehension strategies
active listening, 63
advance organizers, 52
comprehension scoring, 55–56
Cornell notes, 70, *71*
double entry journals, 69
graphic organizers to capture text
information, 68, *69*
graphic summaries, 69, *70*
"one question, one comment," 62–63
one-sentence summaries, 56
quick fixes, 56–58
reciprocal teaching, 63, 64–67, 76
says/means chart, 56, *57*
selective underlining, 56, 60, *61*, 75–76
"something-happened-and-then"
technique, 69
text previewing, 51–52, 53–54, 75
text protocols, 52, *52*, 76–77
think-pair-share, 62, 64
3-2-1 summaries, 68
concept circles, 108
concept ladders, 84–85, *86*
concept maps, 84, *85*, 89–91, *90*, 108
conceptual understanding. *See* critical
literacy and understanding
concept vocabulary, 84–91, 106
concept webs, 68, *69*
concrete spellings, 88
considerate texts, 8

context
Analyzing Words in Context graphic
organizer, 104, *105*
assessing, 41–42
figuring out vocabulary from, 81
in prereading activities, 28
role of, 20–21
science example, 22–27, *26*
context clues, 99–100, 104–6, *105*
core concepts, xx, 4–5
Cornell notes, 70, *71*
coverage problem in textbooks, 14–15
coverage vs. critical learning, 111
cracks, teaching in the, 3–4
creative "re"presentations, 134–35
critical literacy and understanding
analyzing texts (text critic role),
117–25
applying content learning (text user
role), 125–32
assessment *for* learning, 135–38
authentic outcomes and, 132–35
characteristics that support, 114–17
of core concepts, 4
as goal, xix–xx
importance of, 111–13
knowledge vs., xiii–xiv, xix
novice vs. critical readers, 116, 118–19,
119
critical literacy strategies
analytical argument, 134
creative "re"presentations, 134–35
critical thinking guides, 126, *127*
"here I stand" activity, 128, 131–32,
137
how-to analysis guides, 135
learning logs, 127, 131
letters to the editor, 135, 136–37
new perspectives, 120
pro–con analysis charts, 132, *133*
questioning the author (QtA), 120,
121, 122–25, *123*, *124*
read it–try it, 126–27, 128–29, 137
real-world solutions, 134
research proposals, 135
SOAPSTone protocol, 119–20, 130, *130*
Socratic seminars, 120–22

critical thinking guides, 126, *127*
curiosity, 29

dance content, 53–54, 75
demonstrations, 23–25, *26*, 29–30
design, instructional, 2
Dewey, J., 111
dictionaries, 80–81
discourse, discipline-specific, 79
discussions, peer. *See* talk, student-to-student
Donovan, M. S., 115
double entry journals, 69
drama, prereading activities for, 31–34, 43
drill-and-practice approach, 80
Dulce Et Decorum Est (Owen), 31

engagement
    curiosity, 29
        multiple engagement with texts and concepts, 114–15
        to support reading for learning, xxi
English language arts (ELA) and discipline-based texts, xii
English language learners (ELLs), 79–80
Erduran, S., 115
essential questions, xx
ethical dilemmas, 31, 40
"every teacher is a teacher of reading" initiative, xi–xii
exclusion brainstorming, 93–94, *94*
explicit instruction, xxiii–xxv

facts, in textbooks, 14
Fairclough, Norman, 113
fake reading, 47–48
features of texts and comprehension, 50–51
Fisher, Doug, 82, 116
Flint, A. S., 132
flowcharts, 126, *127*, 136
focus. *See* prereading activities and focusing the reader
font size, 10
formative assessment. *See* assessment *for* learning
format of texts, 10
Frayer Model, 84, *85*

Freebody, Peter, 117
Freire, Paulo, 112
Freschi, R., 83
Frey, Nancy, 82, 116
Fry Readability Graph, 6
full concept knowledge, 83

Gallagher, Kelly, 62–63, 79, 100, 107
genres, 50–51
The Grapes of Wrath (Steinbeck), 32
graphic organizers
    Analyzing Words in Context, 104, *105*
    anticipation guides, 30–31, 36, *37*, 44
    cause–effect, *127*
    compare–contrast, *127*
    for comprehension, 68, *69*
    concept ladders, 84–85, *86*
    concept maps, 84, *85*, 89–91, *90*
    concept webs, 68, *69*
    critical thinking guides, 126, *127*
    flowcharts, 126, *127*, 136
    knowledge rating guides, 102–3, *103*
    K-W-L charts, 16, 30, 33–34, *34*, 42, 43
    multiple issues–multiple perspectives, *127*
    Observe, Predict, Verify charts, 25, *26*, 43
    in preparation of texts, 10
    problem–solution, *127*
    pro–con analysis charts, *41*, *127*, 132, *133*
    purpose of, 116
    says/means charts, 56, *57*
    Venn diagrams, 126
graphic summaries, 69, *70*
Graves, Donald, xxii
Griffen, W. L., 14
Gutiérrez, Kris, 112

Hakim, Joy, 33
"here I stand" activity, 128, 131–32, 137
history and humanities
    analytical argument, 134
    comprehension and, 57, 63–67, 76
    critical literacy, 130–32, 137
    importance of historical documents, xiii

Observe, Predict, Verify charts, 25, *26*, 43
Ogle, D., 114
"one question, one comment," 62–63
Osborne, J., 115
Owen, Wilfred, 31

partial concept knowledge, 83
peer talk. *See* talk, student-to-student
Pellegrino, J. W., 115
perspectives, 120, *127*
Pichert, J. W., 21–22
postreading response, previewing, 29
predicting ABCs, 93, *93*
preparation of texts for the classroom,
    10–13
prereading activities and focusing the
    reader
    assessment for learning, 40–45
    characteristics of effective activities,
        28–29
    clear and narrow focus, xxiii
    context, role of, 20–21
    drama example, 31–34, 43
    history example, 39–40, 44
    math example, 34–39, 44
    purpose, importance of, 21–22
    science examples, 22–27, 43
    vocabulary for history, 102–6
prereading strategies
    anticipation guides, 30–31, 36, *37*, 42,
        44
    artistic expressions, 31
    demonstrations, 29–30
    ethical dilemmas, 31, 40
    K-W-L charts, 30, 33–34, *34*, 42, 43
    visual displays, 30
previewing text features, 51–52, 53–54, 75
primary sources, 5–6, *7*
prior knowledge, 9, 20–21, 30
problem–solution guides, *127*
process strategies, 116
pro–con analysis charts, *41*, *127*, 132, *133*
professional development, discipline-
    based, 139
proposals, research, 135
protocols for text, 52, *52*, 76–77
purpose

accountable talk and, 62
assessing, 42
importance of, 21–22
in prereading activities, 28–29
science example, 22–27
writing, purposeful, 67

questioning the author (QtA), 120, *121*,
    122–25, *123*, *124*
questions, guiding, 43
quick-fix strategies, 56–58
quick-write responses, 23

readability and text selection, 6–10
reading aloud for vocabulary, 92–93
read it–try it, 126–27, 128–29, 137
real-world solutions, 134
real-world work. *See* authenticity and
    real-world outcomes
recall, effect of purpose on, 21–22
reciprocal teaching, 63, 64–67, 76
repetitive interaction and vocabulary, 83
research proposals, 135
resistance to reading, and text selection, 5

says/means chart, 56, *57*
scavenger hunts, 85–86
schema activation, 20–21
science
    critical literacy, 122–25, 136–37
    prereading activities, 22–27, *26*, 43
    previous research, importance of, xiii
    protocols for reading journal articles,
        52, *52*, 76–77
    reading for learning case example,
        xiv–xviii, xx, xxi, xxii, xxiv, xxv
    skepticism and evidence
        investigation, xv
    textbooks in, 17
    text selection, 3, *7*
    understanding as goal, xix–xx
    vocabulary, 79, 89–91, 108
    writing to support comprehension,
        71–74
scoring of comprehension, 55–56
secondary sources, 5–6, *7*
section breaks in text, 10
selection of texts

About Heather Lattimer

HEATHER LATTIMER, EdD, is assistant professor at the School of Leadership and Education Sciences at the University of San Diego and a visiting faculty member at High Tech High's Graduate School of Education. Prior to coming to the university, Heather taught history, mathematics, and English in a diverse range of high school and middle school classrooms in both Northern and Southern California. She is the author of *Thinking through Genre: Units of Study in Reading and Writing Workshops, 4–12* and *Choosing to Teach: Lessons from the Lives of Effective Urban Teachers* and editor of a collected volume, *Learning by Design: Projects and Practices at High Tech Middle* (forthcoming). Heather and her husband, Joe, live in San Diego and are the proud parents of three boys, Andy, Matthew, and James.

This book was typeset in TheMix and Palatino by Barbara Frazier.

Typeface used on the cover is FF Eureka Sans.

The book was printed on 50-lb. Opaque Offset paper by Versa Press, Inc.